Microsoft Office 97

PROFESSIONAL EDITION

Carol M. Cram

Capilano College, North Vancouver, B.C.

ONE MAIN STREET, CAMBRIDGE, MA 02142

an International Thomson Publishing company I(T)P®

Cambridge • Albany • Bonn • Boston • Cincinnati • London • Madrid • Melbourne • Mexico City
New York • Paris • San Francisco • Singapore • Tokyo • Toronto • Washington

ILLUSTRATED PROJECTS™

Microsoft® Office 97, Professional Edition — Illustrated Projects™

is published by Course Technology.

Managing Editor: **Nicole Jones Pinard**
Product Manager: **Jeanne Herring**
Production Editor: **Catherine G. DiMassa**
Contributing Author: **Katherine T. Pinard**
Composition House: **GEX, Inc.**
Quality Assurance Tester: **John McCarthy**
Text Designer: **Joseph Lee Design**
Cover Designer: **Joseph Lee Design**

© 1997 by Course Technology
A Division of International Thomson Publishing — I(T)P®

For more information contact:

Course Technology
One Main Street
Cambridge, MA 02142

International Thomson Publishing Europe
Berkshire House 168-173
High Holborn
London WC1V 7AA
England

Thomas Nelson Australia
102 Dodds Street
South Melbourne, 3205
Victoria, Australia

Nelson Canada
1120 Birchmount Road
Scarborough, Ontario
Canada M1K 5G4

International Thomson Editores
Campos Eliseos 385, Piso 7
Col. Polanco
11560 Mexico D.F. Mexico

International Thomson Publishing GmbH
Königswinterer Strasse 418
53277 Bonn
Germany

International Thomson Publishing Asia
211 Henderson Road
#05-10 Henderson Building
Singapore 0315

International Thomson Publishing Japan
Hirakawacho Kyowa Building, 3F
2-2-1 Hirakawacho
Chiyoda-ku, Tokyo 102
Japan

All rights reserved. This publication is protected by federal copyright law. No part of this publication may be reproduced, stored in a retrieval system, or transmitted in any form or by any means, electronic, mechanical, photocopying, recording, or otherwise, or be used to make a derivative work (such as translation or adaptation), without prior permission in writing from Course Technology.

Trademarks

Course Technology and the Open Book logo are registered trademarks of Course Technology.
Illustrated Projects and the Illustrated Series are trademarks of Course Technology.

I(T)P® The ITP logo is a registered trademark of International Thomson Publishing.

Some of the product names and company names used in this book have been used for identification purposes only and may be trademarks or registered trademarks of their respective manufacturers and sellers.

Disclaimer

Course Technology reserves the right to revise this publication and make changes from time to time in its content without notice.

ISBN 0-7600-5133-X

Printed in the United States of America

10 9 8 7 6 5 4

From the Illustrated Series™ Team

At Course Technology we believe that technology will transform the way that people teach and learn. We are very excited about bringing you, instructors and students, the most practical and affordable technology-related products available.

The Development Process

Our development process is unparalleled in the educational publishing industry. Every product we create goes through an exacting process of design, development, review, and testing.

Reviewers give us direction and insight that shape our manuscripts and bring them up to the latest standards. Every manuscript is quality tested. Students whose backgrounds match the intended audience work through every keystroke, carefully checking for clarity and pointing out errors in logic and sequence. Together with our own technical reviewers, these testers help us ensure that everything that carries our name is as error-free and easy to use as possible.

The Products

We show both how and why technology is critical to solving problems in the classroom and in whatever field you choose to teach or pursue. Our time-tested, step-by-step instructions provide unparalleled clarity. Examples and applications are chosen and crafted to motivate students.

The Illustrated Series Team

The Illustrated Series Team is committed to providing you with the most visual introduction to microcomputer applications. No other series of books will get you up to speed faster in today's changing software environment. This book will suit your needs because it was delivered quickly, efficiently, and affordably. In every aspect of business, we rely on a commitment to quality and the use of technology. Each member of the Illustrated Series Team contributes to this process. The names of all our team members are listed below.

Cynthia Anderson	Pam Conrad	Meta Hirschl	Gregory Schultz
Chia-Ling Barker	Mary-Terese Cozzola	Jane Hosie-Bounar	Ann Shaffer
Donald Barker	Carol M. Cram	Steven Johnson	Dan Swanson
David Beskeen	Kim Crowley	Tara O'Keefe	Marie Swanson
Ann Marie Buconjic	Catherine G. DiMassa	Harry Phillips	Jennifer Thompson
Rachel Bunin	Linda Eriksen	Nicole Jones Pinard	Sasha Vodnik
Joan Carey	Jessica Evans	Katherine T. Pinard	Jan Weingarten
Patrick Carey	Lisa Friedrichsen	Kevin Proot	Christie Williams
Sheralyn Carroll	Michael Halvorson	Elizabeth Eisner Reding	Janet Wilson
Pat Coleman	Jamie Harper	Art Rotberg	
Brad Conlin	Jeanne Herring	Neil Salkind	

Preface

Welcome to *Microsoft Office 97—Illustrated Projects*. This highly visual book offers a wide array of interesting and challenging projects designed to reinforce the skills learned in any beginning Office 97 book. The Illustrated Projects Series is for people who want more opportunities to practice important software skills.

Organization and Coverage

This text contains a total of eight units. Four units contain projects chosen for the individual programs: Word, Excel, Access, and PowerPoint. Three other units contain projects that take advantage of the powerful integration capabilities of the suite. The eighth unit contains projects that help students practice gathering and using the information available on the World Wide Web. Each unit contains three projects followed by four Independent Challenges and a Visual Workshop. (A Hot Spots page replaces the Visual Workshop in the World Wide Web unit.)

About this Approach

What makes the Illustrated Projects approach so effective at reinforcing software skills? It's quite simple. Each activity in a project is presented on two facing pages, with the step-by-step instructions on the left page, and large screen illustrations on the right. Students can focus on a single activity without having to turn the page. This unique design makes information extremely accessible and easy to absorb. Students can complete the projects on their own and because of the modular structure of the book, can also cover the units in any order.

Each two-page spread, or "information display," contains the following elements:

Road map—It is always clear which project and activity you are working on.

Introduction—Concise text that introduces the project and explains which activity within the project the student will complete. Procedures are easier to learn when they fit into a meaningful framework.

Hints and Trouble comments—Hints for using Microsoft Office 97 more effectively and trouble shooting advice to fix common problems that might occur. Both appear right where students need them, next to the step where they might need help.

Numbered steps—Clear step-by-step directions explain how to complete the specific activity. These steps get less specific as students progress to the third project in a unit.

Time To checklists—Reserved for basic skills that students should do frequently such as previewing, printing, saving, and closing documents.

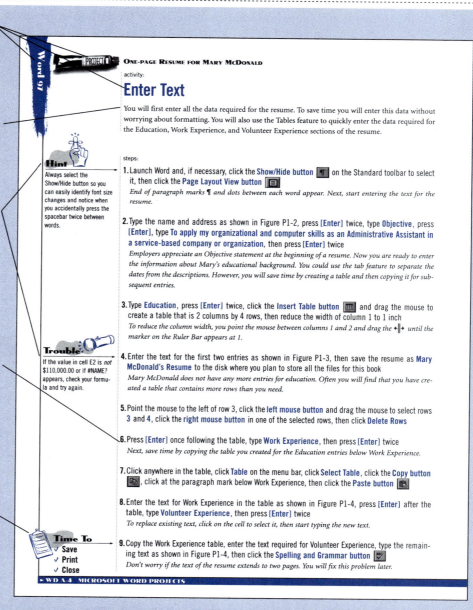

The Projects

The two-page lesson format featured in this book provides students with a powerful learning experience. Additionally, this book contains the following features:

▶ **Meaningful Examples**—This book features projects that students will be excited to create, including a resume, a job search form letter, and a budget to amortize a car loan. By producing relevant documents that will enhance their own lives, students will more readily master skills.

▶ **Different Levels of Guidance**—the three projects in each unit provide varying levels of guidance. In Project 1, the guidance level is high, with detailed instructions keeping the student on track. Project 2 provides less guidance, and Project 3 provides minimal help, encouraging students to work more independently. This approach gets students in the real-world mindset of using their experiences to solve problems.

▶ **Start from Scratch**—To truly test if a student understands the software and can use it to reach specific goals, the student should start from scratch. This adds to the book's flexibility and real-world nature.

▶ **Outstanding Assessment and Reinforcement**—Each unit concludes with four Independent Challenges. These Independent Challenges offer less instruction than the projects, allowing students to explore various software features and increase their critical thinking skills. The Visual Workshop follows the Independent Challenges and broadens students' attention to detail. Students see a completed document, worksheet, database, or presentation, and must recreate it on their own.

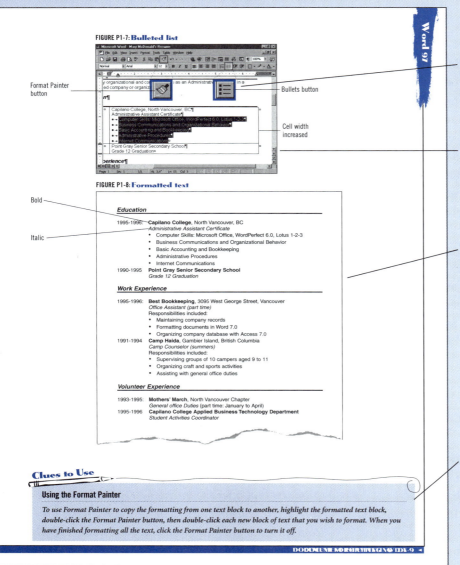

Callouts and enlarged buttons—The innovative design draws the students' eyes to important areas of the screen.

Screen shots—Every activity features large representations of what the screen should look like as students complete the numbered steps.

Completed document—At the end of every project, there is a picture of how the document will look when printed. Students can easily assess how well they've done.

Clues to Use Boxes—Many activities feature these sidebars, providing concise information that either explains a skill or concept that is covered in the steps or describes an independent task or feature that is in some way related to the steps. These often include both text and screen shots.

Instructor's Resource Kit

The Instructor's Resource Kit is Course Technology's way of putting the resources and information needed to teach and learn effectively into your hands. With an integrated array of teaching and learning tools that offer you and your students a broad range of instructional options, we believe this kit represents the highest quality and most cutting edge resources available to instructors today. Visit us on the Web at http://www.course.com. Briefly, the resources available with this text are:

Course Faculty Online Companion
This new World Wide Web site offers Course Technology customers a password-protected Faculty Lounge where you can find everything you need to prepare for class. These periodically updated items include lesson plans, graphic files for the figures in the text, additional problems, updates and revisions to the text, links to other Web sites, and access to Student Disk files. This new site is an ongoing project and will continue to evolve throughout the semester. Contact your Customer Service Representative for the site address and password.

Course Student Online Companion
The appearance and location of specific sites described in the World Wide Web unit may change after publication of this book, due to the dynamic nature of the World Wide Web. To manage this ever-changing environment and to keep the steps for each project as up-to-date as possible, the Student Online Companion provides the most current links to the sites that are described in the projects in this unit. In addition, the Student Online Companion is a place where students can access challenging, engaging, and relevant exercises. They can find a graphical glossary of terms found in the text, an archive of meaningful templates, software, hot tips, and Web links to other sites that contain pertinent information. We offer student sites in the broader application areas as well as sites for specific titles. These new sites are also ongoing projects and will continue to evolve throughout the semester.

Instructor's Manual
This is quality assurance tested and includes:
- *Solutions to end-of-unit material*
- *Lecture notes which contain teaching tips from the author*
- *Extra Projects*

The Illustrated Family of Products

This book that you are holding fits into the Illustrated Projects Series—*one series of three in the Illustrated family of products. The other two series are the* Illustrated Series *and the* Illustrated Interactive Series. *The* Illustrated Series *consists of concepts and applications texts that offer the quickest, most visual way to build software skills.* The Illustrated Interactive Series *is our line of computer-based training multimedia products that offer the novice user a quick, visual and interactive learning experience. All three series are committed to providing you and your students with the most visual and enriching instructional materials.*

Contents

From the Illustrated Series Team   **iii**

Preface   **iv**

Microsoft Word Projects: Document Formatting   WD A-1

- Project 1: **One-Page Resume for Mary McDonald**   WD A-2
- Project 2: **Business Cards for Jacques Dupré**   WD A-10
- Project 3: **Sales Letter for Tokada Software Solutions**   WD A-16
- Independent Challenges   WD A-20
- Visual Workshop   WD A-24

Microsoft Excel Projects: Worksheet Building   EX A-1

- Project 1: **Projected Budget for Cape Cod Arts Council**   EX A-2
- Project 2: **Loan Amortization to Lease or Buy a Car**   EX A-12
- Project 3: **Planning a Budget for a European Vacation**   EX A-16
- Independent Challenges   EX A-20
- Visual Workshop   EX A-24

Microsoft Word and Excel Projects: Document Linking   IN A-1

- Project 1: **Linked Invoice and Letter for Sparkle Catering**   IN A-2
- Project 2: **Guest Survey Results for Royal Palms Hotel**   IN A-10
- Project 3: **Price List for rainbow BATH SALTS**   IN A-16
- Independent Challenges   IN A-20
- Visual Workshop   IN A-24

Microsoft Access Projects: Database Creation   AC A-1

- Project 1: **Inventory for World Crafts**   AC A-2
- Project 2: **Artist Profiles for Pacific Art Gallery**   AC A-12
- Project 3: **Sales Information for Cruise Heaven, Inc.**   AC A-18

- Independent Challenges — AC A-20
- Visual Workshop — AC A-24

Microsoft Access, Word, and Excel Projects: Task Streamlining — IN B-1

- Project 1: **Job Search Database for Mark Leung** — IN B-2
- Project 2: **Company Profile for Dragon Designs** — IN B-10
- Project 3: **Video Catalogue for Home Library** — IN B-16
- Independent Challenges — IN B-20
- Visual Workshop — IN B-24

Microsoft PowerPoint Projects: Presentation Graphics — PPT A-1

- Project 1: **Training Presentation on Oral Presentation Skills** — PPT A-2
- Project 2: **Event Poster for First Night Celebration** — PPT A-12
- Project 3: **Lecture Presentation on Time Management** — PPT A-18
- Independent Challenges — PPT A-20
- Visual Workshop — PPT A-24

Microsoft PowerPoint, Word, Excel, and Access Projects: Integrated Presentations — IN C-1

- Project 1: **Sales Presentation for On the Edge Travel** — IN C-2
- Project 2: **Career Options Presentation** — IN C-12
- Project 3: **Class Party Presentation** — IN C-18
- Independent Challenges — IN C-20
- Visual Workshop — IN C-24

World Wide Web Projects: College and Job Search — WWW A-1

- Project 1: **College Programs for Studying Abroad** — WWW A-2
- Project 2: **Summer Job Opportunities** — WWW A-12
- Project 3: **Resume Posting** — WWW A-16
- Independent Challenges — WWW A-20
- Visual Workshop — WWW A-24

Index — INDEX 1

Microsoft Word Projects

Document Formatting

In This Unit You Will Create:

 **One-page Resume**

 **Business Cards**

 **Sales Letter**

You can use Microsoft Word to produce an enormous variety of documents—from simple one-page letters and resumes to multiple-page reports, newsletters, brochures, and even novels. Once you are comfortable with the many features of Microsoft Word, you can concentrate on how to *use* these features to produce just about any document you can think of. Suppose you wish to create a sheet of business cards. Word does not include a convenient Wizard to help you accomplish this task, so you have to think about the features available and decide which one is best suited to the creation of business cards. Think about what a sheet of business cards resembles. If you thought of *labels*, you are on your way! All you need to do is take a look at the list of label types provided in the Label Options dialog box, find Business Card, and off you go. ► In this unit you will learn how to use Microsoft Word to modify styles, apply Format Painter, create WordArt objects, apply borders, create Headers, and, most importantly, identify the best feature to use to accomplish a specific task.

OVERVIEW

One-Page Resume for Mary McDonald

Mary McDonald recently earned an administrative assistant certificate from Capilano College in North Vancouver, British Columbia. She now needs to create an attractive one-page resume that she will include with her job applications. Three activities are required to complete the one-page resume for Mary McDonald:

Project Activities

Enter Text

When you need to create a document such as a resume that will require a great deal of formatting, you will save time by first entering all the text and *then* applying the required formatting. You can also use the Table function to enter data in columns. The text in the Education, Work Experience, and Volunteer Experience sections of Mary McDonald's resume was created in a table form.

Modify Styles

Once you have entered all the text required for the resume, you can select and then modify the styles you wish to apply to the various parts of the resume. In Mary's resume, the font style and font size in the normal document style were changed to Arial and 12-point, and then an attractive style was created and applied to each of the headings. By using styles to format a document, you save time and attain a consistent look.

Enhance and Print the Resume

At first Mary's resume did not fit on one page. Here the margins are changed so that all the text fits on one page—without reducing the font size, which would affect the overall readability of the resume.

When you have completed Project 1, the resume will appear as shown in Figure P1-1.

FIGURE P1-1: **Mary McDonald's resume**

Resume Heading style — Resume Title style

MARY McDONALD
2131 Dollarton Hwy.
North Vancouver, BC V7H 1A8
Phone/Fax: (604) 929-4431
e-mail: marym@commerce.ca

Objective
To apply my organizational and computer skills as an Administrative Assistant in a service-based company or organization.

Education

1995-1996:   **Capilano College**, North Vancouver, BC
Administrative Assistant Certificate
- Computer Skills: Microsoft Office, WordPerfect 6.0, Lotus 1-2-3
- Business Communications and Organizational Behavior
- Basic Accounting and Bookkeeping
- Administrative Procedures
- Internet Communications

1990-1995:   **Point Gray Senior Secondary School**
Grade 12 Graduation

Work Experience

1995-1996:   **Best Bookkeeping**, 3095 West George Street, Vancouver
Office Assistant (part-time)
Responsibilities included:
- Maintaining company records
- Formatting documents in Word 7.0
- Organizing company database with Access 7.0

1991-1994:   **Camp Haida**, Gambier Island, British Columbia
Camp Counselor (summers)
Responsibilities included:
- Supervising groups of 10 campers aged 9 to 11
- Organizing craft and sports activities
- Assisting with general office duties

Volunteer Experience

1993-1995:   **Mothers' March**, North Vancouver Chapter
General Office Duties (part-time: January to April)
1995-1996:   **Capilano College Applied Business Technology Department**
Student Activities Coordinator

References
Available on request

Margins reduced — Table forms used

DOCUMENT FORMATTING   WD A-3

ONE-PAGE RESUME FOR MARY MCDONALD

activity:

Enter Text

You will first enter all the data required for the resume. To save time you will enter this data without worrying about formatting. You will also use the Tables feature to quickly enter the data required for the Education, Work Experience, and Volunteer Experience sections of the resume.

steps:

Hint
Always select the Show/Hide button so you can easily identify font size changes and notice when you accidentally press the spacebar twice between words.

1. Launch Word and, if necessary, click the **Show/Hide button** on the Standard toolbar to select it, then click the **Page Layout View button**
   End of paragraph marks ¶ and dots between each word appear. Next, start entering the text for the resume.

2. Type the name and address as shown in Figure P1-2, press **[Enter]** twice, type **Objective**, press **[Enter]**, type **To apply my organizational and computer skills as an Administrative Assistant in a service-based company or organization,** then press **[Enter]** twice
   Employers appreciate an Objective statement at the beginning of a resume. Now you are ready to enter the information about Mary's educational background. You could use the tab feature to separate the dates from the descriptions. However, you will save time by creating a table and then copying it for subsequent entries.

Hint
You will see 4 × 2 Table at the bottom of the Table grid as you drag the mouse.

3. Type **Education**, press **[Enter]** twice, click the **Insert Table button** and drag the mouse to create a table that is 2 columns by 4 rows, then reduce the width of column 1 to 1 inch
   To reduce the column width, you point the mouse between columns 1 and 2 and drag the ↔ until the marker on the Ruler Bar appears at 1.

4. Enter the text for the first two entries as shown in Figure P1-3, then save the resume as **Mary McDonald's Resume** to the disk where you plan to store all the files for this book
   Mary McDonald does not have any more entries for education. Often you will find that you have created a table that contains more rows than you need.

5. Point the mouse to the left of row 3, click the **left mouse button** and drag the mouse to select rows **3** and **4**, click the **right mouse button** in one of the selected rows, then click **Delete Rows**

6. Press **[Enter]** once following the table, type **Work Experience**, then press **[Enter]** twice
   Next, save time by copying the table you created for the Education entries below Work Experience.

7. Click anywhere in the table, click **Table** on the menu bar, click **Select Table**, click the **Copy button**, click at the paragraph mark below Work Experience, then click the **Paste button**

8. Enter the text for Work Experience in the table as shown in Figure P1-4, press **[Enter]** after the table, type **Volunteer Experience**, then press **[Enter]** twice
   To replace existing text, click on the cell to select it, then start typing the new text.

9. Copy the Work Experience table, enter the text required for Volunteer Experience, type the remaining text as shown in Figure P1-4, then click the **Spelling and Grammar button**
   Don't worry if the text of the resume extends to two pages. You will fix this problem later.

FIGURE P1-2: **Resume name and address**

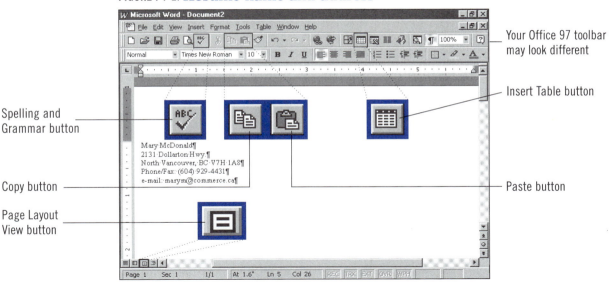

FIGURE P1-3: **Text for Education table**

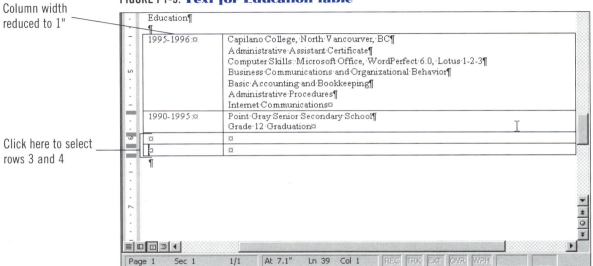

FIGURE P1-4: **Remaining text for resume**

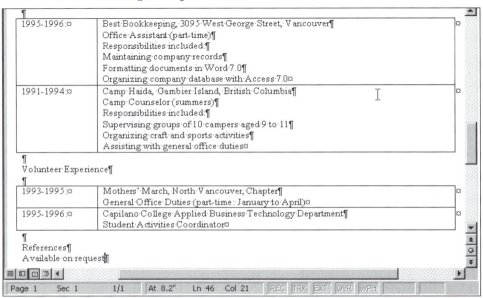

ONE-PAGE RESUME FOR MARY MCDONALD

activity:

Modify Styles

You need to modify the normal document style to change the font and font size for the entire document to 12-point, then create an attractive heading style and use Format Painter to apply the style to each heading in the resume.

steps:

Hint

You can also modify a document style *before* you start typing any text. All the text you type after modifying the style will be displayed with the enhancements you selected.

1. Press **[Ctrl][Home]** to move to the top of the resume, then press **[Ctrl][A]** to select the entire document

   As always you select text first and then you make formatting changes.

2. Click **Format** on the menu bar, click **Style,** click **Modify**, click **Format**, click **Font**, select the **Arial** font and a font size of **12**, click **OK**, click **OK** again, then click **Apply**

   The Normal style for your current document now includes the Arial font and a font size of 12. Next, create an attractive heading style.

3. Click anywhere but in a table in the resume to deselect the text, click **Format** on the menu bar, click **Style**, then click **New**

   You need to give your new style a name and then select the enhancements you require.

4. Type **Resume Heading Style**, click **Format**, click **Font**, select a font size of **16**, click **Bold Italic**, then click **OK**

   Next, add a single border line to the Resume Heading Style.

5. Click **Format**, click **Border,** select a line width of **2¼ pt**, click **Box**, click the **top**, **left**, and **right** borders to remove these lines in the sample Border display as shown in Figure P1-5, click **OK**, click **OK** again, then click **Close**

   Next, see how the new heading style appears when you apply it to a heading in the resume.

6. Double-click **Objective** to select it, click the **Style list arrow**, then click **Resume Heading Style**

   Your heading looks great. Next, apply the Resume Heading Style to the remaining headings.

7. Double-click **Education**, click the **Style list arrow**, click **Resume Heading Style**, repeat the procedure to apply the style to **Work Experience**, **Volunteer Experience**, and **References**, then click anywhere in the text to deselect References

   *Make sure you select only the text required and **not** the previous paragraph marker. If the previous paragraph marker is included in the style, extra space will appear in your document. Next, you create a new style for Mary McDonald's name.*

8. Select **Mary McDonald**, click **Format**, click **Style**, create a new style called **Resume Title Style** that includes the **Arial Black** font, a font size of **18**, **Small Caps**, and a **1½** point **Shadow** border, click **OK**, click **OK**, click **Apply**, click anywhere in the resume to deselect the text, then save the resume

   Compare your screen to Figure P1-6. Mary McDonald's resume is coming along very nicely. Next, go on to add the finishing touches.

FIGURE P1-5: **Borders and Shading dialog box**

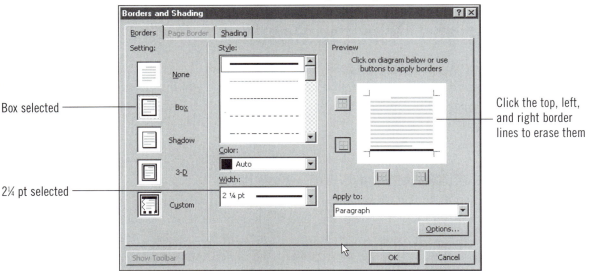

FIGURE P1-6: **Resume styles applied**

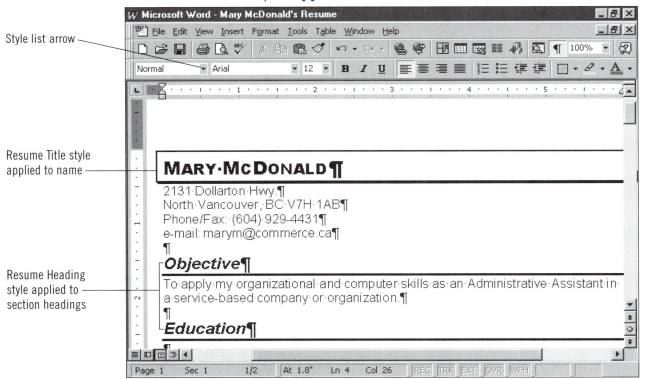

ONE-PAGE RESUME FOR MARY MCDONALD

activity:

Enhance and Print the Resume

You need to view Mary's resume in Whole Page view, decide whether you like the heading styles you created, make some modifications, apply some formatting to the individual sections of the resume, then modify the page setup options to fit the resume on one page, and print a copy.

steps:

1. Click the **Zoom Control list arrow**, then click **Whole Page**

   You can see right away that the resume is considerably longer than one page. Even if you reduce the margins, you will not fit all the text on one page. At present the resume heading style contains a font size of 16 and a 2¼-point border. Start by reducing both the font size and the border size. When you modify a style, the changes are instantly applied to all the text in the document currently formatted with the style.

Hint

Click Close, *not* Apply, when you have finished modifying the style because you do not want to apply the style to the text at your insertion point. Instead you want only the text already formatted with a style to be modified.

2. Click **Format** on the menu bar, click **Style**, select **Resume Heading Style**, click **Modify**, click **Format**, click **Font**, change the font size to **14**, click **OK**, then change the Border size to **1½ pt**, and close the Style dialog box

   A little more text now appears on page 1, but still not enough. Next, you modify the Resume Title Style.

3. Change the font size in the **Resume Title Style** to **16 pt**, then remove the Shadow border

   Next, go into the Page Setup dialog box and reduce the margins to fit the entire resume on one page.

4. Click **File** on the menu bar, click **Page Setup**, set the **Top Margin** to **.7**, the **Bottom Margin** to **.6**, and the **Left** and **Right Margins** to **1**, then click **OK**

   The resume should now fit on one page. If the resume does not fit on one page, reduce the top and bottom margins to .5". Next, enhance the text in the Education section of the resume.

5. Click the **Zoom list arrow**, click **100%**, select the text from **Computer Skills** to **Internet Communications**, click the **Bullets button**, then increase the width of the cell to **6½"**, as shown in Figure P1-7

6. With the text still selected, double-click the **Format Painter button**, drag across the list of responsibilities for Best Bookkeeping, drag across the list of responsibilities for Camp Haida, then click to turn it off

7. Refer to Figure P1-8, then use **Format Painter** to enhance selected text so that it appears as shown

   Mary's resume is looking great. Now all you need to do is center the heading text and print a copy.

8. Select the heading text from **Mary McDonald** to the **e-mail address**, then click the **Center button**

9. Click in each table, click **Format** on the menu bar, click **Borders and Shading**, click **None**, then click **OK** to remove the gridlines

Time To
✓ Save
✓ Close

10. View the resume once more in Whole Page view and check the spacing, then print a copy

FIGURE P1-7: Bulleted list

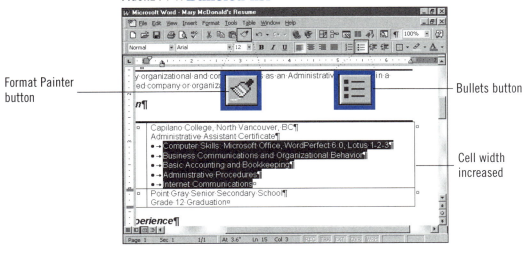

Format Painter button

Bullets button

Cell width increased

FIGURE P1-8: Formatted text

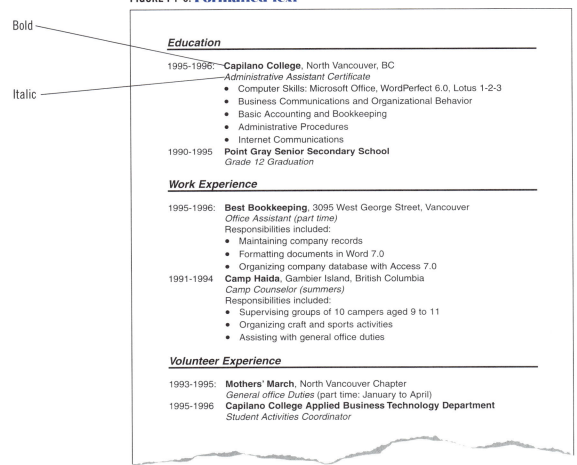

Bold

Italic

Using the Format Painter

To use Format Painter to copy the formatting from one text block to another, highlight the formatted text block, double-click the Format Painter button, then double-click each new block of text that you wish to format. When you have finished formatting all the text, click the Format Painter button to turn it off.

OVERVIEW

Business Cards for Jacques Dupré

Jacques Dupré works from his home in New Orleans as a freelance computer systems analyst. He has decided to create a sheet of business cards that he can then have printed on card stock. In the Labels Options dialog box, he finds a form that he can use to create his business cards. To create Jacques Dupré's business cards, you will **Create Labels and Enter Text**, **Add a WordArt Logo**, and **Format the Label Sheet for Printing**.

activity:

Create Labels and Enter Text

steps:

1. Start a new document, click **Tools** on the menu bar, click **Envelopes and Labels**, then click the **Labels tab**
   You need to select the Business Card label type in the Options dialog box.

2. Click **Options**, then scroll the **Product Number list box** until **5371 - Business Card** appears

3. Click **5371 - Business Card** to select it, click **OK**, then click **New Document**
   You click New Document because you want to display the label sheet as a table in which you can include both the text for the business card and a WordArt object. Next, enter Jacques Dupré and display the Symbol dialog box to insert the accented é.

4. Type **Jacques Dupr**, click **Insert** on the menu bar, click **Symbol**, click **(normal text)** as the Font type, click the **é** as shown in Figure P2-1, click **Insert**, click **Close**, then save the document on your disk as **Business Cards for Jacques Dupre**

5. Press **[Enter]** once, then enter the remaining text for the business card as shown in Figure P2-2.
   Next, you'll center and enhance the text.

6. Select the six lines of text, change the font to **Arial**, click the **Center button**, then enhance **Jacques Dupré** with **Bold** and a font size of **12** and **Computer Systems Analyst** with **Bold**
   Next, see how your business card looks in relation to the rest of the page.

7. Click the **Zoom Control list arrow**, then click **Whole Page view**
   As you can see, 10 labels appear on the screen, although only one label contains text.

8. Click the **Zoom Control list arrow**, click **100%**, then save the business cards
   Compare your screen to P2-3. Next, go on to create a WordArt logo for the business card and then copy both the logo and the text to the remaining nine cards.

FIGURE P2-1: Symbol dialog box

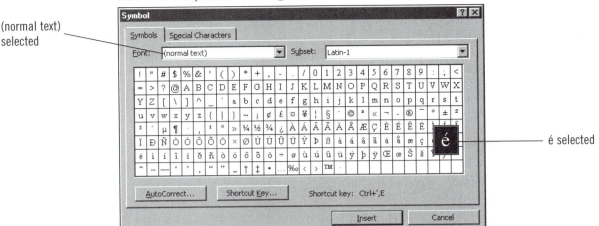

FIGURE P2-2: Text for business card

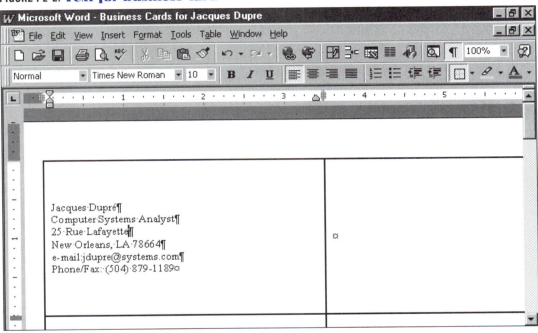

FIGURE P2-3: Label sheet

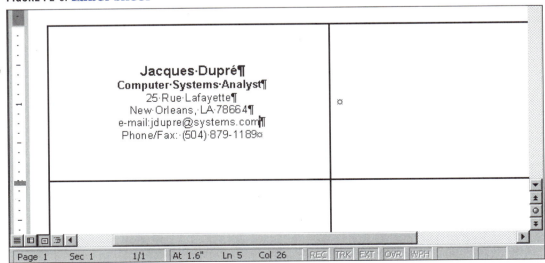

Business Cards for Jacques Dupré

activity:

Add a WordArt Logo

You need to modify the paragraph formatting for the business card text, add a WordArt logo, then copy the logo and text to the remaining nine cards.

steps:

1. Click to the left of the **J** in Jacques, display the **Drawing toolbar**, then click the **WordArt button**
   The WordArt Gallery appears as shown in Figure P2-4.

2. Select the second option from the left, as shown in Figure P2-4, then click **OK**
   The WordArt Gallery closes and you can now type the text for your logo

3. Type **JD**, change the font style to **Bookman Old Style**, then change the font size to **20 point**
   The logo appears on the first business card. Move it to the top-left corner of the business card.

4. Drag the **WordArt object** to the top-left corner of the first business card, as shown in Figure P2-5
   The logo appears on the first business card. Now, you can add a shadow.

5. Click the **Shadow button** on the Drawing toolbar, then click **Shadow Style 9**
   The shadow is applied, but in order for the logo to print across the rows of the business cards, you need to copy and move it.

6. Click the **Copy button** on the Standard toolbar, then click the **Paste button**
   A second logo appears. Next, move it to the business card to the right.

7. Drag the copy of the logo to the top-left corner of the second business card in the row
   Compare your screen to P2-6

8. Save the document

WD A-12   MICROSOFT WORD PROJECTS

FIGURE P2-4: **WordArt dialog box**

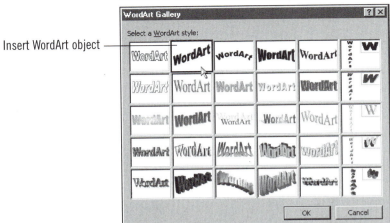

FIGURE P2-5: **Business card with WordArt object inserted**

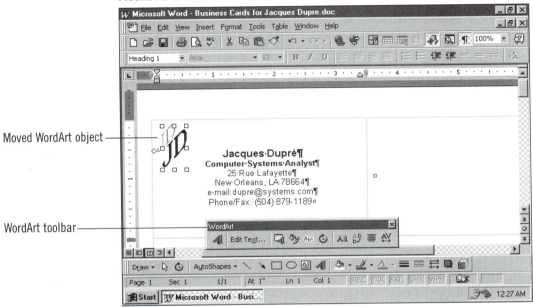

FIGURE P2-6: **Completed business card**

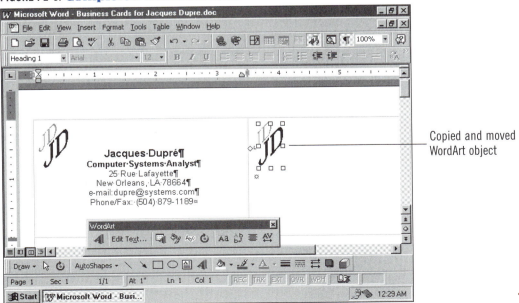

BUSINESS CARDS FOR JACQUES DUPRÉ

activity:

Format the Label Sheet for Printing

Jacques' business card is complete. Now all you need to do is insert the cutting lines and print the label sheet.

steps:

1. Point in the margin to the left of the cell containing the text and logo, then click the left mouse button to select the top two cells

   Next, you will format the text as necessary in the Envelopes and Labels dialog box.

2. Click **Tools**, then be sure the **Full page of the same label option** is selected

3. Right-click the selected text in the Address box, then click **Paragraph** on the pop-up menu

   You will now center the text to print properly on the label sheet.

4. In the alignment section, choose **Centered alignment**, then click **OK**

   Now you need to select the lines of text that need the special formatting you chose earlier.

5. Select the **first line of text** in the Address box, right-click it, click **Font** on the pop-up menu, then choose **Arial font** and **12 point**

6. Select the **second line of text** in the Address box, right-click the pop-up menu, click **Font** on the pop-up menu, then choose **Arial font**

   You can now print the document.

7. Click **Print**

   Compare your completed sheet of cards to Figure P2-7, then close the document.

▶ WD A-14 MICROSOFT WORD PROJECTS

FIGURE P2-7: **Completed sheet of business cards**

Jacques Dupré
Computer Systems Analyst
25 Rue Lafayette
New Orleans, LA 78664
e-mail:dupre@systems.com
Phone/Fax: (504) 879-1189

Jacques Dupré
Computer Systems Analyst
25 Rue Lafayette
New Orleans, LA 78664
e-mail:dupre@systems.com
Phone/Fax: (504) 879-1189

Jacques Dupré
Computer Systems Analyst
25 Rue Lafayette
New Orleans, LA 78664
e-mail:dupre@systems.com
Phone/Fax: (504) 879-1189

Jacques Dupré
Computer Systems Analyst
25 Rue Lafayette
New Orleans, LA 78664
e-mail:dupre@systems.com
Phone/Fax: (504) 879-1189

Jacques Dupré
Computer Systems Analyst
25 Rue Lafayette
New Orleans, LA 78664
e-mail:dupre@systems.com
Phone/Fax: (504) 879-1189

Jacques Dupré
Computer Systems Analyst
25 Rue Lafayette
New Orleans, LA 78664
e-mail:dupre@systems.com
Phone/Fax: (504) 879-1189

Jacques Dupré
Computer Systems Analyst
25 Rue Lafayette
New Orleans, LA 78664
e-mail:dupre@systems.com
Phone/Fax: (504) 879-1189

Jacques Dupré
Computer Systems Analyst
25 Rue Lafayette
New Orleans, LA 78664
e-mail:dupre@systems.com
Phone/Fax: (504) 879-1189

Jacques Dupré
Computer Systems Analyst
25 Rue Lafayette
New Orleans, LA 78664
e-mail:dupre@systems.com
Phone/Fax: (504) 879-1189

Jacques Dupré
Computer Systems Analyst
25 Rue Lafayette
New Orleans, LA 78664
e-mail:dupre@systems.com
Phone/Fax: (504) 879-1189

OVERVIEW

Sales Letter for Tokada Software Solutions

Tokada Software Solutions provides software consulting services to English-speaking companies in Japan. Janet Tokada, the company president, has just met with Aaron Markham, the manager of an American accounting firm in Tokyo. She decides to write him a letter to thank him for their meeting and to inform him of how Tokada Software Solutions can help his business. To create the sales letter you will first **Create the Letterhead** and then **Enter and Format the Letter Text**.

activity:

Create the Letterhead

steps:

1. Start a new document, press **[Enter]** 4 times to be sure the object does not move with your text, press **[Ctrl][Home]**, then save the document as **Sales Letter for Tokada Software Solutions** on your disk

   You are now ready to insert the company letterhead.

2. Click the **Insert WordArt button** on the Drawing toolbar, click the second option from the left, then click **OK**

   The WordArt Gallery appears. Next, enter the text for your letterhead.

3. Type **Tokada Software Solutions**, select the **Arial font**, change the font size to **20 point**, then add **Shadow Style 14**

   Your letterhead appears as shown in Figure P3-1. Next, move and resize the object.

4. Drag the object to the top-left of the document, next to the first paragraph marker, click the **Free Rotate button** on the WordArt toolbar, then rotate the object as shown in Figure P3-2

   Your letterhead appears properly in the document. Your next step is to insert a picture.

5. Deselect the WordArt object, click **Insert** on the menu bar, point to **Picture**, click **Clip Art**, select the Clip Art shown in Figure P3-3 (in the People at Work category), then click **Insert**

   Next, move the picture to a new location in your document.

6. Drag the picture to the top-right of the document as shown in Figure P3-3

   The graphics element of your letterhead are complete.

7. Click in front of the third paragraph marker, enter the address information as shown in Figure P3-3, then add a bottom border

FIGURE P3-1: WordArt object

Formatted WordArt object

FIGURE P3-2: Resized WordArt object

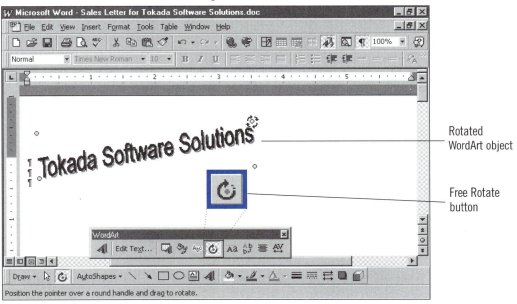

Rotated WordArt object

Free Rotate button

FIGURE P3-3: Address information for letterhead

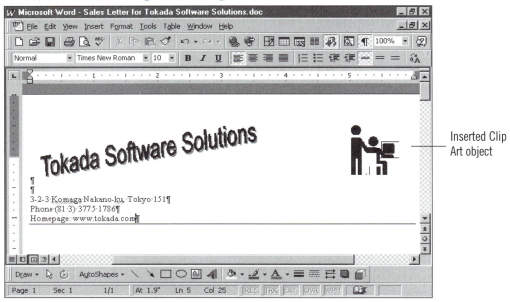

Inserted Clip Art object

SALES LETTER FOR TOKADA SOFTWARE SOLUTIONS

activity:

Enter and Format the Letter Text

You need to insert the current date, type the text for the letter, and then apply formatting to selected paragraphs.

steps:

Hint

You will find the currency symbol for Japanese yen (¥) in the (normal text) font in the Symbol dialog box.

1. At the paragraph marker under the border, press **[Enter]** three times, click **Insert** on the menu bar, click **Date and Time**, select the date format you prefer, then click **OK**

2. Press **[Enter]** twice, then type the text of the letter as shown in Figure P3-4 without including any indents or paragraph numbers, then click the **Spelling and Grammar button** 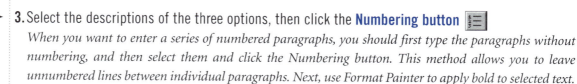 and make any necessary corrections

   Just type the text without formatting. You will apply formatting to selected paragraphs later. Don't even type numbers before each of the three numbered paragraphs. Note that your letter will extend to two pages. You'll fix this problem later. Next, format the numbered paragraphs.

Time To
✓ Save

3. Select the descriptions of the three options, then click the **Numbering button**

   When you want to enter a series of numbered paragraphs, you should first type the paragraphs without numbering, and then select them and click the Numbering button. This method allows you to leave unnumbered lines between individual paragraphs. Next, use Format Painter to apply bold to selected text.

4. Select **Basic Software Setup**, click the **Bold button** **B**, then double-click the **Format Painter button**

5. Refer to the completed letter shown in Figure P3-4, and apply **Format Painter** to the text that appears in bold

6. Click the **Format Painter button** to turn it off when you have finished formatting selected text

   Next, view the letter in Whole Page view, and make the adjustments required to fit it on one page.

7. Click the **Zoom Control list arrow**, click **Whole Page**, display the **Page Setup dialog box**, change the **Left** and **Right Margins** to **1"** and the **Top Margin** to **.9"** (or smaller if necessary to fit on one page), then click **OK**

   You may need to reduce the size of the WordArt object and the picture to fit the letter on one page.

Time To
✓ Save
✓ Print
✓ Close

8. Return to **100% view**, hold down the **Ctrl key** and press **[Home]** to move to the top of the page, then use your mouse to slightly adjust the sizes and positions of the Picture and the WordArt object so that they appear as shown in Figure P3-4

   Your sales letter is complete.

FIGURE P3-4: **Completed letter for Tokada Software Solutions**

Tokada Software Solutions

3-2-3 Komaga Nakano-ku, Tokyo 151
Phone (81 3) 3775 1786
Homepage: www.tokada.com

December 3, 1997

Mr. Aaron Markam
Manager
Tokyo American Accounting, Inc.
3-3-1 Hongo, Bunkyo-ku
Tokyo 143

Dear Mr. Markham:

Thank you for meeting with me last week to discuss how Tokada Software Solutions can help your company maximize its efficiency. As we discussed, Tokada Software Solutions offers the following three packages to meet the needs of Tokyo American Accounting, Inc.

1. **Basic Software Setup**: Purchase and installation of the latest version of AccPac accounting software on your office computers and one day of staff training for **¥105,500** ($1,000 US).

2. **Custom Software Setup**: Design and installation of software customized for all the accounting and office management needs of Tokyo American Accounting, Inc., for **¥530,000** ($5,000 US).

3. **Software Maintenance Plan**: 24-hour-a-day support, monthly staff training sessions, and annual software updating for a monthly fee of **¥21,000** ($200 US).

As you have just recently established your business, Mr. Markham, I feel that a combination of Packages 1 and 3 would be most suitable. Within days, your office will be up and running with AccPac and your staff given some basic training. Our 2-hour support and monthly staff training sessions will provide your staff with all the backup they need to get the most out of your AccPac installation.

The enclosed brochure describes Packages 1 and 3 in more detail. If you have any questions regarding the packages, please call me at 3755 1786 or send me an e-mail at jtokada@tokada.com. You may also wish to explore our new homepage on the World Wide Web. Our URL is www.tokada.com.

Thank you for your interest in Tokada Software Solutions. I hope we may look forward to serving you soon.

Sincerely,

Janet Tokada
President

Encl.

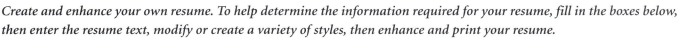

Independent Challenges

INDEPENDENT CHALLENGE 1

Create and enhance your own resume. To help determine the information required for your resume, fill in the boxes below, then enter the resume text, modify or create a variety of styles, then enhance and print your resume.

1. Determine your objective. What kind of position are you looking for that will match your qualifications and experience? Enter your objective in the box below:

   Resume Objective:

2. In the table below, list the components related to your educational background, starting with your most recent school or college. Note the name of the institution, the certificate or degree you received, and a selection of the courses relevant to the type of work you are seeking.

Year(s):	Institution:	Certificate/Degree:	Courses:

3. In the table below, list the details related to your work experience. Use **parallel structure** when listing your responsibilities; that is, make sure that each element uses the same grammatical structure. For example, you can start each point with a verb, such as "maintaining" or "managing," and then follow it with the relevant object, for example, "maintaining company records" and "using Word 97 to create promotional materials."

Year(s):	Company/Organization:	Location:	Position/Title:	Responsibilities:

4. In the table below, describe any volunteer experience you have, awards you have received and, if you wish, your hobbies and interests.

   Volunteer Experience:
   Awards:
   Hobbies/Interests:

5. Set up your resume in Word as follows:
   a. Type all the text required for your resume; use a table form to enter the information for Education, Work Experience, and Volunteer Experience (if appropriate). Remember to use the Copy and Paste features to save time.
   b. Select the entire document [Ctrl][A], and modify the Normal style so that the text displays the font and font size you prefer.
   c. Create styles for the resume headings. If you wish, you can modify the Resume Heading Style you created in Project 1.
   d. Apply the styles then modify them, if necessary.
   e. Use Format Painter to add other enhancements such as bold, italics, and bullets to selected text.
   f. View your resume in Whole Page view, change the margins, if necessary, and make any other changes required to fit the resume attractively on one or two pages. If your resume extends to two pages, include a header at the top of Page 2 that contains your name and the page number.
   g. Save your resume as "My Personal Resume," then print a copy.

INDEPENDENT CHALLENGE 2

Use the Business Card label sheet to create a sheet of business cards for yourself. Here are some tips for creating your business cards:

1. Select Business Cards from the list of available label sheets in the Label Options dialog box, click OK, then click New Document.
2. Click above the text and create an attractive WordArt logo from your own initials.
3. Reduce the size of the logo. Select the text then modify the options in the Paragraph dialog box to position the text in the table cell. Add any enhancements that you would like to the business card text.
4. Save the document as "My Business Cards."
5. Align the business cards in the Address box as you want them to appear when you print.
6. Print your business cards.

INDEPENDENT CHALLENGE 3

Adapt the sales letter you created in Project 3 to promote a product for a company of your choice. For example, you could choose to describe aquarium products for a company called Fish Fantasies or promote Internet services for a company called OnLine OnTime. Once you have decided on a company and product, open the letter for Tokada Software Solutions, delete the current letterhead, create your own letterhead (use WordArt and insert an appropriate picture), then adapt the content to suit your product and company. Save the letter as "Sales Letter for (Your Company Name)," then print the completed letter.

INDEPENDENT CHALLENGE 4

Type the text for the confirmation letter in Figure IC-1, then enhance the letter as directed. Note that the purpose of a confirmation letter is to confirm arrangements related to a specific event or agreement made between two companies or organizations. In the confirmation letter below, Step One Communications confirms a seminar they are hosting for employees of the Midland Counties Bank.

1. Type the text as shown in Figure IC-1. Note that you will find the £ symbol in the (normal text) font in the Symbol dialog box.
2. Use WordArt to create an attractive letterhead, then add a picture if you wish.
3. Modify the Normal style to change the font and font size to the settings you prefer, then apply the style to the entire document.
4. Use your own judgment to enhance the letter so that it appears attractive and fits on one page.
5. View the letter in Whole Page view, then make any spacing or formatting adjustments required.
6. Save the letter as "Confirmation Letter for Challenge 3," then print a copy.

FIGURE IC-1: **Text of confirmation letter**

Step One Communications, Inc.
145 Beaumont Crescent, Reading, Berkshire, M1K 2S0, UK
Phone: (44 181) 877045

[Current Date]

John Shackleton
Personnel Manager
Midland Counties Bank: Basingstoke Branch
24 London Road
Basingstoke, Berkshire
M1K 3P3, UK

Dear Mr. Shackleton:

Thank you for your letter of [specify a date 1 week prior to the current date] confirming a one-day communications seminar at the Basingstoke branch of the Midland Counties Bank. My colleague, Ms. Jenna White, will be conducting the seminar and supplying all the materials the participants will require.

Here again are the seminar details:

> Date: [specify a date one month after the current date]
> Time: 0900 to 1700
> Location: 2nd Floor, Administration Building, Reading University, Whiteknights Campus
> Cost: £1,000 for 20 participants

As we discussed, the communications seminar will include the following activities:

1. Warm-up exercises to stimulate a relaxed atmosphere and to determine the general level of communications skills among the participants.

2. Analysis of various communications situations to assess writing strengths and weaknesses.

3. Intensive "hands-on" practice in the communication of clear and effective sales, training, and informational presentations.

I'm very much looking forward to an exciting seminar. Thank you again, Mr. Shackleton, for your interest in Step One Communications. If you have any further questions, please call me at 877045.

Sincerely,

[Your Name]
President

Visual Workshop

Create the letterhead shown in Figure VW-1 in a document named "Letterhead Practice." For the WordArt object, select the Cascade Up shape and the Impact font, and add a Shadow. Insert the largest border line under the address, then select 30% shading.

FIGURE VW-1: Letterhead

Safari Adventures

1809 West Ridge Road, West Ridge, 7650, Cape Town, South Africa

Microsoft ► Excel Projects

Worksheet Building

In This Unit You Will Create:

► **Projected Budget**

► **Loan Amortization**

► **Planning Budget**

Microsoft Excel provides you with the tools you need to make effective planning decisions. For example suppose you want to take a two-week vacation to the Caribbean. You have allocated $2,000 for all your trip expenses. To find out if you have enough money to cover your expenses, you can set up a simple worksheet that will list all your expenses for airfare, accommodations, food, entertainment, etc. Once you have totaled all your expenses, you may find that they exceed your $2,000 budget. Rather than cancel your trip, you could then try to determine which expenses you can decrease. You could decide to stay at a less expensive hotel or allocate a reduced amount for your shopping needs. When you use a worksheet as a planning tool, you identify and evaluate different courses of action and then select the actions that will best meet your personal or business needs.
► In this unit you will learn how to use Microsoft Excel to determine worksheet categories, build arithmetic formulas, and, most important, ask relevant "What if?" questions designed to help you develop worksheets that you can then use as planning tools.

OVERVIEW

Projected Budget for Cape Cod Arts Council

The Cape Cod Arts Council is a small, nonprofit organization that teaches arts and crafts classes in a converted boathouse located in the Cape Cod area. You will create the Cape Cod Arts Council's budget for the first six months of 1999, based on figures obtained from the 1998 budget, and then ask a series of "What if?" questions to determine realistic planning goals for the second half of 1999.

The following four activities are required to complete the six-month budget for the Cape Cod Arts Council:

Project Activities

Enter and Enhance Labels

You can easily present worksheet data in an attractive and easy-to-read format. In Figure P1-1, the labels in the top five rows are centered across columns and enhanced with various font styles and sizes, while a white-on-black effect is used to highlight two of the worksheet titles.

Calculate Totals

You can either use the AutoSum button or enter a formula when you need to add values in a spreadsheet. You use the AutoSum method when you want to add the values in cells that appear consecutively in a column or row and then display the total directly below or to the right of the added values. You enter a formula when you want to calculate values that do not appear in consecutive cells. For example, you would enter the formula =A1+A3 if you wished to add the values in cells A1 and A3. You can also use the SUM formula. For example, you would enter the function =SUM(A1..A6) if you wished to add all the values in cells A1 through A6 and display the result in a nonadjacent cell.

Ask "What if?" Questions

One of the most useful tasks you can perform with a spreadsheet program is to change values in a worksheet to see how the totals are affected. For example, you can ask yourself: "*If we spend $2,000 a month on payroll instead of $4,500, how much money will we save over six months?*" As soon as you change the values entered in the Payroll row, the totals are automatically updated. To complete Project 1, you will ask three "What if?" questions.

Format and Print the Budget

You will use a variety of the features in the Page Setup dialog box to produce an attractive printed version of your budget that includes a customized header and footer.

When you have completed the activities above, your budget will appear as shown in Figure P1-1.

FIGURE P1-1: **Cape Cod Arts Council projected budget**

Cape Cod Arts Council
North Shore Boathouse, R.R. #2, Mattapoisett, MA 02739

Projected Budget
January to June 1999

10/8/98

	January	February	March	April	May	June	Totals
Income							
Course Fees	$ 26,875.00	$ 26,875.00	$ 26,875.00	$ 26,875.00	$ 34,937.50	$ 34,937.50	$ 177,375.00
Grants	1,000.00	1,000.00	1,000.00	1,000.00	1,000.00	1,000.00	6,000.00
Donations	400.00	400.00	400.00	400.00	400.00	4,800.00	6,800.00
Total Income	$ 28,275.00	$ 28,275.00	$ 28,275.00	$ 28,275.00	$ 36,337.50	$ 40,737.50	$ 190,175.00
Expenses							
Payroll	$ 5,520.83	$ 5,520.83	$ 5,520.83	$ 5,520.83	$ 5,520.83	$ 5,520.83	$ 33,125.00
Lease	600.00	600.00	600.00	600.00	600.00	600.00	3,600.00
Course Supplies	1,200.00	1,200.00	1,200.00	1,200.00	1,000.00	1,000.00	6,800.00
Maintenance	900.00	900.00	900.00	900.00	400.00	400.00	4,400.00
Computer Lease	400.00	400.00	400.00	400.00	400.00	400.00	2,400.00
Advertising	700.00	700.00	3,000.00	700.00	700.00	700.00	6,500.00
Total Expenses	$ 9,320.83	$ 9,320.83	$ 11,620.83	$ 9,320.83	$ 8,620.83	$ 8,620.83	$ 56,825.00
Profit	$ 18,954.17	$ 18,954.17	$ 16,654.17	$ 18,954.17	$ 27,716.67	$ 32,116.67	$ 133,350.00

Labels centered across columns

White text on black background

Currency style

Comma style

Border styles

PROJECTED BUDGET FOR CAPE COD ARTS COUNCIL

activity:

Enter and Enhance Labels

You need to enter and enhance the name and address of the organization, the worksheet title, the current date, and the first series of labels.

steps:

1. Open a new worksheet, click the blank box to the left of the **A** at the top left corner of the worksheet to select the entire worksheet, click the **Font Size list arrow**, then click **12**
   A font size of 12 is selected for the entire worksheet.

2. Click cell **A1**, type **Cape Cod Arts Council**, press **[Enter]**, type the remaining labels as shown in Figure P1-2, then save your worksheet as **Projected Budget for Cape Cod Arts Council** on the disk where you plan to store all the files for this book.
   Next, you can enhance the labels you have typed with new fonts, font sizes, colors, and fills. You'll start by enhancing "Cape Cod Arts Council" in cell A1.

3. Click cell **A1**, click the **Font list arrow**, select **Comic Sans MS**, if it is available, or select **Britannic Bold**, click the **Font Size list arrow**, then select **24**
   Next, enhance cells A4 and A5 with a font size of 18.

4. Select cells **A4** and **A5**, click the **Font Size list arrow**, then select **18**
   Your next step is to center cells A1 to A5 across several columns, then add a fill color to selected cells.

5. Select cells **A1** to **H5** as shown in Figure P1-3, right-click on the selection, click **Format Cells**, click the **Alignment tab**, click the **Horizontal list arrow**, click **Center Across Selection**, click **OK**, select cells **A4** to **H5**, click the **Fill Color list arrow**, click the **black box**, then click away from the cells to deselect them
   You can no longer see the labels in cells A4 and A5. Next, change their color to white.

6. Select cells **A4** and **A5**, click the **Font Color list arrow**, then click the **white box**
   Next, use the Today function to enter the current date.

7. Click cell **A7**, click the **Paste Function button** *fx* on the Standard toolbar, select **Date & Time** from the list under Function Category, select **Today** from the list under Function Name (you'll need to scroll down), click **OK**, click **OK**, select cells **A7** to **H7**, then click the **Merge and Center button** on the Formatting toolbar
   Next, use the automatic fill feature to enter the labels for the months of the year from January to June.

8. Click cell **B9**, type **January**, press **[Enter]**, click cell **B9** again, position the mouse pointer over the handle in the lower, right corner, drag the ✚ to cell **G9**, then click the **Center button** on the Formatting toolbar
   The six months from January to June appear and are centered.

9. Click cell **A10**, enter the labels required for cells **A10** to **A25** and cell **H9** as shown in Figure P1-4, click the **Spelling button** on the Standard toolbar, correct any spelling errors, then save your worksheet
   Next, you will link two sheets in the current workbook, then calculate the total income and expenses.

Although the text extends into columns B and C, you only need to select cells A4 and A5—where the text originated.

FIGURE P1-2: Labels for cells A1 to A5

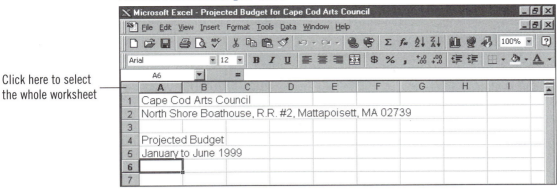

Click here to select the whole worksheet

FIGURE P1-3: Cells A1 to H5 selected

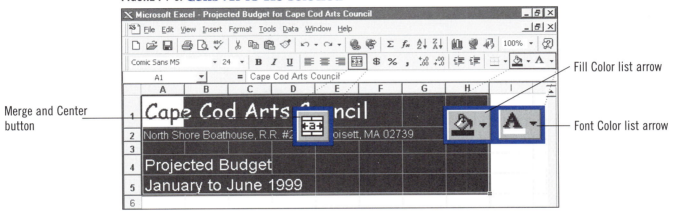

Merge and Center button

Fill Color list arrow

Font Color list arrow

FIGURE P1-4: Labels for cells A10 to A25 and H9

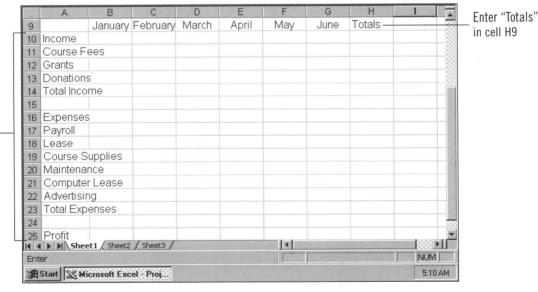

Labels for cells A10 to A25

Enter "Totals" in cell H9

Clues to Use

Merging Cells

A merged cell is a single cell created by combining two or more cells. The cell reference for the merged cell is the upper, left cell in the original selected range. When you merge a range of cells, only the data in the upper, left cell of the range is included in the merged cell. If you want to center several rows of data across columns, select the cells, then use the Alignment tab in the Format Cells dialog box. If you want to center the data in only one cell across several columns, then you can use the Merge and Center button on the Formatting toolbar.

PROJECTED BUDGET FOR CAPE COD ARTS COUNCIL

activity:

Calculate Totals

You now need to enter the income and expenses that Cape Cod Arts Council expects in 1999. After you have entered the values, you will calculate the average monthly course fees collected and then the total income and expenses.

steps:

1. Position the mouse pointer on the column divider line between **A** and **B** on the worksheet frame so it changes to ↔, then double-click to increase the width of column A to fit all the labels in cells A10 to A25

   You are now ready to enter the values required for your budget.

2. Click cell **B12** then enter the values for January as shown in Figure P1-5

   Next, use the Fill feature to enter the same values for all six months.

3. Select cells **B12** to **B22**, position the mouse pointer over the handle in the lower right corner of cell **B22**, then drag across to cell **G22**

   The values in cells B12 to B22 appear in cells C12 to G22. Now you need to estimate the course fees you hope to make each month in 1999. You know that approximately 5,000 people took courses in 1998 in three payment categories: adults, children/seniors, and school groups. You will use a new blank worksheet to calculate the average course fee in each category for 1999, based on the total fees collected in 1998. Use a new worksheet to avoid cluttering the current worksheet with data that won't be printed.

Hint

You will need to use your mouse to widen column A so that the labels are clearly visible and then center and bold the labels in cells A1 to E1.

4. Click the **Sheet2 tab** at the bottom of your worksheet, then enter and enhance the labels and values as shown in Figure P1-6

   Next, calculate the course fees for each category.

5. Click cell **E2**, enter the formula **=B2*C2*D2**, then press **[Enter]**

   You should see 110000 in cell E2. If not, check your formula and try again.

6. With cell **E2** selected, drag the corner handle down to cell **E4**, click cell **E5**, then double-click the **AutoSum button** Σ on the Standard toolbar

   The course fees collected should be 156250 or $156,250. Now you need to display the average course fees for each month in Sheet1. You will first calculate the fees for January by entering a formula in cell B11 of Sheet1 that divides the value in cell E5 of Sheet2 by six (for six months).

7. Click the **Sheet1 tab**, click cell **B11**, enter the formula **=Sheet2!E5/6**, press **[Enter]**, then drag the corner handle of cell **B11** across to cell **G11**

   Ooops! Cells C11 through G11 contain zeroes. Why? If you click cell C11 and look at the formula entered in the formula bar at the top of the worksheet, you will see =Sheet2!F5/6. There is no value in cell F5 of Sheet2. To correct this, you need to enter a formula that designates cell E5 as an absolute value.

8. Click cell **B11**, drag I across **E5** in the formula bar, press **[F4]**, press **[Enter]**, then fill cells **C11** to **G11** with the new formula

   You will see 26042 in cells B11 to G11. Next, calculate the total income and expenses.

9. Select cells **B11** to **H14**, click Σ, select cells **B17** to **H23**, then click Σ again

   The total income in cell H14 is 164650, and the total expenses in cell H23 are 46800, as shown in Figure P1-7. Go on to calculate the profit and ask a series of "What if" questions.

FIGURE P1-5: Values for cells B12 to B22

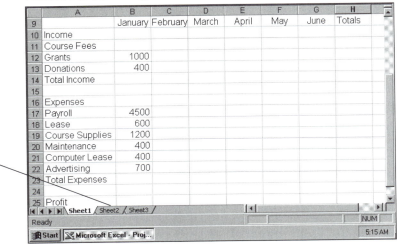

Sheet2 tab

FIGURE P1-6: Sheet2 labels and values

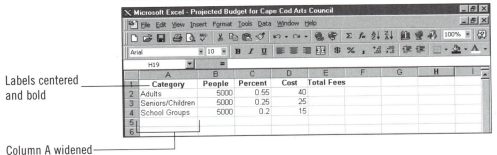

Labels centered and bold

Column A widened

FIGURE P1-7: Worksheet completed with totals

	A	B	C	D	E	F	G	H
9		January	February	March	April	May	June	Totals
10	Income							
11	Course Fees	26042	26042	26042	26042	26042	26042	156250
12	Grants	1000	1000	1000	1000	1000	1000	6000
13	Donations	400	400	400	400	400	400	2400
14	Total Income	27442	27442	27442	27442	27442	27442	164650
15								
16	Expenses							
17	Payroll	4500	4500	4500	4500	4500	4500	27000
18	Lease	600	600	600	600	600	600	3600
19	Course Supplies	1200	1200	1200	1200	1200	1200	7200
20	Maintenance	400	400	400	400	400	400	2400
21	Computer Lease	400	400	400	400	400	400	2400
22	Advertising	700	700	700	700	700	700	4200
23	Total Expenses	7800	7800	7800	7800	7800	7800	46800
24								
25	Profit							

Total income

Total expenses

Clues to Use

Relative and Absolute References

By default Microsoft Excel considers all values entered in formulas as relative values. That is, Excel will change all cell addresses in a formula when you copy it to a new location. If you do not want Excel to change the cell address of a value when you copy it, you must make the value absolute. To do this, you enter a dollar sign ($) before both the column and row designation in the address. You can also press [F4] to insert the symbol. For example, $C$26 tells Excel that the reference to cell C26 must not change, even if you copy the formula to a new location in the worksheet.

PROJECTED BUDGET FOR CAPE COD ARTS COUNCIL

activity:

Ask "What if?" Questions

You need to calculate the profit you expect to make in each of the first six months of 1999, then perform the calculations required to answer three "What if?" questions.

steps:

Hint

To calculate percentage, multiply the total amount by the percentage amount expressed as a decimal. For example 300*.07 will calculate 7% of 300.

Hint

To enter new values in a cell that already contains values, just click on the cell and type the values. They will automatically replace the existing values.

Trouble

If your results are different, ensure that your formula in cell B17 adds 4500 to 24500 divided by 2 *and* 12. Remember to use parentheses to control the order of operations.

1. Click cell **B25**, enter the formula **=B14-B23**, press **[Enter]**, then copy the formula across to cell **H25** as shown in Figure P1-8

   The total profit for the first six months of 1998 is 117850 in cell H25. This profit will change when you make new calculations to answer the "What if?" questions. The first question is, "what if you raise the adult course fee to $60?" To answer this question you need to change the course fee entered in Sheet2.

2. Click the **Sheet2 tab**, click cell **D2**, type **60**, press **[Enter]**, then click the **Sheet1 tab**

   Your total profit in cell H25 is 172850. Good news! However, a course fee increase could result in a 20% drop in the number of students you can expect in 1999. Next, display Sheet2 again and enter a formula that subtracts 20% of 5000 from the total number of adult course fees (5000).

3. Click the **Sheet2 tab**, click cell **B2**, enter the formula **=5000-(5000*.2)**, press **[Enter]**, copy cell **B2** to cells **B3** and **B4** as shown in Figure P1-9, then click the **Sheet1 tab**

   The new profit is 130600—quite a reduction from 172850! Perhaps you shouldn't raise the adult course fees to $60, if the result is a 20% drop in the number of people who take courses.

4. Return to **Sheet2**, change the cost of the adult course fee to **40** and the number of people in cells **B2** to **B4** to **5000**, then return to **Sheet1**

   The results of the first "What if?" question led you to return to your original profit of 117850 in cell H25. The next question is, "What if you launch a $3,000 advertising campaign in March?"

5. Click cell **D22** in Sheet1, type **3000**, then press **[Enter]**

   Your total profit for the six months (cell H25) is now reduced to 115550 from 117850. However, a major advertising campaign launched in March could lead to a 30% increase in revenue from course fees in May and June. Next, edit the formula in cells F11 and G11 to reflect this projected 30% increase.

6. Click cell **F11**, click at the *end* of the formula displayed on the formula bar, type ***1.3**, press **[Enter]**, then copy the formula to cell **G11**

   The new total profit in cell H25 is 131175. The next question is, "What if you hire a full-time administrative assistant for $24,500 per year?" You need to divide this amount by 12 to determine the monthly rate, then add the total to the values entered in the Payroll row.

7. Click cell **B17**, enter the formula **=(24500/12)+4500**, press **[Enter]**, then copy the formula across to cell **G17**

   Your total profit is now 118925. Perhaps you should hire a part-time administrative assistant instead.

8. Change the formula in cell **B17** so that it adds **4500** to *half* of **24500** divided by **12**, press **[Enter]**, then copy the formula across to cell **G17**

   The value in cell B17 will be 5520.8, and the total profit in cell H25 will be 125050. Next, change some more values in the worksheet to reflect anticipated changes to the budget.

9. Increase Maintenance costs to **$900** per month from **January** through **April**, reduce Course Supplies costs to **$1000** per month in **May** and **June**, raise the course fee for School Groups to **$20**, then change the donation for **June** to **$4,800**

   Your total profit in cell H25 should now be 133350. Compare your worksheet with Figure P1-10.

FIGURE P1-8: Formula in cell B25 copied to cell H25

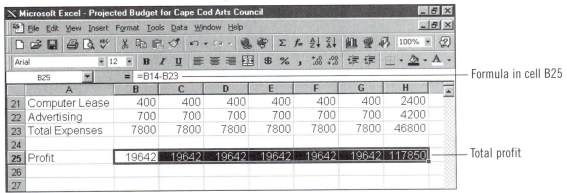

FIGURE P1-9: Formula in cell B2 copied to cells B3 and B4

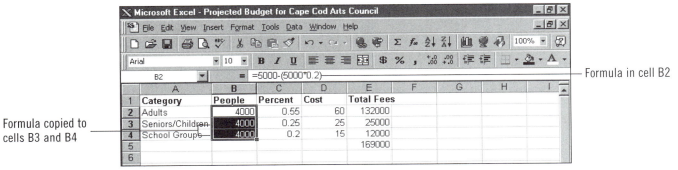

FIGURE P1-10: Worksheet with completed budget

	A	B	C	D	E	F	G	H
9		January	February	March	April	May	June	Totals
10	Income							
11	Course Fees	26875	26875	26875	26875	34937.5	34938	177375
12	Grants	1000	1000	1000	1000	1000	1000	6000
13	Donations	400	400	400	400	400	4800	6800
14	Total Income	28275	28275	28275	28275	36337.5	40738	190175
15								
16	Expenses							
17	Payroll	5520.8	5520.8	5520.8	5520.8	5520.83	5520.8	33125
18	Lease	600	600	600	600	600	600	3600
19	Course Supplies	1200	1200	1200	1200	1000	1000	6800
20	Maintenance	900	900	900	900	400	400	4400
21	Computer Lease	400	400	400	400	400	400	2400
22	Advertising	700	700	3000	700	700	700	6500
23	Total Expenses	9320.8	9320.8	11621	9320.8	8620.83	8620.8	56825
24								
25	Profit	18954	18954	16654	18954	27716.7	32117	133350

PROJECTED BUDGET FOR CAPE COD ARTS COUNCIL

activity:

Format and Print the Budget

Now you need to display values in the Currency or Comma styles, add border lines to selected cells, use a variety of Page Setup features, and then print a copy of your budget.

steps:

Trouble

If the column widths did not automatically increase, click Format on the menu bar, point to Column, then click AutoFit Selection.

1. Select cells **B11** to **H11**, then click the **Currency Style button** on the Formatting toolbar
   The widths of columns B to H automatically increased.

2. Select cells **B12** to **H13**, click the **Comma Style button** on the Formatting toolbar, select cells **B14** to **H14**, then click
   Format the remaining cells.

3. Format cells **B18** to **H22** as **Comma style**, and format cells **B17** to **H17**, **B23** to **H23**, and **B25** to **H25** as **Currency style**
   Next, enclose selected cells with border lines.

Hint

You need to deselect the cell to see the borders.

4. Select cells **B14** to **H14**, click the **Borders list arrow** on the Formatting toolbar, then select the **Single top/Double bottom** border style as shown in Figure P1-11
   A single line appears above cells B14 to H14, and a double line appears below them.

5. Add the **Single top/Double bottom** border style to cells **B23** to **H23**, then add the **Double bottom** border style to cells **B25** to **H25**

6. Center and bold the heading "Totals" in cell **H9**, then enhance cells **B9** to **G9**, **A10**, **A14**, **A16**, **A23**, and **A25** to **H25** with **bold**
   Next, display your budget in the Print Preview screen, then select a variety of options from the Print Setup dialog boxes in order to format your budget attractively on the printed page.

7. Click the **Print Preview button** on the Standard toolbar, click **Setup**, click the **Landscape option button** and the **Fit to 1 page option button**, then click the **Margins tab**
   In the Margins dialog box, you will center the budget horizontally and vertically on the page and then display the Header/Footer dialog box.

Time To

✓ Save
✓ Print
✓ Close the workbook

8. Click the **Horizontal** and **Vertical check boxes**, click the **Header/Footer tab**, click **Custom Header**, enter the text for the header as shown in Figure P1-12, click **OK**, then click **OK** again
   The budget for the Cape Cod Arts Council is complete. Compare your print preview screen with Figure P1-13.

FIGURE P1-11: Border styles

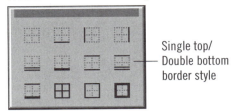

Single top/Double bottom border style

FIGURE P1-12: Custom header

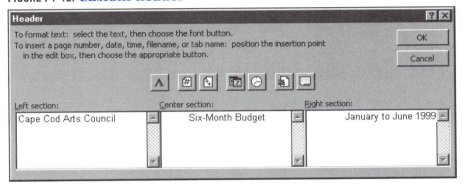

FIGURE P1-13: Completed worksheet in print preview

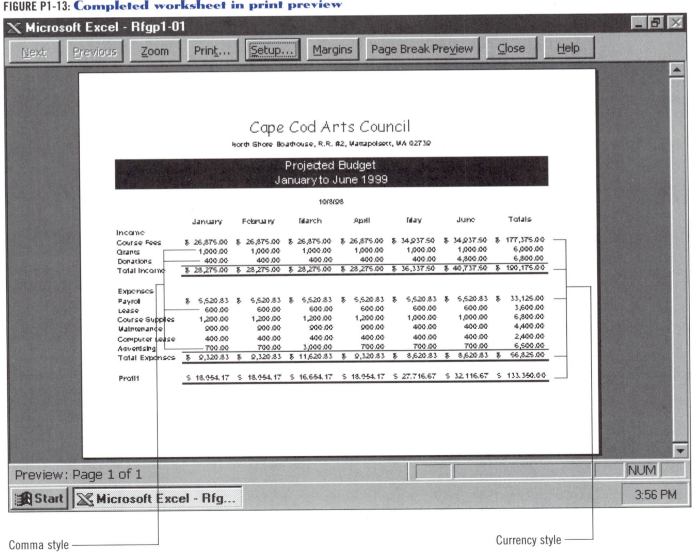

Comma style

Currency style

OVERVIEW

Loan Amortization to Lease or Buy a Car

You have decided to purchase a car that costs $12,400.00. Your monthly net income (after taxes) is $2,024.80. You need to decide whether to lease the car over three years or buy the car with the aid of a bank loan for $12,400.00. You will **Set Up a Loan Worksheet** and **Evaluate Options** to help you make an informed decision.

activity:

Set Up a Loan Worksheet

steps:

Hint

When you want to enter a value that you will then format as a percent, enter the value as a decimal. For example you would enter 10% as .1, then click the Percent Style button.

1. Open a new workbook, then set up the worksheet so that it appears as shown in Figure P2-1

   Next, enter the interest rate percentage for the car lease option in cell B6.

2. Click cell **B6**, type **.18** press **[Enter]**, click cell **B6** again, then click the **Percent Style button** on the Formatting toolbar

   Next, enter the interest rate percentage for the bank loan option in cell G6.

3. Click cell **G6**, type **.11**, press **[Enter]**, then format cell **G6** in the **Percent Style**

   Now that you know the retail price of the car ($12,400.00) and the interest rates for both a three-year lease and a bank loan, you need to calculate the total interest you will pay for each option. To calculate the total interest, you will multiply the Retail Price by the Interest Rate for both options.

4. Click cell **C6**, then enter the formula **=$A$6*B6** to calculate the total interest paid on the retail price for a three-year lease, then widen the column

   The total interest you pay on a three-year lease is $2,232.00.

5. Copy cell **C6** to cell **H6**, then widen the column

   The relative cell reference in the formula adjusted for cell H6, but the absolute reference to cell A6 remained constant. The total interest you will pay on a three-year loan is $1,364.00. Next, determine the monthly payment required for each option by adding the Retail Price to the Total Interest and dividing the total by 36.

6. Click cell **D6**, enter the formula **=($A$6+C6)/36**, press **[Enter]**, then display the value in the **Currency Style**

7. Copy cell **D6** to cell **I6** to calculate the monthly payment on a bank loan

   Compare your worksheet with Figure P2-2. As you can see, the monthly payment for a three-year lease is $406.44, while the monthly payment for a bank loan is $382.33. The monthly payment on a bank loan is less than the monthly payment on a three-year lease. However, what about resale value, and, more important, what about your monthly expenses? Can you really afford a new car?

8. Save your worksheet as **Car Planning Budget**

FIGURE P2-1: Worksheet setup

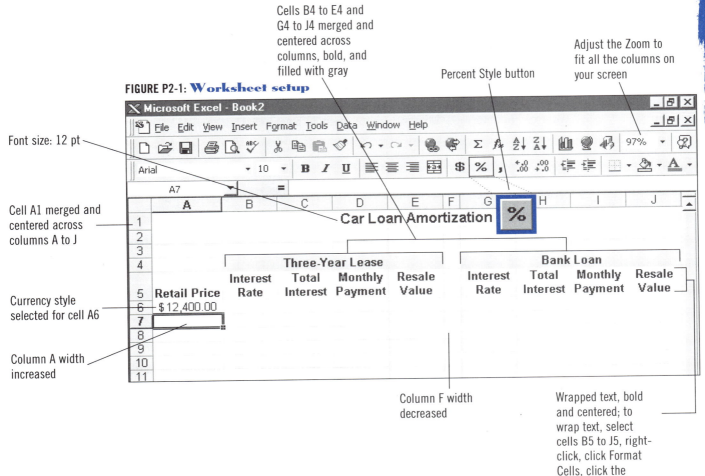

FIGURE P2-2: First row calculations added

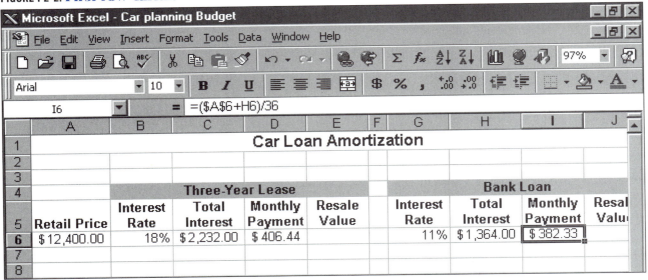

WORKSHEET BUILDING   EX A-13

PROJECT 2 — LOAN AMORTIZATION TO LEASE OR BUY A CAR

activity:

Evaluate Options

The three-year lease plan includes a buyout feature. You can pay $2,000 at the end of three years to own your car. If you purchase the car with a bank loan, you will own the car outright. In both cases you need to determine how much your car will be worth at the end of three years.

Hint

Straight Line Depreciation is based on the assumption that depreciation of an asset (such as a car) depends only on time. The depreciable expense of the asset is therefore spread evenly over a period of time (such as three years). Another method is **accelerated depreciation**, where the expense is higher in the early years of the life of the asset.

steps:

1. Click cell **E6**, enter the formula **=($A$6*0.2*3)-2000**, press **[Enter]**, then display the result in the **Currency Style** and widen the column

   *The resale value is $5,440.00. The formula you entered calculates the **straight line depreciation** by multiplying the Retail Price by 20% and then multiplying this result by 3 (for three years). You subtracted the $2,000 from the resale value because you would pay an extra $2,000 at the end of three years to own the car. Next, calculate the resale value of the car for the bank loan option.*

2. Click cell **J6**, enter the formula to multiply the retail price by **20%** and **3**, then press **[Enter]**

   The resale value will be $7,440.00. Next, calculate the loss you will sustain by selling the car.

3. Right-click in any cell in column **F**, click **Insert**, click the **Entire column option button**, click **OK**, type **Loss** in cell **F5**, then enter a formula in cell **F6** that subtracts the Resale Value from the sum of Total Interest, Retail Price, and $2,000

   The loss you will sustain is $11,192.00.

4. Type and enhance **Loss** in cell **L5**, click cell **L6**, enter the formula **=(A6+I6)-K6** to calculate the loss you will sustain in the bank loan option, then extend the cell merge to cell **L4**

   The three-year lease option allows you to trade in your car at the end of three years and then lease a new car. You will always drive a new or near-new car—which may compensate for never owning a car. You could lose $6,324.00 when you try to sell the car you bought with the aid of a bank loan. But can you afford either option? Answer this question by creating a personal budget.

5. Click cell **A10**, enter and enhance the labels and values as shown in Figure P2-3 for Step 5, then widen columns as necessary

   The insurance on the new car will be $1,100 per year, and gas will be $840 a year. Start by determining whether you can afford to lease a car.

6. Click cell **B19**, type **=D6** (the cell address of the monthly payment for a three-year lease), press **[Enter]**, then enter the formulas shown in Figure P2-3 for cells B20 to B26 and format the cells

   Your surplus in cell B26 is a negative number: ($24.62). You obviously cannot afford to lease a car for $406.44 per month. Can you afford to buy a car with the aid of a bank loan?

7. Click cell **B19**, enter the cell address of the bank loan monthly payment, then press **[Enter]**

   The value in cell B26 is $1.90. Now find out what car you could afford based on your own monthly income and expenses.

8. Enter your own monthly expenses in cells **A14** to **A21** (add new rows if necessary), enter a variety of retail prices in cell **A6** until you find a price that you can afford, add the current date, then format and print your Car Planning Budget in landscape so that it appears similar to the illustration in Figure P2-4

   Note that your totals will differ, depending upon your monthly expenses and the retail price.

Time To
- ✓ Save
- ✓ Close your workbook

FIGURE P2-3: Expense calculations

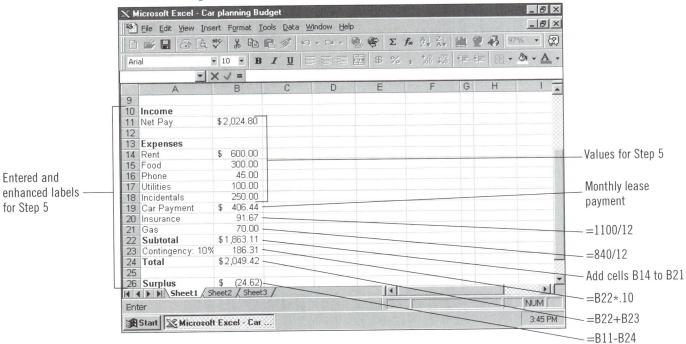

Entered and enhanced labels for Step 5

Values for Step 5
Monthly lease payment
=1100/12
=840/12
Add cells B14 to B21
=B22*.10
=B22+B23
=B11-B24

FIGURE P2-4: Completed car planning budget

Car Loan Amortization   Sheet1   [Your Name]

Car Loan Amortization

		Three-Year Lease						Bank Loan			
Retail Price	Interest Rate	Total Interest	Monthly Payment	Resale Value	Loss		Interest Rate	Total Interest	Monthly Payment	Resale Value	Loss
$ 12,400.00	18%	$ 2,232.00	$ 406.44	$ 5,440.00	$ 11,192.00		11%	$ 1,364.00	$ 382.33	$ 7,440.00	$ 6,324.00

Income
Net Pay $ 2,024.80

Expenses
Rent $ 600.00
Food   300.00
Phone   45.00
Utilities   100.00
Incidentals   250.00
Car Payment $ 382.33
Insurance   91.67
Gas   70.00
Subtotal $ 1,839.00
Contingency: 10%   183.90
Total $ 2,022.90

Surplus $ 1.90

Page 1

OVERVIEW

Planning a Budget for a European Vacation

You are planning a five-week trip to Europe with a friend. Your budget for the trip is $5,000. Before you buy your plane ticket, you need to determine how much you can spend on airfare, accommodations, food, entertainment, and transportation. You may *want* to stay in first-class hotels, but your $5,000 budget may not extend that far. What kind of trip can you really afford? For this project you will **Set Up a Vacation Planning Budget** and **Reduce Trip Costs** to create a spreadsheet that will help you to plan a European vacation that you will remember for a lifetime.

activity:

Set Up a Vacation Planning Budget

Hint
To right align the labels in cells D13 to D15, type the labels in these cells, then select them and click the Align Right button.

Hint
Resize columns if necessary.

steps:

1. Set up your worksheet so that it appears as shown in Figure P3-1
   Next, vertically align the labels in cells B4 to E4.

2. Select cells **B4** to **E4**, click the **right mouse button**, click **Format Cells**, click the **Alignment tab**, make sure **Center** is selected in the Horizontal section, click **Top** in the Vertical section, drag the **red diamond** in the Orientation section down so the spin box shows -90 Degrees, as shown in Figure P3-2, then click **OK**
   Your next step is to enter the formulas required to calculate your total expenses.

3. Click cell **E5**, enter the formula **=C5*D5**, press **[Enter]**, then copy the formula down to cell **E11**

4. Click cell **E13**, then double-click the **AutoSum button** Σ on the Standard toolbar to calculate the Subtotal

5. Click cell **E14**, calculate a **15%** contingency on the **Subtotal**, then click cell **E15** and add the **Subtotal** to the **Contingency** to determine your Total Expenses

6. Display the values in cells **E5**, **E13**, and **E15** in the **Currency Style** and the remaining values in column **E** in the **Comma Style**
   Compare your worksheet with Figure P3-3. Your total expenses in cell E15 are $6,563.05. You are $1,563.05 over your budget of $5,000.

7. Save your budget as **Europe Trip**
   Next, you will go on to perform a series of calculations to reduce your trip expenses to your $5,000 budget.

FIGURE P3-1: Worksheet setup

Font size: 24 pt

Font size: 14 pt

Display the value in cell C5 in the Currency style and the values in cells C6 to C11 in the Comma style

To right-align D13 to D15, select the cells and click the Align Right button

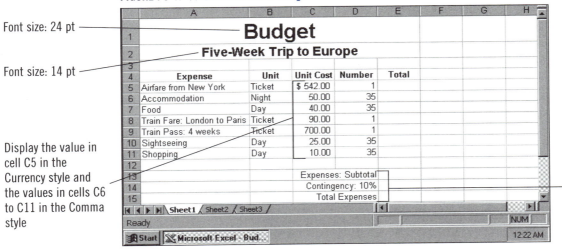

FIGURE P3-2: Format Cells dialog box

Drag diamond to bottom

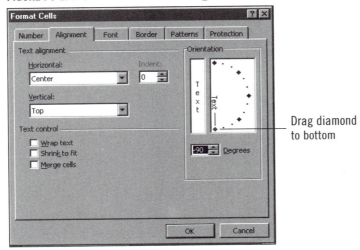

FIGURE P3-3: Worksheet with expenses

4	Expense	Unit	Unit Cost	Number	Total
5	Airfare from New York	Ticket	$ 542.00	1	$ 542.00
6	Accommodation	Night	50.00	35	1,750.00
7	Food	Day	40.00	35	1,400.00
8	Train Fare: London to Paris	Ticket	90.00	1	90.00
9	Train Pass: 4 weeks	Ticket	700.00	1	700.00
10	Sightseeing	Day	25.00	35	875.00
11	Shopping	Day	10.00	35	350.00
12					
13				Expenses: Subtotal	$5,707.00
14				Contingency: 10%	856.05
15				Total Expenses	$6,563.05
16					

PROJECT 3: PLANNING A BUDGET FOR A EUROPEAN VACATION

activity:

Reduce Trip Costs

To reduce the trip cost to $5,000, you will perform a variety of calculations to answer several "What if?" questions, then format and print your trip planning budget. As you perform the calculations in Steps 1 through 8, check the total in cell E15 against the totals provided. You will need to think carefully about the calculations required. For some steps you will need to insert new rows.

Hint

You may want to make a copy of the worksheet in Sheet2 in case you want to start over.

steps:

1. What if you reduce your sightseeing allowance to $20 a day?
   Total expenses are now $6,361.80.

2. What if you book a charter flight that costs $200 less than the current airfare?
   Total expenses are now $6,131.80.

3. What if you lease a car for four weeks at a cost of $435.72 per week, do not buy a train pass, and share the cost of the car lease with a friend?
   Total expenses are now $6,328.96.

4. What if you stay at campsites for 20 days ($22/night for two), stay in youth hostels for 10 days ($28.50/night for one), and then stay in hotels for the remaining 5 days ($120/night for two)?
   Note that you will need to insert two new rows for the various accommodation options. The total expenses are now $5,242.21.

5. What if you buy and cook your own food on the days that you camp, thereby reducing your food costs on those days to $25 a day?
   Note that your food costs will remain the same for the days that you do not camp. The total expenses are now $4,897.21.

6. If you lease a car, you will split gas costs with your friend during the four weeks that you have the car. You plan to drive approximately 3,000 kilometers; the car you plan to rent gets 12 kilometers to the liter; gas in Europe costs approximately $2.00 a liter
   The total expenses are now $5,184.71.

7. What if you decide not to go to England and save the cost of the train fare from London to Paris?
   The total expenses are now $5,081.21.

8. What if you reduce your contingency to 10%?
   The total expenses are now $4,860.28. You can afford to go to Europe now, although you will have to stick carefully to your budget.

9. Change the font size to **14** for cells **A4** to the end of the data, format and print your budget so that it appears similar to the illustration in Figure P3-4, then save and close the workbook

FIGURE P3-4: Completed Europe Trip budget

Trip Planning Budget [Your Name]

Budget
Five-Week Trip to Europe

Expense	Unit	Unit Cost	Number	Total
Airfare from New York	Ticket	$ 342.00	1	$ 342.00
Hotels	Night	60.00	5	300.00
Campsites	Night	11.00	20	220.00
Youth Hostels	Night	28.50	10	285.00
Food	Day	40.00	15	600.00
Food: Camping	Day	25.00	20	500.00
Car Lease	Week	217.86	4	871.44
Gas	Liter	1.00	250	250.00
Sightseeing	Day	20.00	35	700.00
Shopping	Day	10.00	35	350.00

Expenses: Subtotal	$ 4,418.44
Contingency: 10%	441.84
Total Expenses	$ 4,860.28

Independent Challenges

INDEPENDENT CHALLENGE 1

Create your own personal budget for the next six months, then ask a series of "What if?" questions to help you make decisions regarding how you will spend your money. Fill in the boxes below with the required information, then set up your budget in an Excel worksheet, and perform the calculations required to answer a variety of "What if?" questions.

1. Determine your sources of income. You may receive money from a paycheck, from investment dividends, or from a student loan. Each income source requires a label and a row on your budget worksheet. In the box below list the income labels you will require:

   Income labels:
   1. ....
   2. ....
   3. ....
   4. ....
   5. ....

2. Determine your expenses. At the very least you will probably need to list your rent, food, utilities, and phone. You may also need to list transportation costs such as car payments, gas, insurance, and bus fares. In addition include labels for entertainment, incidentals, and savings. In the box below list the expense labels you have identified:

   Expense labels:
   1. ....   6. ....
   2. ....   7. ....
   3. ....   8. ....
   4. ....   9. ....
   5. ....   10. ....

3. Even a personal budget should be created for a specific purpose. For example you may wish to save for a vacation or to buy a car, or even just to live within a set income. Identify the goal of your budget in the box below:

   Budget Goal: ....
   ....

4. Set up your budget in Excel as follows:
   a. Enter and enhance a title for your budget in cell A1.
   b. Enter the current date (use the Today function).
   c. Enter the Income and Expense labels in column A.
   d. Determine the time frame of your budget (e.g., monthly, weekly, annual), then enter the appropriate labels starting in column B.
   e. Enter the values required for your income and expenses. Adjust expenses according to the time of year. For example, your utilities costs will probably be less in the summer than in the winter, while your entertainment and holiday expenses may rise in the summer.
   f. Calculate your total income and expenses.

g. Ask yourself at least ten "What if?" questions, and then make the calculations required to answer them. Here are some sample "What if?" questions:
- What if I move in March to a new apartment where my rent is 30% more than the current rent?
- What if I eat out in restaurants only twice a month?
- What if I take the bus or subway to work twice a week?
- What if I join a fitness club with monthly dues?
- What if I buy a car with payments of $250/month? Remember to factor in costs for insurance and gas.
- What if I start taking violin lessons?

Try to formulate questions that will help you to plan your finances to achieve the goals you have set.
h. Save your worksheet as "Personal Budget."
i. Format and print a copy of your budget.

INDEPENDENT CHALLENGE 2

Create a planning budget to help you determine your expenses for a vacation of your choice. The following tasks will help get you started.

1. Before you create the worksheet in Excel, answer the questions listed below:
   a. Where do you plan to go for your vacation?
   b. What is your proposed budget?
   c. How long is your planned vacation?
   d. What kind of activities do you plan to do on your vacation (e.g., sightseeing, guided tours, horseback riding, skiing, etc.)?
2. Set up your worksheet with labels for transportation costs (airfare, car rental, train fares, etc.), accommodations, food, sightseeing, shopping, and any other expense categories appropriate to the kind of vacation you plan to take.
3. Include a contingency amount for emergency expenses that is 10% to 15% of your total expenses.
4. Try to make your budget as realistic as possible. You can choose to base your budget on a vacation you have already taken or on a vacation you hope to take.
5. Save your vacation planning budget as "My Vacation Plan," then format and print a copy.

INDEPENDENT CHALLENGE 3

You have decided to purchase a computer system that costs $3,100 plus 8% sales tax. The computer system includes a laser printer, a modem, and all the software you require. You have to choose between buying the computer with the aid of a bank loan (11% annual interest) or leasing it at 20% interest per month for 36 months.

1. Create a worksheet that will help you to determine which option you should choose. Base your worksheet on the Car Loan Amortization you created in Project 2.
2. Take into account the probable resale value of your computer at the end of three years, given the continually changing computer market. Calculate the straight line depreciation at 25% per year for 3 years.
3. Copy the worksheet into Sheet2 of the worksheet you created for Project 2, then study the personal budget you created in Sheet1 to determine the payment options you can afford. Include formulas that link the two worksheets. For example if you enter =Sheet2!B6 in cell A10 of Sheet 1, the value in cell B6 of Sheet 2 will appear. If you change the value in cell B6 of Sheet2, the value in cell A10 of Sheet1 will also change.
4. Try to reduce some of your expenses in your personal budget so you can afford to purchase the computer.
5. Save your modified personal budget and the worksheet containing your Computer Purchase Plan as "Computer Purchasing Plan," then print a copy of both sheets.

INDEPENDENT CHALLENGE 4

Create the worksheet in Figure IC-1, then perform the calculations required to answer the questions provided.

FIGURE IC-1: Personal budgeting

	A	B
1		January
2	Income	
3	Pay Check	2,397.35
4	Investment Dividends	
5	Total Income	
6		
7	Expenses	
8	Rent	600.00
9	Food	400.00
10	Phone	60.00
11	Utilities	110.00
12	Car Payment	350.00
13	Gas	80.00
14	Car insurance	100.00
15	Total Expenses	
16		
17	Total Savings	

1. Use the AutoFill function to fill in the months from February to June.
2. Copy the values for January across to June.
3. Add a column labeled "Totals," then calculate the row totals and display all the values in the Comma Style.
4. Calculate the Monthly and Total Income and the Monthly and Total Expenses. Your total income is 14,384.10, your total expenses are 10,200.00, and your total savings are 4,184.10.
5. You will need to think carefully about the calculations required. For some questions you will need to insert new rows.

Questions

1. If you take a vacation that costs $2,200, how much money will you have left?

2. What would your total income be if you sold your car in March for $1,875?

3. What would your total expenses be for March if your phone bill increased by 25%?

4. What would your total savings be if you bought a car in April that required payments 15% higher than your current payments for the remaining months including April?

5. If you buy a new car in April, your gas costs will increase by 30% for the remaining months including April. What would your total savings be?

6. What if you received investment dividends of $100 a month?

7. What if you took a new job in May that paid 20% more than your current job?

8. If you take a new job, you will need to move to a new apartment in a new city. The rent for the new apartment will be $800/month.

6. When you have completed the questions above, add a title to the budget, format it attractively, save it as "Budget Practice," then print a copy.

Visual Workshop

Create the six-month budget as shown in Figure VW-1 for Web Wonders, a new company that provides Internet users with quick and easy access to the World Wide Web. Save the budget as "Web Wonders Budget" on your disk, then answer the following questions. Excel 5 Users: Save as WEB.XLS.

FIGURE VW-1: Web Wonders budget

	A	B	C	D	E	F	G	H
1				Web Wonders				
2			Proposed Six-Month Budget: July to September 1999					
3				[Current Date]				
4								
5		July	August	September	October	November	December	Totals
6	REVENUE							
7	Internet Subscriptions							
8	Homepage Server Space							
9	Total Revenue							
10								
11	EXPENSES							
12	Salaries	4500	4500	4500	7000	7000	4500	
13	Rent	1500	1500	1500	3500	3500	3500	
14	Equipment Leases	1000	1000	1500	2500	2500	2500	
15	Advertising	150	250	350	1200	1800	3500	
16	Operating Costs	350	350	350	780	780	780	
17	Total Expenses							
18								
19	PROFIT							
20								

1. In July you estimate that 1000 Internet subscribers will join Web Wonders at a cost of $30 per subscriber. You project that the subscription revenue generated in July will increase by 5% in August, 10% in September, then 20% for each of the remaining months. Calculate all increases based on July revenue. What is the total revenue in cell H9?
2. In July you estimate that 50 subscribers will purchase space on the server for their homepages at a cost of $100 each. This revenue should increase by 30% each month to December. (Enter =B8*1.3 in cell C8, then copy the formula to cell G8.) What is the total revenue in cell H9?
3. Triple the October Salaries and Advertising expenses for November and December. What is the total Salaries expense? What is the total Advertising expense?
4. Quadruple the October equipment lease for November and December. What is the total Equipment Lease expense?
5. What is the total projected profit in cell H19?
6. Save the worksheet again, then preview and print it.

Microsoft
► Word and Excel
Projects

Document Linking

In This Unit You Will Create:

Linked Invoice and Letter

Guest Survey Results

Price List

You can perform arithmetic calculations in a Word table and enter text in an Excel spreadsheet. By doing so, however, you do not maximize the integration capabilities of Office. To increase your efficiency you need to use the program best suited to perform a specific task and then create links between the programs to produce the documents you require. For example, suppose that every few months you want to send your customers a letter that contains a price list you have created and frequently update in Excel. You can create a form letter in Word, switch to Excel, copy the price list, then paste it as a link into the Word letter. Every time you make a change to the price list in Excel, the price list you copied into Word will also change. ► In this unit you will learn how to link documents that combine elements created in both Word and Excel.

OVERVIEW

Linked Invoice and Letter for Sparkle Catering

Sparkle Catering provides full catering services for weddings, parties, conferences, and other special events. As the owner of Sparkle Catering, you have decided to include a personalized thank-you letter with every invoice you send out to your customers. To save time you've decided to link each invoice with its accompanying letter so that you can quickly and easily update the letter when changes occur to the invoice. Three activities are required to complete the invoice form and letter for Sparkle Catering:

Project Activities

Create the Invoice in Excel

The invoice form lists the products and services that Ms. Darlene Siu purchased from Sparkle Catering for her daughter's wedding. Note that the invoice form consists of four principal types of information: the company name and location, shipping and billing information, a list of the items purchased, and the prices. When you create the invoice form, you will enter a formula in the Amount column that will multiply the Quantity by the Unit Price to determine the total Amount owed for each item.

Create the Letter in Word

You will create the letterhead in Word, type the text for the letter, then copy elements of the Word letterhead to the Excel invoice.

Link Invoice and Letter in Word

You will copy selected prices directly from Excel and paste them into Word as links. When you change the prices in the Excel invoice, the prices displayed in the Word letter will also change.

When you have completed Project 1, your invoice form and letter will appear as illustrated in Figures P1-1 and P1-2.

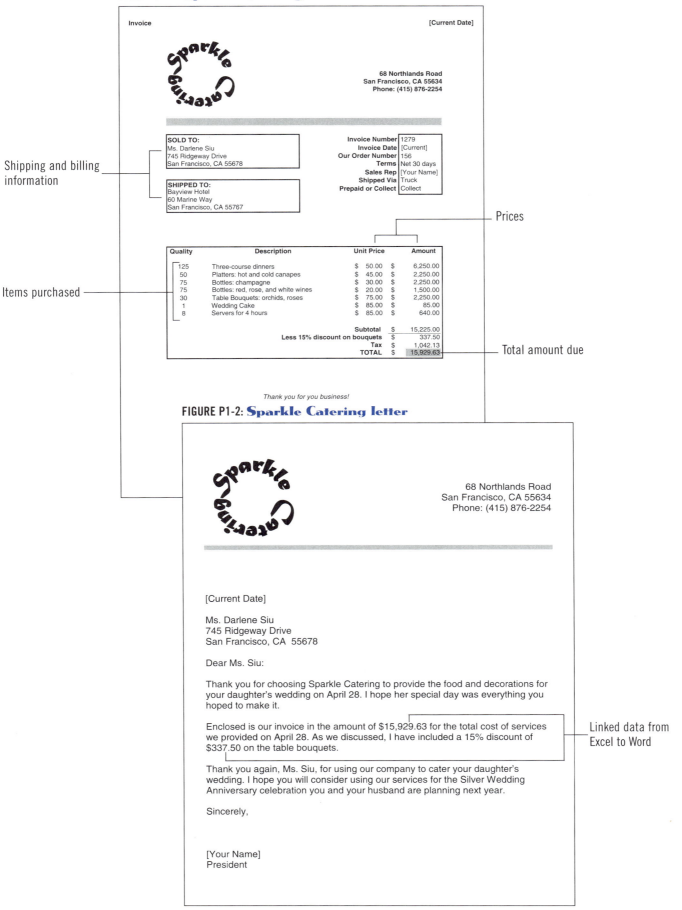

FIGURE P1-1: Sparkle Catering invoice

FIGURE P1-2: Sparkle Catering letter

PROJECT 1: LINKED INVOICE AND LETTER FOR SPARKLE CATERING

activity:

Create the Invoice in Excel

You will first create and enhance the Invoice form in Excel then perform the required calculations.

Hint

To open a new workbook, you can click the New Office Document button on the Office Shortcut bar

steps:

1. Open a new, blank Excel workbook

   Start by entering the labels for the name and address of the invoice recipient and the shipping location.

2. Click cell **A12**, enter and enhance the labels for cells **A12** to **A20** to match Figure P1-3, then save your worksheet as **Invoice for Sparkle Catering** on the disk where you plan to save all of your files for this book

   You start in cell A12 because you want to leave plenty of room for the heading elements you will later copy from Word. Next, enter the billing information, starting in cell G12.

3. Click cell **G12**, then enter, align, and enhance the labels for cells **G12** to **G18** and cells **H12** to **H18**, as shown in Figure P1-3

   Next, enter the list of items purchased by Ms. Siu, starting in cell A25.

4. Click cell **A25**, enter the labels and values, as shown in Figure P1-4, center the values in column A, then right-align and bold the labels in cells **G34** to **G37**

   Next, enhance selected labels.

5. Select cells **A25** to **H25**, click the **Bold button**, click the **Center button**, select cells **B25** to **F25**, click the **Merge and Center button** on the Formatting toolbar, select cells **G26** to **H37**, then click the **Currency Style button** on the Formatting toolbar

   Next, enter the formulas required to extend the invoice. You just multiply the Quantity by the Unit Price to determine the total amount due for each item.

6. Click cell **H26**, enter the formula **=A26*G26**, press **[Enter]**, click cell **H26** again, then drag the corner handle of cell **H26** down to cell **H32** to copy the formula

   Next, you'll calculate the Subtotal, 7% Sales Tax, the 15% discount, and the total due.

7. Select cells **H26** to **H34**, click the **AutoSum button** on the Standard toolbar, click cell **H35**, enter the formula **=H30*.15**, press **[Enter]**, enter the formula **=(H34-H35)*.07** in cell H36, press **[Enter]**, enter the formula to subtract the discount from the sum of cells **H34** and **H36** in cell H37, then press **[Enter]**

   You should see $16,186.43 in cell H37. Next, enclose selected cells in solid borders, and save your worksheet.

8. Select cells **A12** to **D15**, click the **Borders list arrow**, click the **Thick Solid Outside border** (last column, last row), apply the same border style to cells **A17** to **D20**, cells **H12** to **H18**, and cells **A25** to **H37**, add a bottom border to cell **H34** and shading to cell **H37**, then save your worksheet

   Compare your worksheet to Figure P1-5 (you may need to scroll to see it all). Go on to create the letter in Word that you will then link to the Invoice worksheet.

FIGURE P1-3: **Labels for cells A12 to H18**

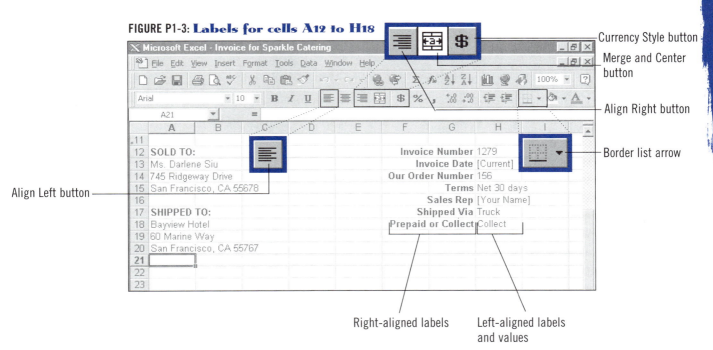

FIGURE P1-4: **Labels and values for cells A25 to H37**

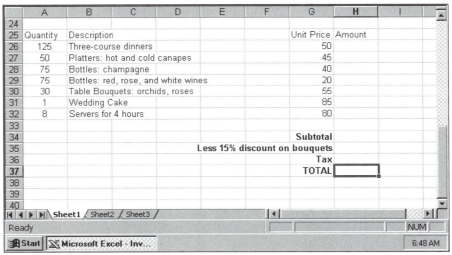

FIGURE P1-5: **Worksheet with invoice data**

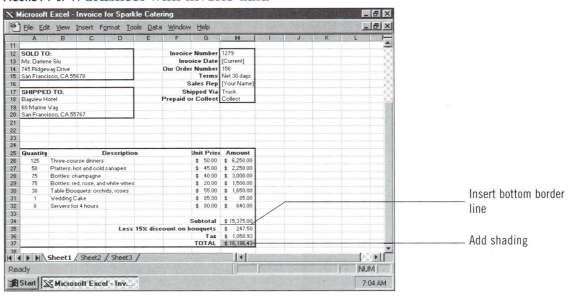

DOCUMENT LINKING IN A-5

LINKED INVOICE FORM AND LETTER FOR SPARKLE CATERING

activity:

Create the Letter in Word

You need to modify the document style, create an attractive letterhead for the Word letter, then enter the text for the letter.

Hint
Click the New Office Document button on the Office Shortcut bar.

steps:

1. Open a new Word document, switch to **Page Layout View** and display the paragraph marks
   Next, modify the document style.

2. Click **Format** on the menu bar, click **Style**, click **Modify**, click **Format**, click **Font**, select the **Arial** font and a font size of **12**, click **OK**, click **OK**, click **Apply**, then save the document as **Letter for Sparkle Catering**
   Next, create the WordArt object for the letterhead.

Trouble
If the Drawing toolbar is not visible, click View on the menu bar, point to Toolbars, then click Drawing.

3. Press **[Enter]** three times, click the first paragraph mark, click the **Insert WordArt button** on the Drawing toolbar, select the third WordArt style in the first row, click **OK**, type **Sparkle Catering**, click the **Font list arrow**, select **Matura MT Script Capitals**, then click **OK**
   The WordArt object and the WordArt toolbar appear.

4. Click the **WordArt Shape button** on the WordArt toolbar, then select the **Circle (Pour) shape**
   Next, reduce the size of the WordArt object.

5. Drag the bottom right corner handle up to reduce the size of the object to approximately **1.5"** high and wide, then click away from the object to deselect it
   Next, enter the address of Sparkle Catering at the right side of the document.

Time To Save ✓

6. Click the fourth paragraph mark, press **[Ctrl][R]**, then type the address, as shown in Figure P1-6
   Next, insert a thick gray border line under the WordArt object and the company address.

7. Press **[Enter]** four times, press **[Ctrl][L]** to return to the left margin, click **Format** on the menu bar, click **Borders and Shading**, click the **Width list arrow**, select **6 pt**, click the **Color list arrow**, select **Gray-25%**, click at the top of the Preview box, then click **OK**
   Next, enter the current date and type the text for the letter.

Hint
If the Office Assistant appears asking if you want help typing the letter, you can click Cancel or click Just type the letter without help.

8. Press **[Enter]** four times, click **Insert** on the menu bar, click **Date and Time**, select the date format you prefer, click **OK**, press **[Enter]** twice after the date, enter the text for the letter, as shown in Figure P1-6, then save the document
   Go on to copy the elements of the letterhead to the invoice in Excel, and then link the invoice with the letter.

FIGURE P1-6: Company address and letter text

68 Northlands Road
San Francisco, CA 55634
Phone: (415) 876-2254

— Right-align the company address

— Insert a 6-point, gray, top border

[Current Date] — Insert the current date

Ms. Darlene Siu
745 Ridgeway Drive
San Francisco, CA 55678

Dear Ms. Siu:

Thank you for choosing Sparkle Catering to provide the food and decorations for your daughter's wedding on April 28. I hope her special day was everything you hoped to make it.

Enclosed is our invoice in the amount of for the total cost of services we provided on April 28. As we discussed, I have included a 15% discount of on the table bouquets.

— Total price will be inserted here

— Discount will be inserted here

Thank you again, Ms. Siu, for using our company to cater your daughter's wedding. I hope you will consider using our services for the Silver Wedding Anniversary celebration you and your husband are planning next year.

Sincerely,

[Your Name]
President

DOCUMENT LINKING   IN A-7

PROJECT 1

LINKED INVOICE AND LETTER FOR SPARKLE CATERING

activity:

Link Invoice and Letter in Word

You will need to switch back and forth between the letter in Word and the invoice in Excel. To do this, you can click on the Microsoft Word or Microsoft Excel buttons at the bottom of the screen or you can also press [Alt][Tab] to switch between the programs. First you will copy the elements of the letterhead from Word to Excel, then copy selected amounts from Excel and paste them as links into Word.

steps:

1. With the Word letter displayed, click the **WordArt** object, click the **Copy button** on the Standard toolbar, switch to Excel, right-click cell **A1**, then click **Paste**

    The WordArt object appears in Excel. Next, drag the logo into the upper-left corner of the worksheet.

2. Position the pointer on the logo so it changes to ⇔, then drag the logo as far to the left and top of the worksheet as possible

    Next, copy the company address from Word to Excel.

3. Switch to Word, select the three lines of the company address, click 📋, switch to Excel, right-click cell **H4**, click **Paste**, then click the **Bold** **B** and **Align Right** buttons

    Finally you will add a shaded line under the letterhead in Excel by reducing the height of row 10, then enhancing cells A10 to H10 with a gray fill.

4. Point the mouse between the **10** and **11** on the worksheet frame, drag the mouse up to reduce the height of row 10 to approximately 4.50, as shown in Figure P1-7, select cells **A10** to **H10**, click the **Fill Color list arrow**, then click the **Light Gray box**

    Next, copy selected prices from Excel to Word.

5. Click cell **H37**, click 📋, switch to Word, then click after the first occurrence of the word "of" in the second paragraph of the letter, as shown in Figure P1-8

    Next, you'll use the Paste Special command to paste the price as a link. Note that you cannot use the Paste button to create links.

6. Click **Edit** on the menu bar, click **Paste Special**, click the **Paste link option button**, click **Unformatted Text**, click **OK**, then delete the extra space after the link

    The value in cell H37 appears. Next, copy the discount Ms. Siu received on the table bouquets from cell H35 in Excel.

7. Switch to Excel, click cell **H35**, click 📋, switch to Word, click after **15% discount of** in the second paragraph, as shown in Figure P1-8, paste the value as a **link (unformatted text)**, then delete the extra space after the link

    Next, see what happens when you change the values in the Excel worksheet.

8. Switch to Excel, reduce the price for the champagne to **$30.00**, increase the price for the table bouquets to **$75.00**, note the new totals, then switch to Word

    The new total amount is $15,929.63, as shown in Figure P1-8. Next, refer to Figures P1-8 and P1-9 to format the invoice and letter for printing.

9. Switch to Excel, type **Thank you for your business!** in cell A44, format it with italics, then center it across cells **A44** to **H44**, click **File**, click **Page Setup**, select the **Horizontally** and **Vertically check boxes** on the Margins tab, create a **Custom Header** on the Header tab, then print a copy

    The text for the header appears in Figure P1-9.

10. Switch to Word, view the letter in **Whole page view**, add some blank lines above the date to center the letter attractively on the page, then print a copy

Time To
✓ Save all documents
✓ Close

FIGURE P1-7: Row 9 height reduced

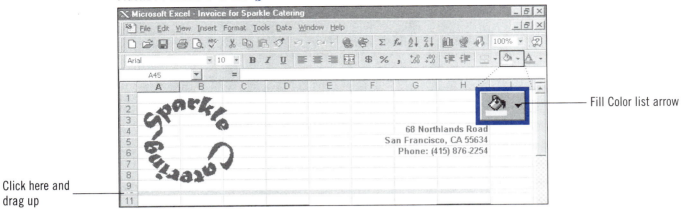

FIGURE P1-8: Completed letter

FIGURE P1-9: Completed invoice

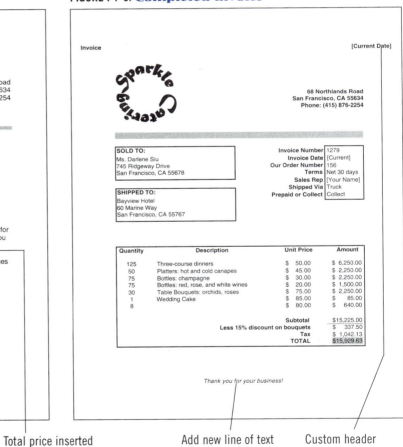

OVERVIEW

Guest Survey Results for Royal Palms Hotel

As the manager of the Royal Palms Hotel on Harbour Island in the Bahamas, you have compiled the results of a Guest Satisfaction Survey completed by 2000 guests. You want to use Excel to organize these results into charts and then create a one-page summary of the results in a Word document that includes the charts you created in Excel. To create the Guest Survey Results you will **Create Charts in Excel, Create the Summary in Word**, and then **Link the Excel Charts with the Word Summary**.

activity:

Create Charts in Excel

Hint
To wrap the text in cells B3 to G3, select cells B3 to G3, right-click, click Format Cells, click the Alignment tab, then click the Wrap text check box.

steps:

1. Display a new blank workbook in Excel, set up the Survey Results worksheet, as shown in Figure P2-1, then save it as **Royal Palms Survey Charts**
   The values entered in cells B4 to G7 represent the total *number of responses to each of the four criteria in each category. You need to convert these values to percentages.*

2. Select cells **A3** to **G7**, click the **Copy button**, click cell **A10**, click the **Paste button**, click cell **B11**, enter the formula **=B4/$B$8*100%**, then press **[Enter]**
   You will see 0.31 in cell B11. Next, copy the formula to cells B12 through B14 and then across to cell G14.

3. Click cell **B11**, drag the corner handle down to cell **B14**, then drag the corner handle of cell **B14** across to cell **G14**, and click the **Percent Style button** on the Formatting toolbar
   Next, you'll create a column chart from the data in cells A10 to G14.

Trouble
If the Office Assistant offers help, click No.

4. Select cells **A10** to **G14**, click the **ChartWizard button** on the Standard toolbar, click **Next** to accept the Column chart, then click **Next** to accept the selected data range
   Next, enter the chart title and titles for the X-axis and Y-axis, and move and resize the chart.

5. Enter **Guest Survey Results** as the chart title, **Guest Facilities** as the X-axis title, and **Response Percentages** as the Y-axis title, click **Next**, click **Finish**, use the mouse to move and resize the chart so it occupies **B21** through **G40**, right-click on any x-axis label, click **Format Axis**, click the **Font tab**, change the font size to **10 pts**, then click **OK**
   Next, remove the chart border.

Hint
You might need to move the Chart Wizard dialog box to select the columns.

6. Double-click the **chart**, click the **Patterns tab** in the Format Chart Area dialog box, click the **None option button** in the Border section, then click **OK**, then click away from the column chart to deselect it
   Next, create a pie chart that displays the breakdown of responses in the Overall Rating column.

7. Click [icon], click **Pie**, click **Next**, click the **Collapse dialog box button** at the end of the Data range text box, select cells **A11** through **A14**, type a comma, select cells **G11** through **G14**, then click the **Restore dialog box button** in the Source Data-Data range window
   Compare your screen to Figure P2-2.

Time To
✓ Save

8. Click **Next**, enter **Overall Rating Breakdown** as the chart title, click **Next**, click **Finish**, drag and resize the pie chart so it occupies approximately the range **H21** through **M37**, as shown in Figure P2-3, then double-click the chart and remove the chart border

FIGURE P2-1: Worksheet setup

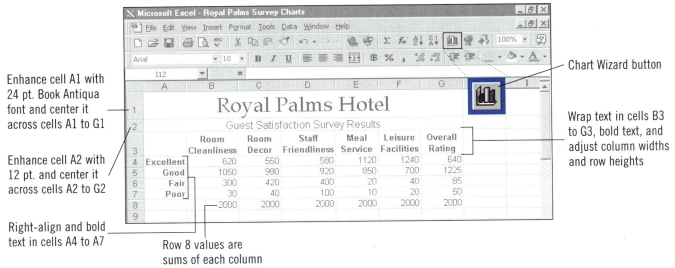

- Enhance cell A1 with 24 pt. Book Antiqua font and center it across cells A1 to G1
- Enhance cell A2 with 12 pt. and center it across cells A2 to G2
- Right-align and bold text in cells A4 to A7
- Row 8 values are sums of each column
- Chart Wizard button
- Wrap text in cells B3 to G3, bold text, and adjust column widths and row heights

FIGURE P2-2: Data range selected in Chart wizard

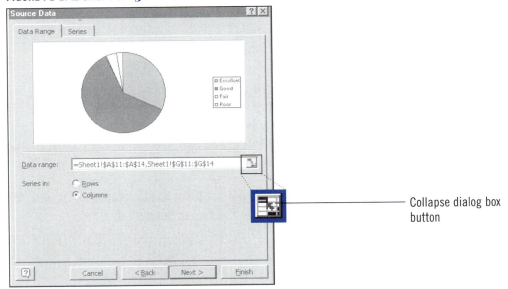

- Collapse dialog box button

FIGURE P2-3: Completed column and pie charts

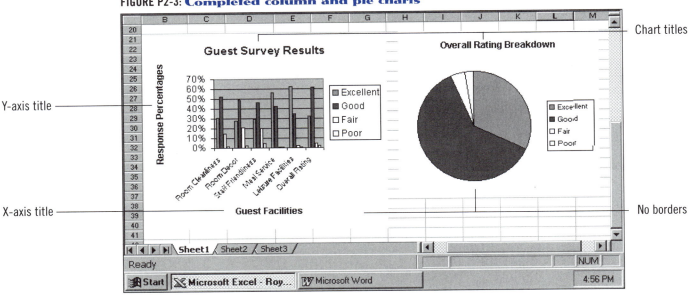

- Y-axis title
- X-axis title
- Chart titles
- No borders

Figure P2-3 shows the charts at 75% zoom. Go on to create a summary of the survey results in Word.

GUEST SURVEY RESULTS FOR ROYAL PALMS HOTEL

activity:

Create the Summary in Word

To create the summary in Word, you will first change the margins and select landscape orientation, then you will create a text box and enter the title of the document, and finally you will turn on columns and enter the text.

steps:

Trouble
If an alert box appears warning you that a margin is set outside the printable area of the page, click fix to fix the problem and close the alert box.

1. Switch to a blank document in Word, click **File** on the menu bar, click **Page Setup**, click the **Margins tab**, change all four margins to **.5"**, click the **Paper Size** tab, click the **Landscape option button**, then click **OK**

   Next, use the Text Box button to draw the box and enter the name of the hotel.

2. If necessary click the **Drawing button** on the Standard toolbar to display the Drawing toolbar, press **[Enter]** five times, click the **AutoShapes menu button**, point to **Basic Shapes**, select the **Rounded Rectangle** (first column, second row), drag to create a rectangle about ½" high by 4½" wide next to the top paragraph mark, then save your document as **Royal Palms Hotel Survey Results**

   Next, add text to the shape and format the text.

3. Click the **Text Box button** on the Drawing toolbar, click in the rectangle you just drew, change the font to **Arial** and the font size to **18**, click the **Bold button** on the Formatting toolbar, type **Royal Palms Hotel Survey Results**, click the **Center button** on the Formatting toolbar, select **Royal Palms Hotel**, change the font to **Algerian**, then widen the rectangle if necessary

   Next, you will change the fill color of the rectangle.

4. Click the text box to select it, click the **Fill Color list arrow** on the Drawing toolbar, click one of the **Light Gray boxes**, then click outside the logo to deselect it

   Your text box looks quite snazzy! Next, you'll turn on columns and enter the text describing the survey results.

5. Click in the last paragraph below the text box, click **Format** on the menu bar, click **Columns**, select the **Two Column** format, click the **Line between check box**, click the **Apply to list arrow**, click **This point forward**, then click **OK**

6. Type the text for the first column, as shown in Figure P2-5, then press **[Enter]**

Time To
√ Save

7. Click **Insert** on the menu bar, click **Break**, click the **Column Break option button**, click **OK**, then type the text for column 2, as shown in Figure P2-5

   Now go on to copy the charts from Excel into Word, and then format the Word summary for printing.

FIGURE P2-4: Completed text box

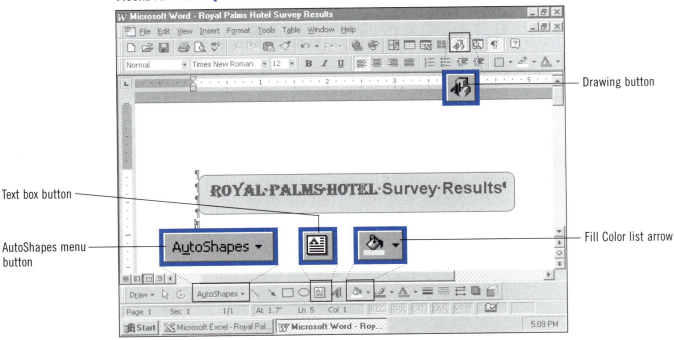

FIGURE P2-5: Text for columns 1 and 2

ROYAL PALMS HOTEL Survey Results

The Royal Palms Hotel is proud to announce the results of its annual survey. This year, 2,000 guests participated in the survey. The guests were asked to rate the following categories of service in terms of four criteria: Excellent, Good, Fair, and Poor.

- Room Cleanliness
- Room Decor
- Staff Friendliness
- Meal Service
- Leisure Facilities
- Overall Rating

As displayed in the column chart below, our Leisure Facilities received the highest rating. However, a significant percentage of our guests rated Staff Friendliness as Poor. The Royal Palms Hotel will initiate a series of staff training seminars to ensure that next year's survey shows a more favorable rating.

The pie chart displayed below breaks down the Overall Rating in terms of the four rating criteria: Excellent, Good, Fair, and Poor.

We can be proud that an overwhelming majority of our guests rated the Royal Palms Hotel as either Excellent or Good.

PROJECT 2

GUEST SURVEY RESULTS FOR ROYAL PALMS HOTEL

activity:

Link the Excel Charts with the Word Summary

You need to copy the column chart and the pie chart from Excel and then paste them as links into Word. You will then add a picture from the ClipArt Gallery, format the Word summary for printing, update the chart information in Excel, then print the Word summary.

steps:

Trouble
If the column chart appears at the top of column 2, drag the handles to reduce the chart size slightly so that it appears at the bottom of column 1. If this doesn't work, you might have inserted the chart after the column break. Try again.

1. Switch to Excel, click the **Column chart** to select it, click the **Copy button** on the Standard toolbar, switch to Word, click below **more favorable rating** in column 1, click **Edit** on the menu bar, click **Paste Special**, click the **Paste link option button** then click **OK**

   Next, you'll insert the pie chart in column 2.

2. Switch to Excel, click the **Pie chart** to select it, then copy and paste it as a link into Word, as shown in Figure P2-6

   Next, you need to format the Word document for printing. Your first step is to change the font of the text.

3. Press **[Ctrl][A]** to select all the text, select the **Arial** font, select **10 pt**, click the text to deselect it, then, if necessary, drag the column chart down a little so the last line of text in the first column appears above it

   Next, view the document in Whole Page view.

4. Click **View** on the menu bar, click **Zoom**, click the **Whole page option button**, then click **OK**

   Insert a picture from the Microsoft ClipArt Gallery.

Trouble
If you do not have this ClipArt image, choose another one.

5. Click after the text in column 2, press **[Enter]**, click **Insert** on the menu bar, point to **Picture**, click **Clip Art**, click **Entertainment**, select the **Fireworks picture** (called **Success Celebration Fireworks Sparks**), then click **Insert**

   Next, adjust the columns.

6. Click at the end of the paragraph before the column chart, and press **[Enter]**, then, if necessary, adjust the size and position of the two charts so that they appear as shown in Figure P2-6

7. Click the picture to select it, position the picture as shown in Figure P2-6, then change the zoom back to **100%**

   You've discovered that the Overall Rating results are incorrect. Fortunately you linked the survey data displayed in the Excel charts with the Word summary. When you change the values related to the charts in Excel, the charts in Word will also be updated.

Time To
✓ Save
✓ Print
✓ Close all documents

8. Look at the pie chart in Word, switch to Excel, change the value in cell **G5** to **800** and the value in cell **G6** to **510**, then switch back to Word

   As you can see, the "Fair" slice in the pie chart has increased considerably as a result of the new values you entered in Excel. Your Survey Results Summary is complete. Compare it with Figure P2-6.

Integration

FIGURE P2-6: Completed summary of Royal Palms Hotel Survey Results

ROYAL PALMS HOTEL Survey Results

The Royal Palms Hotel is proud to announce the results of its annual survey. This year, 2,000 guests participated in the survey. The guests were asked to rate the following categories of service in terms of four criteria: Excellent, Good, Fair, and Poor.

- Room Cleanliness
- Room Decor
- Staff Friendliness
- Meal Service
- Leisure Facilities
- Overall Rating

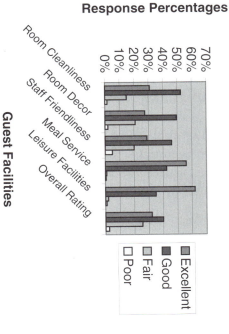

As displayed in the column chart below, our Leisure Facilities received the highest rating. However, a significant percentage of our guests rated Staff Friendliness as Poor. The Royal Palms Hotel will initiate a series of staff training seminars to ensure that next year's survey shows a more favorable rating.

The pie chart displayed below breaks down the Overall Rating in terms of the four rating criteria: Excellent, Good, Fair, and Poor.

Overall Rating Breakdown

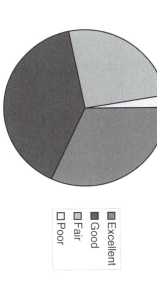

We can be proud that an overwhelming majority of our guests rated the Royal Palms Hotel as either Excellent or Good.

DOCUMENT LINKING IN A-15

OVERVIEW

Price List for rainbow BATH SALTS

You are the owner of rainbow BATH SALTS, a small, home-based business in Auckland, New Zealand, that sells uniquely scented bath salts in 100-gram and one-kilo packages. You distribute your bath salts to gift shops, department stores, and bath specialty stores all over New Zealand. You have now decided to start shipping your bath salts to stores in Australia. To advertise your product you will create an attractively formatted price list in Word that includes a worksheet created in Excel. First you will **Create the Price List in Excel** and then you will **Set Up the Price List in Word**.

activity:

Create the Price List in Excel

As you create the price list in Excel, you will take advantage of the AutoComplete feature to save you from typing similar labels more than once.

steps:

1. Display a blank Excel workbook, type **Product** in cell A1, type **Size** in cell B1, type **Price** in cell C1, then save your worksheet as **Rainbow Bath Salts Worksheet**

   Next, enter data for the first product in cell A2.

2. Click cell **A2**, type **Raspberry Swirl**, press **[Tab]**, type **100 grams**, press **[Tab]**, type **4.50**, then widen column A, as shown in Figure P3-1

   Next, use some time-saving methods to enter the remaining data.

3. Click cell **A3**, type **R**, press **[Tab]**, type **1 kilo**, press **[Tab]**, type **=C2*10**, then press **[Enter]**

   The formula in cell C3 multiplies the value in cell C2 by 10 to determine the cost of one kilo of the Raspberry Swirl bath salts, because 100 grams multiplied by 10 is equal to one kilo. Therefore the cost of one kilo of Raspberry Swirl is ten times the cost of 100 grams. Next, you'll copy this formula down to cell C17.

4. Click cell **C3** then drag the corner handle down to cell **C17**

   Some of the cells contain values displayed in scientific notation because the formula has continually multiplied the value in cell C2 by 10. Don't worry! As you enter the 100-gram price for each of the products, these numbers will change to the correct amounts.

5. Click cell **A4**, type **Citrus Heaven**, press **[Tab]**, type **100 g**, press **[Tab]**, type **3.75**, then press **[Enter]**

   "100 grams" appears in cell B4 thanks to the handy AutoComplete feature. Also note that the one-kilo price (37.5) appears in cell C5. Pressing [Enter] move the active cell to the next empty cell in the table. Next, go on to enter the remaining data for the price list.

6. Enter the remaining data for the price list, as shown in Figure P3-1, then format cells **C2** to **C17** in the **Currency Style**

   Note that you still need to enter the 100-gram prices in column C. The one-kilo prices appear automatically. Your next step is to display the list in alphabetical order.

Time To
✓ Save

7. Click anywhere in column A, then click the **Sort Ascending button** on the Standard toolbar

   The price list appears in alphabetical order, as seen in Figure P3-2.

FIGURE P3-1: **Price list data**

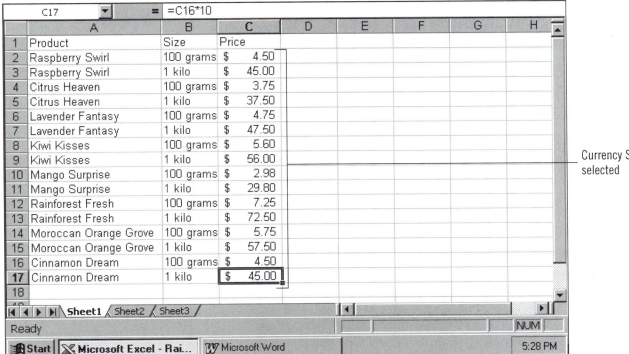

Currency Style selected

FIGURE P3-2: **Sorted price list**

Clues to Use

AutoComplete Feature

When you start to type a label into a cell, Excel checks the surrounding cells for similar data. If Excel finds similar data, it automatically completes the entry for you. For example if you have entered "Bath Salts" in cell A1, then type "B" in cell A2, Excel immediately enters "Bath Salts."

PRICE LIST FOR RAINBOW BATH SALTS

activity:

Set Up the Price List in Word

You need to set up a Word document, copy the price list from Excel to Word, then use the Word Table AutoFormat features to display the price list information attractively. You will first create a WordArt object for Price List.

steps:

1. In a blank Word document, press **[Enter]** five times, display the Drawing toolbar, click at the first paragraph mark, click the **Insert WordArt button** on the Drawing toolbar, create **rainbow BATH SALTS Price List** as a WordArt object as shown in Figure P3-3 using the **Arial Rounded MT Bold font, 28 pts**, then use the left, yellow adjustment handle to make the curve more pronounced
   Next, view the document in page width to make sure the WordArt is centered.

2. Click **View** on the menu bar, click **Zoom**, click the **Page width option button**, click **OK**, then position the WordArt so it is centered horizontally on the page
   Next, you'll type and format the two paragraphs of text.

3. Type the two paragraphs of text, as shown in Figure P3-3, press **[Ctrl][A]**, change the font size to **14**, then save the document as **Rainbow Bath Salts Price List**
   Next, position the insertion point where you want to insert the Excel worksheet.

4. Click the selected text to deselect it, click under the text, then press **[Enter]** four times

5. Display Excel, select cells **A1** to **C17**, then press **[Ctrl][C]**
   [Ctrl][C] is the Copy command used in all Windows applications.

6. Display Word, click at the last insertion point, click **Edit** on the menu bar, click **Paste Special**, click the **Paste link option button**, then click **OK** and save your document
   The Excel worksheet appears in the Word document. Next, you need to use Table AutoFormat to display the data attractively.

7. Click anywhere in the table, click **Table** on the menu bar, click **Table AutoFormat**, click **Contemporary** (you will need to scroll down), click the **AutoFit check box** to deselect it, then click **OK**

8. Use your mouse to select the table, change the font size to **12**, adjust the column widths so all the text fits as shown in Figure P3-3, click **Table** on the menu bar, click **Cell Height and Width**, click the **Row tab**, click the **Center radio button**, then click **OK**
   Next, you will update the price list in Excel.

9. Switch to Excel, change the 100-gram price for Cinnamon Dream, Lavender Fantasy, and Rainforest Fresh to **6.50**, switch back to Word, display the **Whole page view**, and adjust the spacing as required to match Figure P3-3
   Your rainbow BATH SALTS price list is complete.

Time To
- ✓ Save
- ✓ Print
- ✓ Close all documents

FIGURE P3-3: Completed price list for rainbow BATH SALTS

rainbow BATH SALTS Price List

Nothing can compare to a long, hot soak in a bath perfumed by rainbow BATH SALTS. Imagine yourself floating through a *Moroccan Orange Grove* or contemplating a *Cinnamon Dream* or even luxuriating in a *Raspberry Swirl*. The daily stresses and strains of modern life dissolve as you attain a new level of relaxation.

The price list displayed below contains just a sample of the fifty different fragrances distributed by rainbow BATH SALTS. Both 100-gram and 1-kilo sizes are available. To order a selection of rainbow BATH SALTS, call us in Auckland, New Zealand at (64) (9) 335-8890.

Product	Size	Price
Cinnamon Dream	100 grams	$ 6.50
Cinnamon Dream	1 kilo	$ 65.00
Citrus Heaven	100 grams	$ 3.75
Citrus Heaven	1 kilo	$ 37.50
Kiwi Kisses	100 grams	$ 5.60
Kiwi Kisses	1 kilo	$ 56.00
Lavender Fantasy	100 grams	$ 6.50
Lavender Fantasy	1 kilo	$ 65.00
Mango Surprise	100 grams	$ 2.98
Mango Surprise	1 kilo	$ 29.80
Moroccan Orange Grove	100 grams	$ 5.75
Moroccan Orange Grove	1 kilo	$ 57.50
Rainforest Fresh	100 grams	$ 6.50
Rainforest Fresh	1 kilo	$ 65.00
Raspberry Swirl	100 grams	$ 4.50
Raspberry Swirl	1 kilo	$ 45.00

Independent Challenges

INDEPENDENT CHALLENGE 1

Create an invoice in Excel, and then link it to a letter you create in Word. Fill in the boxes below with the required information, then set up your invoice in an Excel worksheet, create a letter in Word, copy some of the graphic elements in the Word letter to Excel, then copy some of the values in Excel, and paste them as links into the Word letter.

1. Determine the company name and type of business that will send the invoice. The type of company you select will determine the kinds of items you will list on the invoice form. For example, a ski touring company called Powder Trails could list items such as skis, boots, and poles, and services such as ski waxing and ski touring lessons. In the box below write the name of your company and five items or services that it sells:

   Company Name:

   Items to Sell:

   1.
   2.
   3.
   4.
   5.

2. In the box below identify the name and address of the company that has purchased the products or services listed in your invoice. You can include a different address under Shipped to: if the products will not be sent directly to the purchaser.

   Sold to:

   Shipped to:

3. Set up your invoice in Excel as follows:
   a. Leave about ten rows blank at the top of the invoice so that you can paste in elements from the letterhead you will create in Word.
   b. Right-align the labels in the billing section of your invoice.
   c. Enter the formulas required to make the following calculations:
      - Multiply the Quantity values by the Unit Price values, and display the results in the Amount column.
      - Add the values in the Amount column to determine the Subtotal.
      - Calculate a 15% discount on one of the items.
      - Calculate tax as 7% of the Subtotal value.
      - Add the Subtotal and Tax values.
      - Subtract the discount from the Subtotal and add Tax to determine the Total Amount Due.
   d. Save the invoice as "Invoice for [Company Name]" on your disk.
   e. Switch to Word, create an attractive letterhead (use WordArt and insert a picture, if you wish), then create and format a letter similar to the letter you created for Project 1.
   f. Switch to Excel, copy the total amount, then switch to Word, and paste the amount into the appropriate sentence in the letter.
   g. Copy elements of the WordArt letterhead to Excel.
   h. Save the letter as "Letter for [Company Name]" on your disk, then print a copy of both the Invoice and the Letter.

INDEPENDENT CHALLENGE 2

Create a Survey Results Summary for a company or organization of your choice. Refer to the summary you created in Project 2 for formatting ideas. Here are some tips for creating your summary:

1. Set up a Survey Results worksheet in Excel. Select categories appropriate to your company or organization. For example, if your company is a neighborhood restaurant, you could select such categories as Food Quality, Selection, Service, and Ambiance, or, if you choose to analyze a course you're taking at college, you could select such categories as Instructor Presentation, Relevance of Assignments, Course Materials, and Grading System. You can use the rating criteria used in Project 2 (i.e., Excellent, Good, Fair, and Poor) or select different rating criteria.
2. Convert the values that represent the total number of responses to each of the criteria in each category to percentages.
3. Create a column chart or a line chart based on the data in your worksheet.
4. Create a pie chart that shows the breakdown of responses in the Overall Rating column.
5. Switch to Word, set up a document with landscape orientation, include a WordArt object and a text box in the heading, select a two-format column, then enter three or four paragraphs of text that describe the survey and its results. Refer to Project 2 for ideas.
6. Copy the charts from Excel into the Word Summary. Remember to paste the charts as links into Word.
7. Make some changes to the data in the Excel worksheet. The charts copied into Word will also change.
8. Format the Word summary in Whole page view, add an appropriate picture, if you wish, then print a copy.
9. Save both the Excel worksheet and the Word summary as "Survey Results for [Company Name]". The appropriate extension (i.e., XLS or DOC) will be added automatically to differentiate the two files.

INDEPENDENT CHALLENGE 3

Create a price list in Excel for a selection of products sold by a company of your choice. As you create the price list, let the AutoComplete feature help minimize your typing time. When you have completed the price list, set up a Word document as you did in Project 3, then copy the Excel price list, and paste it as a link into Word. Format the Word price list attractively, include a WordArt object and a picture, and use the Table AutoFormat feature to present the data in the Excel price list attractively. Save the Excel and Word files as "Price List for [Company Name]."

INDEPENDENT CHALLENGE 4

Create an Excel worksheet that displays the projected income and expenses for Paradise Landscaping, a small home-based landscaping business in Atlanta. You will then use the data in the worksheet to create two charts, which you will link to a Projected Sales Summary you will create in Word.

1. Display a blank workbook in Excel, then set up a worksheet using data from the worksheet in Figure IC-1. To save time copy the values entered in column B across to column E.

FIGURE IC-1: Paradise Landscaping worksheet

	A	B	C	D	E	F
1		*Paradise Landscaping*				
2		Projected Income and Expenses: April to July 1998				
3		April	May	June	July	Totals
4	**Income**					
5	Landscaping Services	$12,500.00	$12,500.00	$12,500.00	$12,500.00	
6	Sales	$ 5,000.00	$ 5,000.00	$ 5,000.00	$ 5,000.00	
7	**Total Income**					
8						
9	**Expenses**					
10	Salaries	$ 5,000.00	$ 5,000.00	$ 5,000.00	$ 5,000.00	
11	Rent	$ 800.00	$ 800.00	$ 800.00	$ 800.00	
12	Advertising	$ 400.00	$ 400.00	$ 400.00	$ 400.00	
13	Equipment Lease	$ 800.00	$ 800.00	$ 800.00	$ 800.00	
14	Operating Costs	$ 500.00	$ 500.00	$ 500.00	$ 500.00	
15	Cost of Sales					
16	**Total Expenses**					
17						
18	**Total Profit**					
19						

2. Enter and copy the formulas required to calculate the following amounts:
   a. Total Monthly Income (cells B7 to E7)
   b. Total Four-month Income (cells F5 to F7)
   c. Cost of Sales: Value of Sales multiplied by 60% (i.e., B6*.6)
   d. Total Monthly Expenses (cells B16 to E16)
   e. Total Four-month Expenses (cells F10 to F16)
   f. Total Profit (cells B18 to F18): subtract the total expenses from the total income for each month
3. Create a pie chart that shows the breakdown of expenses by total amount. You will need to click the Chart Wizard button, and select cells A10 to A15 and cells F10 to F15. Call the pie chart "Breakdown of Expenses."
4. Switch to Word, create an attractive heading for a document called "Paradise Landscaping: Projected Sales Summary," include a picture if you wish, then write a paragraph or two of text to introduce the chart you created in Excel. Leave space in the paragraph for amounts (such as the total expenses and total income) that you will paste as links from Excel. For example you could include a sentence such as "The total projected expenses for April through July, 1998 are:" and then leave a space for the copied total expenses.
5. Copy the pie chart and any totals required from Excel, and paste them as links into Word.
6. Switch to Excel and modify the income and expense amounts for each month. For example you could increase the salaries expense for April and decrease it for July. Note the changes to the pie chart. Print the worksheet.
7. Switch to Word, update the pie chart, add a paragraph or two describing the actions you plan to take to increase sales and/or reduce expenses, and then format and print the Projected Sales Summary.
8. Save the Word document as "Paradise Landscaping Projected Sales Summary.DOC" and save the Excel document as "Paradise Landscaping Projected Sales Summary.XLS."

Visual Workshop

Create the Price List shown in Figure VW-1 in Excel, calculate the prices where indicated, sort cells A2 through A15 ascending, paste the worksheet as a link into Word, then modify the Word document so that it appears as shown in Figure VW-2. Note that some of the values are different in the Word version of the price list. Make the changes in Excel, and then update the link.

Save the worksheet and document as "Price List for SGN", print the worksheet and the document, then close all files.

FIGURE VW-1 *Price List worksheet*

	A	B	C
1	Product	Quantity	Price
2	Spicy Corn Fritters	10	$ 2.25
3	Spicy Corn Fritters	50	$ 11.25
4	Cilantro Rice Balls	10	$ 3.50
5	Cilantro Rice Balls	50	
6	Crab Stuffed Mushrooms	10	$ 5.50
7	Crab Stuffed Mushrooms	50	
8	Spinach and Pine Nut Quiches	10	$ 6.75
9	Spinach and Pine Nut Quiches	50	
10	Creamy Scallop Quiches	10	$ 8.50
11	Creamy Scallop Quiches	50	
12	Black Bean Stuffed Peppers	10	$ 2.50
13	Black Bean Stuffed Peppers	50	
14	Cheesy Potato Croquettes	10	$ 1.50
15	Cheesy Potato Croquettes	50	

— Calculate the required prices

CURRENT PRICE LIST

Product	Quantity	Price
Black Bean Stuffed Peppers	10	$ 2.50
Black Bean Stuffed Peppers	50	$ 12.50
Cheesy Potato Croquettes	10	$ 1.50
Cheesy Potato Croquettes	50	$ 7.50
Cilantro Rice Balls	10	$ 5.50
Cilantro Rice Balls	50	$ 27.50
Crab Stuffed Mushrooms	10	$ 8.00
Crab Stuffed Mushrooms	50	$ 40.00
Creamy Scallop Quiches	10	$ 8.50
Creamy Scallop Quiches	50	$ 42.50
Spicy Corn Fritters	10	$ 4.50
Spicy Corn Fritters	50	$ 22.50
Spinach and Pine Nut Quiches	10	$ 6.75
Spinach and Pine Nut Quiches	50	$ 33.75

FIGURE VW-2 *Suzy's Gourmet Nirvana Price List*

Microsoft ► Access Projects

Access 97

Database Creation

In This Unit You Will Create:

 ► **Inventory**

 ► **Artist Profiles**

 ► **Sales Information**

To survive and compete in the contemporary business world, companies and organizations need reliable information about their products or services, their customers, their suppliers, and their personnel. Suppose you run a fitness center and have decided to offer a special incentive plan to all the clients who joined the center in January of 1998. You could comb through all your paper files to find the clients, or you could use a relational database program, such as Access, to print out a list of all the clients who joined your center in January of 1998—or during any other time period you choose. A relational database program stores information in a variety of tables that you can link in order to find the information you need to perform a specific task. To use a database program effectively, you first determine appropriate categories of information (called fields), and then you formulate questions that help you retrieve the information you need. ► In this unit you will learn how to use Microsoft Access to set up a variety of databases and then ask questions that will lead Access to find the information you need to perform specific tasks.

DATABASE CREATION   AC A-1 ◄

OVERVIEW

Inventory for World Crafts

World Crafts is a nonprofit organization based in Toronto that sells crafts made by artisans all over the world. The profits from the sales are invested back into the artisans' communities to be used to build schools and hospitals, finance agricultural projects, and operate social programs. You are in charge of monitoring the inventory levels and placing orders with the suppliers who work directly with the artisans to distribute their products. For this project you will create a small database consisting of a Products table that contains 15 records and a Suppliers table that contains four records. Your principal goal in this project is to find out which products you need to order and the supplier you need to contact to place the order. Four activities are required to build an inventory database for World Crafts and then produce a list of the products to order.

Project Activities

Set Up Products Table

The Products table shown in Figure P1-1 lists 15 of the products sold by World Crafts. This table consists of six fields, including a field for Units in Stock. You will use the Table Wizard to create the Products table.

Set Up Suppliers Table

The Suppliers table lists the four suppliers who obtain the products from the artisans and then ship them to World Crafts. You will use the Form Wizard to enter the data required for the Suppliers table. Figure P1-2 shows a form created for one of the suppliers.

Create Queries

You will create queries to find information listed in the Products table and Suppliers table of the World Crafts database. You will be most concerned with the data entered in the Units in Stock field.

Format and Print an Order Report

You will create a query that lists all the products that you need to order, along with the distributors you need to contact. You will then create and format a report that presents this information in an easy-to-read and attractive format. Figure 1-3 shows the Order report you will create.

FIGURE P1-1: Datasheet view of Products table for World Crafts database

Field names ⎯⎯⎯

Records ⎯⎯⎯

Product ID	Product Name	Region	Supplier ID	Units In Stock	Unit Price
1	Jade Earrings	Asia	1	15	$45.50
2	Soapstone Walrus	Arctic	2	9	$220.00
3	Zebra Mobile	Africa	3	5	$15.00
4	Rainforest Jigsaw	South America	4	8	$22.95
5	Bamboo Wind Chimes	Asia	1	12	$25.95
6	Teak Carving: Elephant	Africa	3	15	$180.00
7	Batik Silk Scarf	Asia	1	8	$40.00
8	Soapstone Seal	Arctic	2	4	$220.00
9	Woven Wall Plaque	South America	4	8	$55.00
10	Walrus Ivory Earrings	Arctic	2	15	$80.00
11	Pottery Tea Set	South America	4	12	$120.00
12	Stuffed Hippo	Africa	3	9	$55.00
13	Embroidered Caftan	Asia	1	13	$85.00
14	Carved Lion Bookends	Africa	3	7	$110.00
15	Wooden Flute	South America	4	18	$95.00

FIGURE P1-2: Form for Supplier 1

Field names ⎯⎯⎯

World Crafts Suppliers

- Supplier ID: 1
- Supplier Name: Far East Imports
- Region: Asia
- Email Address: fareast@pacific.com

⎯⎯⎯ 1 record

FIGURE P1-3: Completed Order report

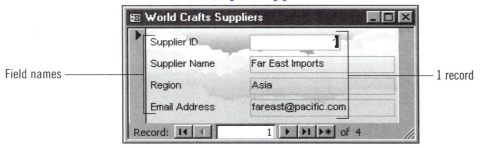

Clues to Use

Database Design

A "real" database for a viable company such as World Crafts would, of course, contain considerably more records because the company would need to sell more than 15 products to stay in business. However, the number of products has been reduced to minimize the amount of time you need to spend entering data.

INVENTORY FOR WORLD CRAFTS

activity:

Set Up Products Table

You first need to enter the data required for the Products table.

Hint

You can also click the New Office Document button on the Office Shortcut bar, or if Access is already running, click the New Database button on the Standard toolbar.

steps:

1. Start Access, click the **Blank Database option button** in the Microsoft Access startup dialog box, click **OK**, display the directory containing your disk (if necessary), double-click the **Filename text box**, type **World Crafts Inventory**, then click **Create**

   You need to create a table that lists information about World Crafts' products.

2. Click the **Tables tab**, if necessary, click **New**, click **Table Wizard**, then click **OK**

   You'll need to wait a few seconds while Access loads the Table Wizard. You could go directly to a blank datasheet; however, the Table Wizard automatically enters selected fields into your table, thereby saving you time.

3. Click **Products** in the Sample Tables list box, make sure **ProductID** is selected in the **Sample fields** list box, then click the **Select Single Field button**

   The ProductID field appears in the "Fields in my new table" list box. Next, enter the Product Name field, then enter and change the name of the CategoryID field.

Hint

If you select the wrong field, click the Remove Single Field button to return the field to the Sample Fields list.

4. Click to select **ProductName**, click **CategoryID**, click , click **Rename Field** under the Fields in my new table list box, type **Region**, click **OK**, then select the following fields: **SupplierID**, **UnitsInStock**, and **UnitPrice**

   You are ready to continue creating the Products table.

5. Click **Next**, type **World Crafts Products** for the table name, accept the default to let the Wizard set a primary key, click **Next**, accept the default to enter data directly into the table, then click **Finish**

   The Datasheet View appears. At present, no data appears in the six fields. Start by entering the data for the first record.

6. Press **[Tab]**, type **Jade Earrings**, press **[Tab]**, type **Asia**, then press **[Tab]**

   A warning message appears because you have entered the wrong kind of data into the Region field. Originally this field was called CategoryID, which Access formats as a field that contains only numbers. To enter text into this field, you need to display the Design view of the table and change the data type.

7. Click **OK** to remove the message, press **[Backspace]** until you erase "Asia," click the **View button** on the toolbar, click **Design View**, click **Number** in the Data Type column for Region, click the **Data Type list arrow**, then click **Text** as shown in Figure P1-4

   Next, return to Datasheet view.

Hint

You can press [Shift][Tab] if you need to move backwards to a previous cell.

8. Click the **View button** on the toolbar to switch to **Datasheet View**, click **Yes** to save the table, press **[Tab]** twice, type **Asia** in the Region field, then enter the remaining data for Record 1, as shown in Figure P1-5

   Just type the numbers for the Unit Price field. Access automatically formats the number in the Currency style. Next, enter the data for the next 14 records.

9. Enter the data for records 2 to 15, as shown in Figure P1-5, double-click on each column divider to resize the columns, click **File** on the menu bar, click **Close**, then click **Yes** if a save message appears

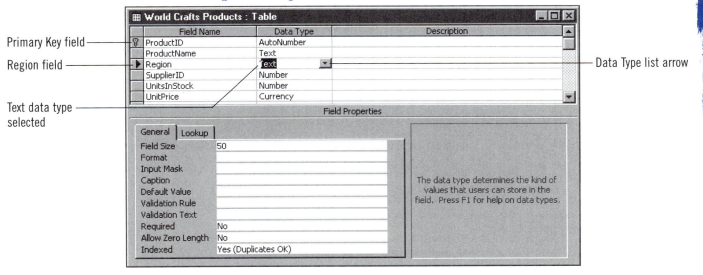

FIGURE P1-4: **Design view of Products table**

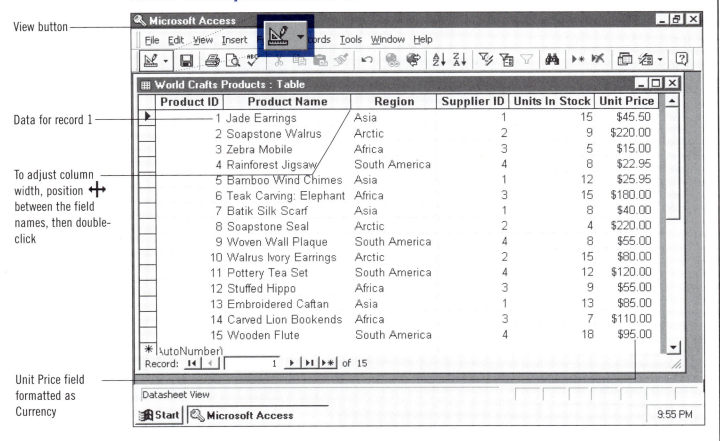

FIGURE P1-5: **Data for records 1 to 15**

INVENTORY FOR WORLD CRAFTS

activity:

Set Up Suppliers Table

The Suppliers table you created for a "real" business would include the address, phone numbers, and even e-mail address of each supplier. For the World Crafts Suppliers table, you'll save time by including only the name, region, and e-mail address of each of the four suppliers who send you the crafts made by the artisans in their region. You can use the Table Wizard to enter data for a table into a datasheet, or you can use the Form Wizard to enter the data into a form. You will use the Table Wizard to set up the Suppliers table, then use the Form Wizard to enter the data required.

steps:

1. Click the **Tables tab** in the Database window if it isn't already in front, click **New**, click **Table Wizard**, then click **OK**

   Next, select the fields you wish to include in the Suppliers table.

2. Click **Suppliers** in the list of Sample Tables (you will need to scroll down), then add **SupplierID**, **Supplier Name**, and **ContactName** to the Fields in my new table list box

   Next, change the name of the ContactName field to Region.

3. Click **Rename Field**, type **Region**, click **OK**, add **EmailAddress** to the table, click **Next**, type **World Crafts Suppliers**, then click **Next**

   Access asks you if your new table is related to any other tables in your current database. Tables that contain at least one common field can be related. Both the Products table and the Suppliers table contain two common fields: Region and Supplier ID. Next, you need to tell Access to relate these two tables.

4. Click **Relationships**, click the **One record in the 'World Crafts Suppliers' table option button**, as shown in Figure P1-6, click **OK**, click **Next**, check that the **Enter data directly into the table option button** is selected, then click **Finish**

   In a few moments the Datasheet view of the Suppliers table appears. However, you want to enter the data into Forms. Next, close the Datasheet view and use the Form Wizard to enter the data.

5. Click **File** on the menu bar, click **Close**, click the **Forms tab** in the Database window, click **New**, click **Form Wizard**, click **OK**, click the **Tables/Queries list arrow**, click **Table: World Crafts Suppliers**, click the **Select All Fields button** [>>], click **Next**, click **Next** to accept the **Columnar** layout, click **Clouds**, click **Next**, make sure the **Open the form to view or enter information option button** is selected, then click **Finish**

   In a few seconds a blank form appears. Next, enter the data required for the first supplier.

6. Press **[Tab]**, type **Far East Imports**, press **[Tab]**, type **Asia**, press **[Tab]**, type **fareast@pacific.com**, then press **[Tab]** twice to move to the Supplier Name field in form 2

   Next, complete the remaining forms.

7. Enter the data for the next three forms, as shown in Figures P1-7, P1-8, and P1-9, then close the last form

   You can now view the data for the World Crafts Suppliers in both individual forms and in a datasheet. Next, go on to create a variety of queries.

FIGURE P1-6: Relationships dialog box

Click here

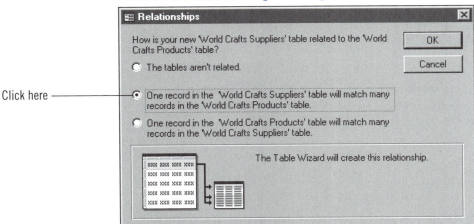

FIGURE P1-7: Data for Supplier 2

FIGURE P1-8: Data for Supplier 3

FIGURE P1-9: Data for Supplier 4

INVENTORY FOR WORLD CRAFTS

activity:

Create Queries

Now that you've set up the two tables for the World Crafts database, you will ask three questions—called **queries** in database language. These queries relate to specific actions you wish to perform using the data stored in the two tables. First you want to make a quick count of the products made in Asia. The fastest method of obtaining this information is to use the Filter tool in the Datasheet view of the World Crafts Products table.

steps:

1. Click the **Tables tab** in the Database window, double-click **World Crafts Products** to open it, click the first **Asia** entry in the Region field, then click the **Filter By Selection button** on the toolbar
   As you can see, four of the products are made in Asia. Next, remove the filter.

2. Click the **Remove Filter button** on the toolbar
   Next, you want to know how many of the products made in the Africa region are toys. You can't answer this query because you don't know which products are toys. Add a new field in the World Crafts Products table that designates each product's category (e.g., toy, jewelry, clothing, etc.) and then make the query.

3. Click the **View button** on the toolbar to switch to **Design View**, click the row selector to the left of SupplierID, click the **right mouse button**, click **Insert Rows**, click the blank **Field Name cell**, type **Category**, then press **[Tab]**
   The default data type is Text, which is fine in this case. You can always add new fields to a table just by displaying Design view. Next, return to Datasheet view, and enter the Category data for each record.

4. Click the **View button** on the toolbar to switch to **Datasheet View**, click **Yes** to save the table, enter the category for each product as shown in Figure P1-10, click **File** on the menu bar, then click **Close**
   Next, create a query that will list all the African products that are toys.

5. Click the **Queries tab** in the Database window, click **New**, click **Simple Query Wizard**, click **OK**, click the **Select All Fields button** to select all the fields in the World Crafts Products table, click **Next**, click **Next** to accept a Detail query, click the **Modify the query design option button**, then click **Finish**
   The design grid appears. Next, you need to tell Access to list only toys from Africa.

6. As shown in Figure 1-11, click the **Region Criteria cell**, type **Africa**, click the **Category Criteria cell** (you may need to scroll right to view it), type **Toy**, then click the **Run button** on the toolbar
   Two of the products from Africa are toys—the stuffed hippo and the zebra mobile.

Hint
You don't save this query because you will not use it again. Often you create queries to find a specific piece of information that you read off the screen before closing the query. If you need to view the information again, you can easily create a new query.

7. Click **File** on the menu bar, click **Close**, then click **No**
   World Crafts likes to keep at least 10 units of each product in their inventory. Next, you need to create a query to determine which products in the World Craft Products table have stock levels below 10.

8. Double-click **World Craft Products Query**, switch to **Design View**, scroll to and click the **UnitsInStock Criteria cell**, type **<10**, then click
   A datasheet listing all the products with fewer than 10 units in stock appears, as shown in Figure P1-12. These are the items that you need to order.

9. Click **File** on the menu bar, click **Close**, then click **No**
   You do not need to save the query table because you will next create a query table that lists all the products to order, along with the names of the suppliers that sell them.

FIGURE P1-10: Category records for World Crafts Products table

Product ID	Product Name	Region	Category	Supplier ID	Units
1	Jade Earrings	Asia	Jewelry	1	
2	Soapstone Walrus	Arctic	Art	2	
3	Zebra Mobile	Africa	Toy	3	
4	Rainforest Jigsaw	South America	Toy	4	
5	Bamboo Wind Chimes	Asia	Art	1	
6	Teak Carving: Elephant	Africa	Art	3	
7	Batik Silk Scarf	Asia	Clothing	1	
8	Soapstone Seal	Arctic	Art	2	
9	Woven Wall Plaque	South America	Art	4	
10	Walrus Ivory Earrings	Arctic	Jewelry	2	
11	Pottery Tea Set	South America	Household	4	
12	Stuffed Hippo	Africa	Toy	3	
13	Embroidered Caftan	Asia	Clothing	1	
14	Carved Lion Bookends	Africa	Household	3	
15	Wooden Flute	South America	Instrument	4	

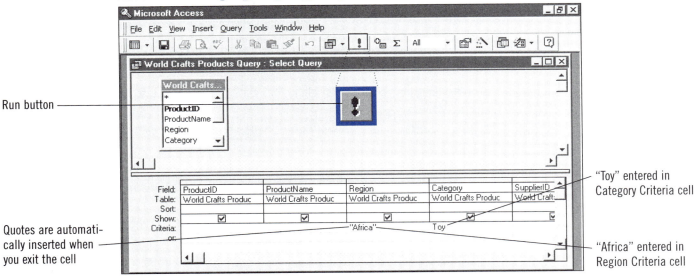

FIGURE P1-11: Design grid for Query 2

- Run button
- Quotes are automatically inserted when you exit the cell
- "Toy" entered in Category Criteria cell
- "Africa" entered in Region Criteria cell

FIGURE P1-12: Datasheet view of Query 3 results

Product ID	Product Name	Region	Category	Supplier ID	Units In
2	Soapstone Walrus	Arctic	Art	2	
3	Zebra Mobile	Africa	Toy	3	
4	Rainforest Jigsaw	South America	Toy	4	
7	Batik Silk Scarf	Asia	Clothing	1	
8	Soapstone Seal	Arctic	Art	2	
9	Woven Wall Plaque	South America	Art	4	
12	Stuffed Hippo	Africa	Toy	3	
14	Carved Lion Bookends	Africa	Household	3	

INVENTORY FOR WORLD CRAFTS

activity:

Format and Print an Order Report

You will create a query from both the World Crafts Products table and the Suppliers table to list the products you need to order and the names of the suppliers you need to contact, and then you will format and print an Order report.

steps:

1. Click **New** on the Queries tab in the Database window, click **Simple Query Wizard**, click **OK**, click the **Tables/Queries list arrow**, click **Table: World Crafts Products**, click the **Select All Fields button**, click the **Tables/Queries list arrow**, click **Table: World Crafts Suppliers**, then select **SupplierName** and **EmailAddress** for inclusion in the table

   Next, continue to build the query.

2. Click **Next**, click **Next** again, type **Items to Order** as the Query table name, then click **Finish**

   You need to display Design view, then tell Access to list all the items with fewer than 10 units in stock and to sort the results alphabetically by region.

Scroll right to view all the fields in the query table.

3. Switch to **Design View**, click the **UnitsInStock Criteria cell**, type **<10**, click the **Region Sort cell**, click the **Sort Cell list arrow**, click **Ascending**, then click the **Run button** on the toolbar

   You have your list of eight products to order and the names and e-mail addresses of the suppliers to contact. Next, format the query table as a report.

4. Click **File** on the menu bar, click **Close**, click **Yes**, click the **Reports tab**, click **New**, click **Report Wizard**, then click **OK**

   When the Report Wizard is loaded, you will select the Items to Order table you created in Step 2.

5. Click the **Tables/Queries list arrow**, click **Query: Items to Order**, then select the following fields: **ProductName**, **Region**, **Category**, **UnitPrice**, **SupplierName**, and **EmailAddress**

6. Click **Next**, click **by World Crafts Products**, if necessary, click **Next**, click **Region** in the list of groupings, click the **Select Single Field button** as shown in Figure P1-13, click **Next**, click **Next**, click the **Align Left 1 option button**, click the **Landscape option button**, click **Next**, click **Corporate**, click **Next**, type **1998 Inventory Items to Order**, then click **Finish**

   Next, view the entire page so you can see if all the field names and records are attractively positioned.

7. Click the **Zoom list arrow** on the toolbar, then click **Fit**

   The Unit Price field heading appears too far to the right. Next, switch to Report Design view, and move the field farther to the left.

8. Click the **View list arrow** on the toolbar, click **Design View**, click the top **Unit Price** label, press and hold **[Shift]**, click the bottom **Unit Price** label, move the mouse over a selected label until the appears, then drag the to move the two selected labels to the left, as shown in Figure P1-14

9. Click the **Print Preview button** on the toolbar, check the positioning of the Unit Price labels as shown in Figure P1-15, click the **Print button** on the toolbar, close the report, click **Yes**, then close the database

FIGURE P1-13: Grouping levels

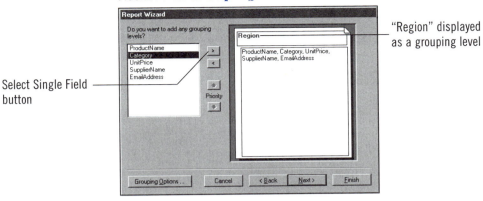

Select Single Field button

"Region" displayed as a grouping level

FIGURE P1-14: Position of Unit Price labels in Design View

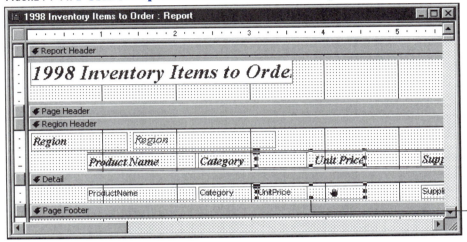

Unit Price labels selected and dragged to the left

FIGURE P1-15: Completed report in Print Preview screen

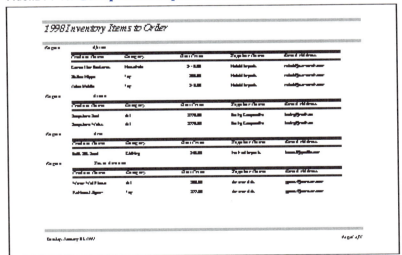

Clues to Use

Formatting Reports

If you want to modify the positioning of the Unit Price labels or any other labels, switch back to Design view, make the adjustments required, then view the results in the Print Preview screen. To format a report in Access, you need to switch frequently between Design view and the Print Preview screen.

OVERVIEW

Artist Profiles for Pacific Art Gallery

The Pacific Art Gallery in northern California exhibits paintings by local and international artists. As the manager of the Pacific Art Gallery, you decide to set up a database that you can use to identify the artists who have sold the most paintings, the most popular styles of art purchased, and which artists sold paintings for more than $2,000. You will **Create the Painting Sales and Artists Tables**, **Create and Modify a Query**, and then **Format and Print a Report**.

activity:

Create the Painting Sales and Artists Tables

Your first task is to create the two tables in the Pacific Art Gallery Client database.

steps:

1. Click the **New Database button** on the toolbar, double-click **Blank Database** on the General tab, save the database as **Pacific Art Gallery Client Database**, then click **Create**

   You cannot find an appropriate sample table and fields in the Table Wizard for the Painting Sales table, so you will list the fields required in Design view.

Hint

Press [↓] to move from record to record, not the [Tab] key.

2. Click the **Tables tab** (if necessary), click **New**, click **Design View**, click **OK**, then enter the following field names: **Painting Title**, **Artist Name**, **Buyer Name**, and **Price**

   Access automatically assigns Text as the data type for each field. Next, you need to select Currency as the data type for the Price field.

3. Click **Text** next to the Price field, click the **Data Type list arrow**, then click **Currency**

   Next, you will enter the records for the Painting Sales table.

Hint

If the AutoCorrect features are turned on, "and" in record 12 will automatically be changed to "And." After typing "Mrs." press [←] as needed and correct the error.

4. Switch to **Datasheet View**, save the table as **Painting Sales**, click **Yes** to create a Primary Key, then enter the data and increase the column widths as shown in Figure P2-1

   Next, sort the table in alphabetical order by Artist Name.

5. Click **Artist Name**, then click the **Sort Ascending button** on the toolbar

   Next, go on to create a table that lists all the artists who exhibited at Pacific Art Gallery last year, along with their style of work. To save time you will copy records from the Painting Sales table.

6. Click the **Artist Name** field, click the **Copy button** on the toolbar, close the table, click **Yes** to save changes, click **New**, then click **OK** to accept Datasheet View

7. Click the **Field1** field, click the **Paste button** on the toolbar, click **Yes**, double-click **Field1**, type **Artist Name**, press **[Enter]**, then widen the column so that you can see all the names

   Next, delete the duplicate names.

8. Right-click the row selector to the left of the second occurrence of Bess Davidson, click **Delete Record** on the pop-up menu, click **Yes**, then repeat the process to delete duplicate occurrences of the remaining artists, as shown in Figure P2-2

9. Rename **Field2** as **Style**, enter the style for each artist, as shown in Figure P2-2, close the table, click **Yes** to save the changes, name it **Artists**, then click **Yes** to create a Primary Key

   Next, go on to create and modify a query based on the Painting Sales and Artists tables.

FIGURE P2-1: Records for Painting Sales table

ID	Painting Title	Artist Name	Buyer Name	Price
1	Striated Landscape	Simpson, G.C.	Alta Vista Corporation	$4,000.00
2	Chasms	Gordon, Lily	Crook, Barry	$2,000.00
3	Presumption	Scheilman, Doris	Barts, Dr. J.	$2,000.00
4	Aztec Sunrise	Simpson, G.C.	Lo, Henry	$3,500.00
5	Santa Ana Winds	Ng, Allan	Lo, Henry	$2,500.00
6	Fiesta	Valenti, Teresa	Holm, Karen	$1,500.00
7	Pacific Moon	Valenti, Teresa	Holm, Karen	$1,500.00
8	Horizons	Ng, Allan	Holm, Karen	$1,200.00
9	Redwoods	Pacheco, Maria	Holm, Karen	$2,000.00
10	Jewels in the Sand	Ng, Allan	Schwartz, Martin	$800.00
11	Last Fanfare	Davidson, Bess	Schwartz, Martin	$1,500.00
12	Sparkle Light	Pacheco, Maria	Prentis, Mr. and Mrs.	$3,000.00
13	Ocean	Lahr, David	Pacific Shores	$2,200.00
14	Mirage	Davidson, Bess	Sun Corporation	$1,500.00
15	Heat Glaze	Simpson, G.C.	Sun Corporation	$3,000.00
(AutoNumber)				$0.00

FIGURE P2-2: Records for Artists table

Artist Name	Style	Field3	Field4	Field5
Davidson, Bess	Landscape			
Gordon, Lily	Abstract			
Lahr, David	Abstract			
Ng, Allan	Abstract			
Pacheco, Maria	Abstract			
Scheilman, Doris	Minimalist			
Simpson, G.C.	Abstract			
Valenti, Teresa	Landscape			

ARTIST PROFILES FOR PACIFIC ART GALLERY

activity:

Create and Modify a Query

You need to create a query to determine the most popular style of art purchased and then modify this query to list only those artists who sold paintings for more than $2,000. Before you can create the query, you need to establish a relationship between the Painting Sales and Artists tables.

steps:

1. Click **Tools** on the menu bar, click **Relationships**, click **Add** in the Show Table dialog box, click **Painting Sales** in the Show Table dialog box, click **Add**, then click **Close**

2. As shown in Figure P2-3, click **Artist Name** in the Artists table, drag it across to **Artist Name** in the Painting Sales table, then click **Create** in the Relationships dialog box that appears
   A link now exists between the two tables. Next, use the Simple Query Wizard to find the most popular style of art purchased and the top-selling paintings in this style.

3. Click the **Close button** in the Relationships window, then click **Yes** to save the changes

4. Click the **Queries tab**, click **New**, click **Simple Query Wizard**, click **OK**, click the **Tables/Queries list arrow**, click **Table: Painting Sales**, then click the **Select All Fields button** to insert all the fields

5. Click the **Tables/Queries list arrow**, click **Table: Artists**, add the **Style** field to the selected fields, click **Next**, click **Next**, name the query **Top Sales**, click the **Modify the query design option button**, then click **Finish**
   You want to sort the query by style to quickly see how many paintings of each style were sold.

6. Click the **Style Sort cell** (you may need to scroll to view it), click the **Sort cell list arrow**, click **Ascending**, then click the **Run button** on the toolbar
   The abstract style is by far the most popular, as shown in Figure P2-4. Next, modify the query to list all the artists who have sold paintings that cost more than $2,000.

7. Click the **View button** on the toolbar to switch to **Design View**, click the **Price Criteria cell**, type **>2000**, then click
   Next, sort the table so that the prices range from the least to the most expensive, and remove the ID field from the query.

8. Switch to **Design View**, click the **Price Sort cell**, click the **Price Sort list arrow**, click **Ascending**, click the **ID Show cell** to remove the check mark, then click
   Compare your screen with Figure P2-5.

9. Click the **Close button** in the Query Results window, then click **Yes** to save the modified query
   Next, go on to create a report from the data in the Top Sales query table.

FIGURE P2-3: **Creating the table relationship**

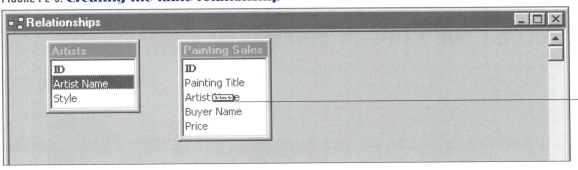

Artist Name dragged to the Painting Sales table

FIGURE P2-4: **Results of Most Popular Styles query**

Top Sales : Select Query

ID	Painting Title	Artist Name	Buyer Name	Price	Style
15	Heat Glaze	Simpson, G.C.	Sun Corporation	$3,000.00	Abstract
4	Aztec Sunrise	Simpson, G.C.	Lo, Henry	$3,500.00	Abstract
1	Striated Landscape	Simpson, G.C.	Alta Vista Corporation	$4,000.00	Abstract
12	Sparkle Light	Pacheco, Maria	Prentis, Mr. and Mrs.	$3,000.00	Abstract
9	Redwoods	Pacheco, Maria	Holm, Karen	$2,000.00	Abstract
10	Jewels in the Sand	Ng, Allan	Schwartz, Martin	$800.00	Abstract
8	Horizons	Ng, Allan	Holm, Karen	$1,200.00	Abstract
5	Santa Ana Winds	Ng, Allan	Lo, Henry	$2,500.00	Abstract
13	Ocean	Lahr, David	Pacific Shores	$2,200.00	Abstract
2	Chasms	Gordon, Lily	Crook, Barry	$2,000.00	Abstract
7	Pacific Moon	Valenti, Teresa	Holm, Karen	$1,500.00	Landscape
6	Fiesta	Valenti, Teresa	Holm, Karen	$1,500.00	Landscape
14	Mirage	Davidson, Bess	Sun Corporation	$1,500.00	Landscape
11	Last Fanfare	Davidson, Bess	Schwartz, Martin	$1,500.00	Landscape
3	Presumption	Scheilman, Doris	Barts, Dr. J.	$2,000.00	Minimalist

Record: 1 of 15

FIGURE P2-5: **Results of Top Sales query**

Top Sales : Select Query

Painting Title	Artist Name	Buyer Name	Price	Style
Ocean	Lahr, David	Pacific Shores	$2,200.00	Abstract
Santa Ana Winds	Ng, Allan	Lo, Henry	$2,500.00	Abstract
Heat Glaze	Simpson, G.C.	Sun Corporation	$3,000.00	Abstract
Sparkle Light	Pacheco, Maria	Prentis, Mr. and Mrs.	$3,000.00	Abstract
Aztec Sunrise	Simpson, G.C.	Lo, Henry	$3,500.00	Abstract
Striated Landscape	Simpson, G.C.	Alta Vista Corporation	$4,000.00	Abstract

Record: 1 of 6

ARTIST PROFILES FOR PACIFIC ART GALLERY

activity:

Format and Print a Report

You need to create a report that appears as shown in Figure P2-6.

steps:

1. Click the **Reports tab**, click **New**, click **Report Wizard**, click **OK**, click the **Tables/Queries list arrow**, click **Query: Top Sales**, then click the **Select All Fields button**

   Next, designate Artist Name as a header, and tell Access to calculate the total sales for each artist.

2. Click **Next**, click **Artist Name**, click the **Select Single Field button** to insert **Artist Name** as a header, click **Next**, click **Summary Options**, click the **Sum check box**, then click **OK**

   Next, select a format and style for your report.

3. Click **Next**, click the **Align Left 1 option button**, click **Next**, click **Formal**, click **Next**, type **Pacific Art Gallery Top Sales**, then click **Finish**

   Next, display Report Design view, and make the changes required to display the report as shown in Figure P2-6. You will first insert the picture of the artist.

Hint

If you work on a network, check with your instructor to find the correct folder for ClipArt.

4. Click the **View list arrow** on the toolbar, click **Design View**, click **Report Header**, click **Insert** on the menu bar, click **Object**, click **Microsoft Clip Gallery** in the Object Type list box, click **OK**, select the **People** category, select the **Artist at Easel** image, then click **Insert**

   Next, resize the clip art, move the report title to the right, and enhance it with a gray fill.

5. Drag the right, middle selection handle to the left until the frame around the clip art is approximately 1½" wide, click **Pacific Art Gallery Top Sales**, move the mouse until the 👋 appears, drag the 👋 to move the title to the right so that all the text is visible, click the **Fill/Back Color list arrow** on the Formatting toolbar, select a **light gray** fill, click the **Line/Border Color list arrow** on the Formatting toolbar, then select **Transparent**

   Next, increase the font size of the text in both of the Artist Name boxes.

6. Click the first **Artist Name** box in the Artist Name Header, press and hold **[Shift]**, click the second **Artist Name** box, click the **Font Size list arrow** on the Formatting toolbar, then click **14**

   Next, see how your changes appear in the Print Preview screen.

7. Click the **Print Preview button** on the toolbar, then change the Zoom to **75%**, then scroll down to view the report

   As you can see, the Price and Style labels appear too close together and the Price and Sum areas are not large enough. Next, switch back to Report Design view, center the text in the Style boxes, and increase the size of the Price and Sum boxes.

8. Click **Close** on the Print Preview toolbar, select the two **Style** boxes (use **[Shift]**), then click the **Center button** on the toolbar, press and hold **[Shift]**, click both **Price** boxes, drag the selected boxes to the right approximately ½", select only the two **Price** boxes, drag the left middle sizing handle to the left approximately ½", then resize the two **Sum** boxes

   Next, view the report in the Print Preview screen, then print a copy.

9. Click , click the **Zoom list arrow** on the Print Preview toolbar, click **Fit**, click the **Print button** , close and save the report, then close the database

   The Pacific Art Gallery Top Sales report is complete. Compare your printed report with Figure P2-6.

FIGURE P2-6: Completed report for Pacific Art Gallery

Pacific Gallery Top Sales

Artist Name   Lahr, David

Painting Title	Buyer Name	Price	Style
Ocean	Pacific Shores	$2,200.00	Abstract

Summary for 'Artist Name' = Lahr, David (1 detail record)
Sum $2,200.00

Artist Name   Ng, Allan

Painting Title	Buyer Name	Price	Style
Santa Ana Winds	Lo, Henry	$2,500.00	Abstract

Summary for 'Artist Name' = Ng, Allan (1 detail record)
Sum $2,500.00

Artist Name   Pacheco, Maria

Painting Title	Buyer Name	Price	Style
Sparkle Light	Prentis, Mr. and Mrs.	$3,000.00	Abstract

Summary for 'Artist Name' = Pacheco, Maria (1 detail record)
Sum $3,000.00

Artist Name   Simpson, G.C.

Painting Title	Buyer Name	Price	Style
Heat Glaze	Sun Corporation	$3,000.00	Abstract
Aztec Sunrise	Lo, Henry	$3,500.00	Abstract
Striated Landscape	Alta Vista Corporation	$4,000.00	Abstract

Summary for 'Artist Name' = Simpson, G.C. (3 detail records)
Sum $10,500.00
Grand Total $18,200.00

Tuesday, January 06, 1998   Page 1 of 1

PROJECT 3 OVERVIEW

Sales Information for Cruise Heaven, Inc.

Cruise Heaven, Inc. offers clients in the Philadelphia area a wide variety of cruise trip packages. As the Sales Manager of Cruise Heaven, Inc., you have decided to set up a database that contains information about all the cruises sold during March of 1998. You want to use the information in the database to print a report based on the results of three queries. You will **Create the Database, Queries, and Report**.

activity:

Create the Database, Queries, and Report

steps:

1. Create a database called **Cruise Heaven Sales**, click the **Tables tab**, click **New**, then click **OK**

   You enter all the data in Datasheet view because the Table Wizard doesn't supply the needed field names.

2. Double-click **Field1**, type **Cruise ID**, double-click **Field2**, type **Cruise Name**, then enter the remaining field names, as shown in Figure P3-1

   Switch to Design view and designate the data type for selected fields.

3. Switch to **Design View**, name the table **March Cruise Sales**, answer **No** to create a Primary Key, designate the **Cruise ID** field as an **AutoNumber** field, the **Duration (in Days)** field as a **Number** field, the **Cruise Cost** field as a **Currency** field, and the **Bookings** field as a **Number** field

   Next, designate the Cruise ID as a primary key.

4. Click **Cruise ID**, click **Edit** on the menu bar, then click **Primary Key**

Hint
Press [Ctrl]['] to enter duplicate information.

5. Switch back to **Datasheet View**, enter the data for the table, as shown in Figure P3-1, then close the table

   Now you are ready to create queries. First, which cruises cost $2,500 or more?

6. Use the **Simple Query Wizard**, select all the fields from the **March Cruise Sales table**, call the query table **Cruises from $2,500**, modify the query design by entering **>=2500** in the **Cruise Cost Criteria cell**, run the Query, then close and save it

   Ten of the cruises cost $2,500 or more. Next, find out how many of the Inside Passage and Alaskan Adventure cruises that cost $2,500 or more have bookings of more than 10.

Hint
The greater than 10 entry must appear on both of the criteria rows (next to both "Inside Passage" and "Alaskan Adventures").

7. Use the **Simple Query Wizard**, select all the fields in the **Cruises from $2,500** query, call the query **Alaskan Cruise Sales**, modify the query design by entering **Inside Passage** in the **Cruise Name Criteria cell**, **Alaskan Adventures** in the **Cruise Name or cell**, and **>10** in the **Bookings Criteria cell** on both rows, then run the query

   Four of the Alaskan cruises that cost $2,500 or more have bookings of more than 10.

8. Return to Design View, sort the Bookings field in **Ascending** order, then run the query

Time To
✓ Save
✓ Close
✓ Exit

9. Close and save the Alaskan Cruise Sales query table, then use the Report Wizard to create a report named "Alaskan Cruise Sales" from the Alaskan Cruise Sales query that appears similar to the report shown in Figure P3-2 by using **Cruise Name** as a grouping level selecting **Sum** for the Bookings field, selecting the **Stepped** layout and the **Soft Gray** format, and adjusting the layout in Design View, then print the report and close the database

   Your report is complete.

FIGURE P3-1: Field names and records for March Cruise Sales table

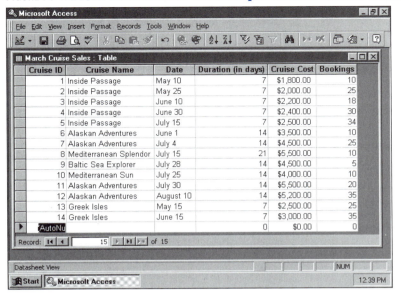

FIGURE P3-2: Completed Alaskan Cruise Sales report

Alaskan Cruise Sales

Cruise Name	Cruise ID	Date	Duration	Cruise Cost	Bookings
Alaskan Adventures					
	12	August 10	14	$5,200.00	35
	11	July 30	14	$5,500.00	20
	7	July 4	14	$4,500.00	25
Summary for 'Cruise Name' = Alaskan Adventures (3 detail records)					
Sum					80
Inside Passage					
	5	July 15	7	$2,500.00	34
Summary for 'Cruise Name' = Inside Passage (1 detail record)					
Sum					34
Grand Total					**114**

More Formatting Hints

Experiment with the many features available in Report Layout view. Remember that you press and hold the [Shift] key to select multiple labels. Formatting the report for printing requires quite a lot of time and patience. Remember to check your progress frequently in the Print Preview screen.

Independent Challenges

INDEPENDENT CHALLENGE 1

Create a report based on tables that contain information about 20 to 30 products stocked by a company of your choice. For example, you could create a report for a small company that sells classic videos or gourmet coffee. Follow the steps provided to create the database, create a Products table and a Suppliers table, make two or three queries, then create a report.

1. You need to know the name of your company and the type of products it sells. For example, you could call your company Waves and describe it as a retail operation that sells water sports equipment, such as surfboards, bathing suits, and inflatable water toys. Write the name of your company and a brief description of it in the box below:

   Company Name: ....
   Description: ....
   ....
   ....

2. Create a database called [Company name] Inventory.
3. Create a Products table. Use the Table Wizard to create a Products table similar to the table you created for Project 1. Include at least six fields, including the UnitsInStock field. If necessary, rename some of the fields to match the type of data you plan to enter.
4. Create a Suppliers table. Use the Form Wizard to enter the data for a Suppliers table. Include at least four or five fields. Make sure that at least one of the fields in the Suppliers table is the same as a field in the Products table. Use the Copy and Paste commands to minimize typing time.
5. Instruct Access to create relationships between the two tables.
6. In the box below, write four queries you plan to make based on the Products and Suppliers tables. For example, you could ask which products are handled by a certain supplier, which products conform to a specific category, and which suppliers are located in a specific area. The queries you make will depend upon the type of data you included in your Products and Suppliers tables and the relationships you have created between the two tables.

   Query 1: ....
   Query 2: ....
   Query 3: ....
   Query 4: ....

7. Use the Query Wizard to create the queries. Make sure you specify the criteria for each query in Design View.
8. Select the query table that you will use to create your Inventory Report.
9. Use the Report Wizard to create your report. Experiment with the many features available in Report Design view. Remember that you will need to switch frequently between Report Design view and the Print Preview screen to check your progress.
10. Print the report then close the database.

INDEPENDENT CHALLENGE 2

Create an Event database that contains information about an event of your choice. For example, you could create tables that contain information about a concert or a conference that you are helping to organize. Plan and then create the database as follows:

1. Create a database called [Event Name]. For example, a database for a local computer users conference could be called "Seattle Computer Users Conference."
2. Display the Table Wizard and select the Events sample table.
3. Plan your database on paper:
   a. Write down the fields from the Events sample table that you plan to include in a table.
   b. Determine additional fields for a second table.
   c. List a few of the records you plan to include in the two tables.
   d. Determine two or three queries that you could make based on the data in the two tables.
   e. Identify the information that you would like to display in a report. For example, you could create a report that displays the total amount of money made at the event from three categories of people who attended (e.g., adults, seniors, and students).

   Spend a fair bit of time planning your Events database so that when you begin working in Access, you will know exactly what kinds of fields and records you need to enter in order to create the type of report you require.
4. Create the tables required for your database.
5. Establish relationships between the tables.
6. Make two or three queries based on the data in the two tables.
7. Create and print an attractively formatted report based on one of the query tables you created.

INDEPENDENT CHALLENGE 3

Create a database that contains information about all the sales made in the past month by a company of your choice. Suppose, for example, that you owned a pet store. You could create three tables related to sales: Pet Sales, Buyers, and Accessories. The Pet Sales table, for example, could look similar to the table shown in Figure IC-1:

FIGURE IC-1: Pet Sales table

ID	Sale Date	Animal	Category	Sales Price
1	5/1/98	Beagle Puppy	Dog	$250.00
2	5/2/98	Siamese Kitten	Cat	$300.00
3	5/3/98	Gerbils: three	Rodent	$75.00
4	5/3/98	Pygmy Boa Constrictor	Reptile	$275.00
5	5/3/98	Hamsters: two	Rodent	$50.00
6	5/4/98	Dachshund Puppy	Dog	$400.00
7	5/5/98	Basset Hound Puppy	Dog	$350.00
8	5/7/98	Fox Terrier Puppy	Dog	$300.00
9	5/8/98	Malamute Puppy	Dog	$500.00
10	5/10/98	Iguana	Reptile	$75.00
(AutoNumber)				$0.00

Spend some time designing your Sales Information database, then create three tables, make two or three queries, and create a report based on one of the queries. Use your imagination and Access skills to create a database that you can use to produce an informative and useful report regarding some aspect of your product sales. Refer to the database you created for Cruise Heaven in Project 3 for ideas.

INDEPENDENT CHALLENGE 4

You are a freelance travel photographer with a large collection of slides and photographs that you want to sell to various travel magazines. To help you determine which magazines would be interested in your photographs, you've decided to create a database consisting of two tables: Picture File and Magazines. The Picture File table will contain data about your photographs, such as subject, location, and format, and the Magazines table will contain data related to the type of photographs purchased (e.g., preferred subjects, locations, and formats). Once you have completed the two tables, make three queries designed to help you choose which magazines may be interested in your photographs.

1. Create a database called Photography Database.
2. Create the Picture File and Magazines tables in Datasheet view, as shown in Figures IC-2 and IC-3. Make sure you click Yes when Access asks you to create a Primary Key so that relationships are automatically created between the two tables.

FIGURE IC-2: Picture File table

ID	Subject	Location	Country	Format	Category
1	El Capitan	Yosemite	USA	Monochrome	Mountains
2	Gondolas	Venice	Italy	Color Slide	People
3	Ocean Waves	Oregon	USA	Color Slide	Seascape
4	Otters	Alaska	USA	Color Slide	Animals
5	Mount Everest	Himalayas	Nepal	Color Photograph	Mountains
6	Denali Sunset	Alaska	USA	Color Photograph	Mountains
7	Eiffel Tower	Paris	France	Monochrome	Architecture
8	Lavender Fields	Provence	France	Color Slide	Rural
9	Ruined Church	Provence	France	Monochrome	Architecture
10	Matterhorn	Alps	Switzerland	Color Photograph	Mountains
11	Alpes Maritimes	Provence	France	Color Photograph	Mountains
12	Half Dome	Yosemite	USA	Color Photograph	Mountains
13	Pont du Gard	Languedoc	France	Monochrome	Architecture
14	Grand Canyon	Arizona	USA	Color Slide	Mountains
15	Notre Dame Cathedral	Paris	France	Monochrome	Architecture
16	Rainforest	Washington	USA	Monochrome	Rural
17	Carnac Alignments	Brittany	France	Monochrome	Architecture

FIGURE IC-3: **Magazines table**

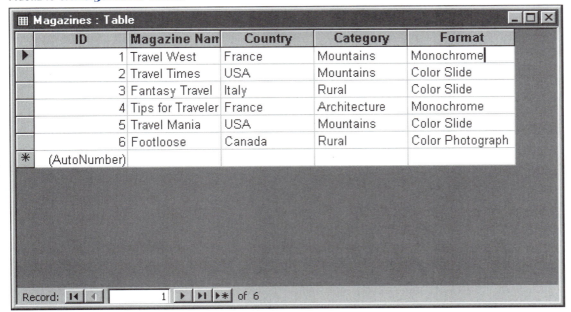

3. Fill in the boxes below with your answers to the following queries:

   Query 1: Which magazines want monochrome photographs of mountains?
   (HINT: Insert all the fields from the Magazines table; enter "Monochrome" in the Format Criteria cell and "Mountains" in the Category Criteria cell.)

   Query 2: Which magazines want color slides?
   (HINT: Change the design of Query 1 so that "Color Slide" appears in the Format Criteria cell; delete "Mountains" in the Category Criteria cell.)

   Query 3: Which of your photos would Tips for Travelers want?
   (HINT: Insert all the fields from Table: Magazines; insert "Tips for Travelers" in the Magazine Name Criteria cell; run the query; note the Country, Category, and Format requirements; close the query; run a query from the Picture File table called "Photographs for Tips for Travelers" that finds all the records containing the Country, Category, and Format requirements noted for Tips for Travelers. Save the query as "Photographs for Tips for Travelers.")

4. Create a report from the Photographs for Tips for Travelers query that lists the photographs you plan to send to *Tips for Travelers*. Format the report attractively, then print a copy.
5. Close the Photography database.

Visual Workshop

Create a database called Staff Travel using the table shown in Figure VW-1. Create a query to find all the staff members who spent more than $2,500 on travel and who traveled to either Europe or Asia, sort the Region field in the query in ascending order, then create a report that appears as shown below. Use the Outline 1 and Soft Gray formats.

FIGURE VW-1: Travel Expenses table

ID	Last Name	First Name	Destination	Region	Expenses
1	Smith	Donna	Berlin	Europe	$2,480.00
2	Allenby	George	New York	USA	$1,300.00
3	Perez	Maria	Tokyo	Asia	$4,890.00
4	Lee	Grace	London	Europe	$3,800.00
5	Dansen	Gregory	St. Louis	USA	$1,800.00
6	Saunders	Marianne	Hong Kong	Asia	$5,800.00
7	Hallstein	Doris	Hong Kong	Asia	$4,500.00
8	Williams	Elizabeth	Vancouver	Canada	$1,400.00
9	Jefferson	Walter	Rome	Europe	$2,400.00
10	Ferrars	Robert	Singapore	Asia	$3,800.00
(AutoNumber)					$0.00

FIGURE VW-2: Travel Expenses report

Travel Expenses Query

Region Asia

Last Name	First Name	Destination	Expenses
Ferrars	Robert	Singapore	$3,800.00
Hallstein	Doris	Hong Kong	$4,500.00
Saunders	Marianne	Hong Kong	$5,800.00
Perez	Maria	Tokyo	$4,890.00

Summary for 'Region' = Asia (4 detail records)
Sum $18,990.00

Region Europe

Last Name	First Name	Destination	Expenses
Lee	Grace	London	$3,800.00

Summary for 'Region' = Europe (1 detail record)
Sum $3,800.00

Grand Total $22,790.00

Microsoft
▶ Access, Word, and Excel
Projects

Integration

Task Streamlining

In This Unit You Will Create:

 **Job Search Database**

 **Company Profile**

 **Video Catalogue**

In a typical day as the administrator of a business, you could send out form letters, create sales charts, identify new inventory to order, complete purchase orders, and produce a proposal to secure a new contract—and all before lunch. To accomplish such a wide diversity of tasks quickly and easily, you need to use each program in the Office suite to maximum efficiency. You would start by building an extensive Access database that contains the names and addresses of all your customers and suppliers, information about your inventory, and sales records. You would then combine the information in this database with Word to produce mail-outs, labels, and catalogues and with Excel to produce charts and spreadsheets. ▶ In this unit you will create three databases in Access that provide you with the information you need to create business documents in both Word and Excel.

OVERVIEW

Job Search Database for Mark Leung

Mark Leung has just graduated from Portland Community College in Oregon with a certificate in business administration. He now wants to find a job in the Portland area as an office manager, sales and marketing coordinator, or management trainee. To coordinate his job search efforts, Mark will enter all the names and addresses of his employment contacts in an Access database, which he will then merge with a job application form letter he creates in Word. Finally, Mark will analyze the results of his job search efforts by creating a chart in Excel. Three activities are required to complete Mark's Job Search Database:

Project Activities

Set Up the Job Search Database

Mark uses Access to create two related tables for his Job Search database. The First Contacts table contains the names and addresses of all the employers he has contacted. He will merge this table with the job application form letter he creates in Word. The Search Results table contains information about the responses Mark received after sending out the form letters. Figure P1-1 shows the data in the First Contacts table. Mark writes to Allison Blenheim to inquire about the marketing analyst position that he saw advertised in the May 2nd edition of the *Oregon Times*.

Create the Job Application Form Letter

Mark switches to Word, creates the job application form letter as a main document, then merges the letter with the names and addresses in the First Contacts table he created in Access. He then prints the form letters. Figure P1-2 shows a portion of the form letter he will send to Ms. Blenheim, the personnel manager at First Fashions.

Analyze the Job Search Results

Mark receives several positive responses to the form letters he sent. He decides to rate each job offer in terms of four criteria: Location, Pay, Benefits, and Advancement. He creates a Ratings table in Access, then switches to Excel, where he creates a pie chart based on the Ratings table. Figure P1-3 shows the Ratings table Mark copies into Excel, and Figure P1-4 shows the pie chart he creates from columns B and H.

FIGURE P1-1: First Contacts table for form letter

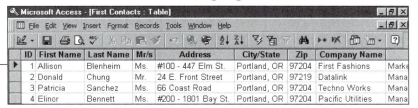

The data in the first record appears in the form letter

FIGURE P1-2: Form letter created in Word for Ms. Blenheim

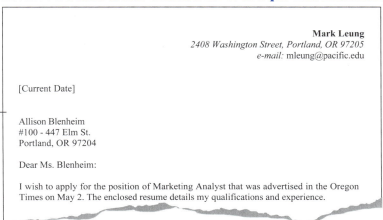

FIGURE P1-3: Ratings table copied from Access to Excel

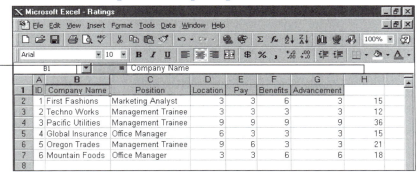

The data in columns B and H appears in the pie chart

FIGURE P1-4: Pie chart created in Excel

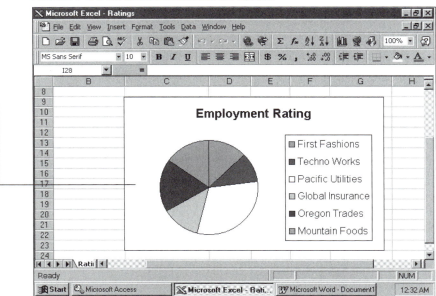

TASK STREAMLINING   IN B-3

JOB SEARCH DATABASE FOR MARK LEUNG

activity:

Set Up the Job Search Database

Mark will create the First Contacts and Search Results tables from the data he has for ten employers. He will use the Table Wizard to create the First Contacts table, then create the Search Results table in Datasheet view.

steps:

1. Create a database in Access called **Job Search Database** on the disk where you plan to store all your files for this book, click the **Tables tab**, click **New**, click **Table Wizard**, then click **OK**

   Mark will base the First Contacts table on the Contacts sample table.

2. Click **Contacts** in the Sample Tables list, click **ContactID**, click the **Select Single Field button** **>**, click **Rename Field**, type **ID**, click **OK**, then select and rename the following fields for the table

Field Name	Rename	Field Name	Rename
FirstName	(Don't rename)	PostalCode	Zip
Last Name	(Don't rename)	CompanyName	(Don't rename)
Dear	Mr/s	Title	Position
Address	(Don't rename)	Title	Newspaper
City	City/State	LastMeetingDate	Date

3. Click **Next**, name the table **First Contacts**, click **Next**, click the **Modify the table design option button**, then click **Finish**

   Next, you need to change the input mask for the Zip and Date fields.

4. Click the **Data Type cell** for Zip, drag your mouse across **00000\-9999** in the current **Input Mask** to select it, press **Delete**, click the **Data Type list arrow** for Date, click **Text**, delete the current input mask, switch to **Datasheet view**, then click **Yes**

Hint
Press [Ctrl]['] to enter duplicate information.

5. Enter the records as shown in Figure P1-5

   Next, create the Search Results table in Datasheet view. This table will include the company names and positions you entered in the First Contacts table.

6. Close the **First Contacts** table, click **New**, click **Design View**, click **OK**, enter the field names as shown in Figure P1-6, close and save the table as **Search Results**, then answer **Yes** to create a Primary Key

   To save time you will open the First Contacts table, then copy the records in the Company Name and Position fields to the Search Results table.

7. Open the **First Contacts** table, select the **Company Name** and **Position** fields, click the **Copy button** on the toolbar, close the **First Contacts** table, open the **Search Results** table, select the **Company Name** and **Position** fields, click the **Paste button** on the toolbar, then click **Yes**

8. Enter the remaining data for the Search Results table as shown in Figure P1-7, then close and save the table

   Next, go on to create a form letter in Word, which you will then merge with the First Contacts table.

FIGURE P1-5: Records for First Contacts table

ID	First Name	Last Name	Mr/s	Address	City/State	Zip	Company Name	Position	Newspaper	Date
1	Allison	Blenheim	Ms.	#100 - 447 Elm St.	Portland, OR	97204	First Fashions	Marketing Analyst	Oregon Times	May 2
2	Donald	Chung	Mr.	24 E. Front Street	Portland, OR	97219	Datalink	Management Trainee	Oregon Times	May 3
3	Patricia	Sanchez	Ms.	66 Coast Road	Portland, OR	97204	Techno Works	Management Trainee	Portland Echo	May 2
4	Elinor	Bennett	Ms.	#200 - 1801 Bay St.	Portland, OR	97204	Pacific Utilities	Management Trainee	Portland Echo	May 5
5	Graham	Eliot	Mr.	455 Byron Court	Portland, OR	97219	A-1 Videos	Sales Trainee	Portland Echo	May 4
6	Tony	Rosselli	Mr.	16 S.W. Water St.	Portland, OR	97201	Express Freight	Office Manager	Oregon Times	May 2
7	John	Edwards	Mr.	120 W. 6th Street	Portland, OR	97214	Global Insurance	Office Manager	Oregon Times	May 6
8	Karen	Morgan	Ms.	33 E. 18th Street	Portland, OR	97201	Lakeside Travel	Office Manager	Oregon Times	May 9
9	Marianne	Tilney	Ms.	450 E. Front Street	Portland, OR	97205	Oregon Trades	Management Trainee	Oregon Times	May 4
10	Kurt	Weber	Mr.	180 Main Street	Portland, OR	97206	Mountain Foods	Office Manager	Portland Echo	May 2

FIGURE P1-6: Field names for Search Results table

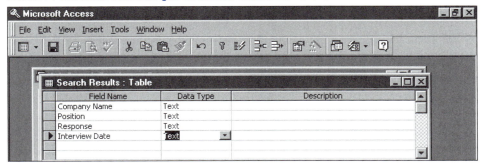

FIGURE P1-7: Records for Search Results table

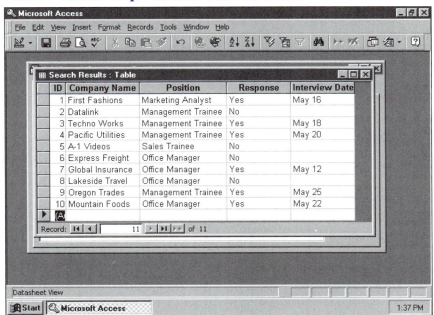

Clues to Use

Using Input Masks

*An **input mask** ensures that the data you enter in a field will fit the format you define. For example, the input mask defined for a telephone number requires that you enter only the digits required to make up a U.S. area code and telephone number. You can change an input mask either by deleting it or by using the Input Mask Wizard to define a new input mask.*

PROJECT 1 — JOB SEARCH DATABASE FOR MARK LEUNG

activity:

Create the Job Application Form Letter

steps:

1. Open a new, blank document in Word

   Next, display the Mail Merge Helper and select Form Letters as the main document type.

2. Click **Tools** on the menu bar, click **Mail Merge**, click **Create**, click **Form Letters**, then click **Active Window**

   Next, select the data for the merge from the Job Search database.

3. Click **Get Data**, click **Open Data Source**, select the drive containing your files for this book (if necessary), click the **Files of type list arrow**, click **MS Access Databases**, click **Job Search Database**, click **Open**, then click **OK** to select the **First Contacts** table

   Next, you are ready to create the form letter in Word.

4. Click **Edit Main Document**, click the **Align Right button** on the Formatting toolbar, type and enhance the return address of Mark Leung as shown in Figure P1-8, press **[Enter]** three times, then click the **Align Left button** on the Formatting toolbar

   Next, enter the date as a field so the current date will appear every time you open the form letter.

5. Click **Insert** on the menu bar, click **Date and Time**, select the date format you prefer, click the **Update automatically check box** to select it, click **OK**, press **[Enter]** three times, then save the main document as **Job Search Form Letter**

   Next, enter the field names for the inside address.

Hint
Mr/s in Access will appear as Mrs in Word.

6. Click **Insert Merge Field** on the Merge toolbar, click **FirstName**, press **[Spacebar]**, click **Insert Merge Field**, click **LastName**, then press **[Enter]**

   The name fields are inserted in the letter. You use the same procedure to enter each field required for the form letter.

7. Enter all the fields and type the text for the form letter as shown in Figure P1-8, right–click the e–mail address in the return address, point to **Hyperlink**, click **Edit Hyperlink**, click **Remove Link**, then correct any spelling errors

   Next, increase the font size for the entire letter, then perform the merge.

8. Press **[Ctrl][A]** to select all the text, click the **Font Size list arrow** on the Formatting toolbar, click **12**, click the **Mail Merge button** on the Merge toolbar, then click **Merge**

   When the merged letters appear, scroll through them to ensure that the records from the First Contacts table appear correctly. Next, print the first two merged letters.

Hint
You don't save merged documents because you can easily re-create them and because they take up unnecessary space on your hard drive or disk.

9. Click **File** on the menu bar, click **Print**, click the **Pages option button**, type **1,2** and click **OK**, compare the printed pages to Figure P1-9, close the merged letters without saving them, then save and close the main document

   Now that you have created the main document and linked it to the First Contacts table in the Job Search Database, you can run the merge at any time and print either all the merged letters or just a few of them, as required.

▶ IN B-6 MICROSOFT ACCESS, WORD, AND EXCEL PROJECTS

FIGURE P1-8: Return address, fields, and text for form letter

Mark Leung
2408 Washington Street, Portland, OR 97205
e-mail: mleung@pacific.edu — Return address

[Current Date]

«FirstName» «LastName»
«Address»
«CityState» «Zip»
— Merge fields

Dear «Mrs» «LastName»:
— Merge fields

I wish to apply for the position of «Position» that was advertised in the «Newspaper» on «Date». The enclosed resume details my qualifications and experience.

I recently graduated from Pacific Community College in Portland with a certificate in business administration. During the two-year program, I took courses in computer applications, marketing, communications, and management. I am familiar with all the Microsoft Office programs, as well as AccPac and Lotus 1-2-3. In my final year, I took several courses in Internet communications and am familiar with the procedures required to create and launch a company homepage on the World Wide Web.

For the past three years, I have also worked part-time as an Assistant Manager of the Janus Clothing Shop in Portland. My duties included supervising sales staff, managing the accounts receivable and accounts payable, and maintaining the inventory and customer database.

I am very interested in the employment opportunity at «CompanyName» and feel that I could apply my skills effectively to the position of «Position». Please contact me at 723-7789 if you wish to discuss my suitability for the position. Thank you for your attention to my applications; I look forward to hearing from you.
— Merge fields

Sincerely,

Mark Leung

FIGURE P1-9: Two merged letters

Mark Leung
2408 Washington Street, Portland, OR 97205
e-mail: mleung@pacific.edu

[Current Date]

Allison Blenheim
#100 - 447 Elm St.
Portland, OR 97204

Dear Ms. Blenheim:

I wish to apply for the position of Marketing Analyst that was advertised in the Oregon Times on May 2. The enclosed resume details my qualifications and experience.

Mark Leung
2408 Washington Street, Portland, OR 97205
e-mail: mleung@pacific.edu

[Current Date]

Donald Chung
24 E. Front Street
Portland, OR 97219

Dear Mr. Chung:

I wish to apply for the position of Management Trainee that was advertised in the Oregon Times on May 3. The enclosed resume details my qualifications and experience.

Project 1: Job Search Database for Mark Leung

activity:

Analyze the Job Search Results

All of the companies that interviewed Mark have offered him employment. Now he needs to decide which company to accept. To help himself make a wise decision, Mark will create a query table that lists only those companies that interviewed him, then add several new fields that will rank each company in terms of its location, pay, benefits, and opportunities for advancement. Mark decides on a rating scale as follows: 3 = Poor; 6 = Good; 9 = Excellent. Once he has completed the table, he will switch to Excel and create a chart that graphically illustrates his overall ranking for each company.

steps:

1. Display the Access Database window, click the **Queries tab**, click **New**, click **Simple Query Wizard**, click **OK**, click the **Tables/Queries list arrow**, click **Table: Search Results**, select the **Company Name**, **Position**, and **Response** fields, click **Next**, type **Positive Results** as the query table title, click the **Modify the query design option button**, then click **Finish**

   Next, select only those records that contain "Yes" in the Response field.

2. Click the **Response Criteria cell**, type **Yes**, then click the **Run button** on the toolbar

   All the companies that responded positively to Mark's form letter appear. Next, Mark needs to create a new table that will include the Company Name and Position fields from the Positive Results query along with his ratings for each company.

3. Select the **Company Name** and **Position** fields, click the **Copy button** on the toolbar, click the **Close button**, click **Yes**, click the **Tables tab**, click **New**, click **OK** to accept Datasheet View, select **Field1** and **Field2**, click the **Paste button** on the toolbar, then click **Yes**

4. Double-click the **Field1** label, type **Company Name**, double-click the **Field2** label, type **Position**, increase the column widths, then enter the labels and records for Fields 3 to 6 as shown in Figure P1-10

   Mark next wants to display the data in a pie chart. He will switch to Excel to create the pie chart.

5. Click the **Close button**, click **Yes**, save the table as **Ratings**, click **Yes** to create a Primary Key, click **Ratings**, click the **OfficeLinks list arrow** on the toolbar, then click **Analyze It with MS Excel**

   In a few moments the table appears in Excel. You will add all the values in the cells that contain ratings, then create a pie chart that shows the ratings breakdown by company.

6. Select cells **D2** to **H7**, click the **AutoSum button** on the Standard toolbar, then click away from the selected cells

   Next, create the pie chart from the data in column B and column H.

7. Click the **Chart Wizard button**, click **Pie**, click **Next**, click the **Collapse Dialog button**, select cells **B2** to **B7**, type a comma (,), select cells **H2** to **H7**, click the **Restore Dialog button**, click **Next**, type **Employment Rating** as the chart title, click **Next**, then click **Finish**

8. Increase the size of the pie chart so that all the data is clearly visible as shown in Figure P1-11, print a copy of the worksheet, save and close the worksheet, then close the database

   Mark can see at a glance that he should accept the job offered by Pacific Utilities.

Trouble

If you get a message telling you that the worksheet was created in a previous version of Excel, click Yes to save it in the updated format.

FIGURE P1-10: **Records for Ratings table**

Copied records

New field names and records

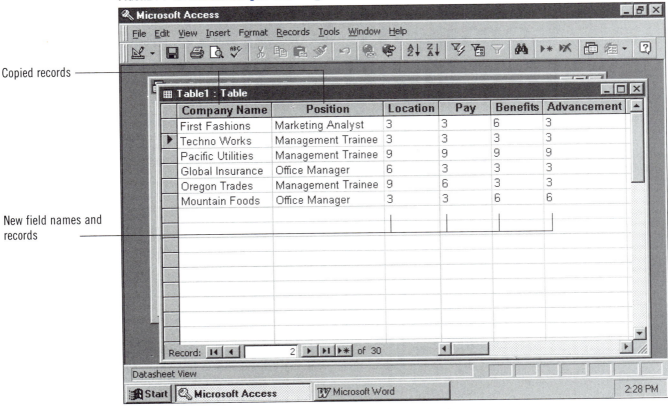

FIGURE P1-11: **Completed pie chart in Excel**

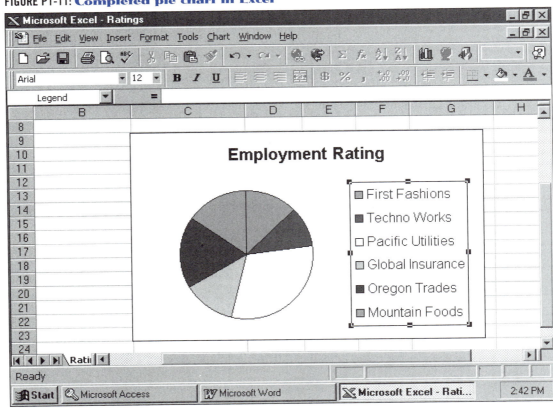

TASK STREAMLINING IN B-9

OVERVIEW

Company Profile for Dragon Designs

As the owner of a small desktop-publishing and homepage design company in Honolulu, Hawaii, you've decided to upgrade your computer system, move into an office, and hire an assistant. Gillian Dane, one of your clients, is so pleased with your work that she is thinking of lending you $15,000 to finance your expansion. To help her make her decision, she has asked you to put together a two-page profile of your company that includes information about your recent jobs and a pie chart that illustrates the most popular—and profitable—services you offer. You will **Create the Dragon Designs Database, Create a Pie Chart in Excel**, and then **Create a Company Profile in Word**.

activity:

Create the Dragon Designs Database

You will create a database that contains information about the contracts completed by Dragon Designs in June 1997, then you will create a query table that lists all the contracts to design homepages.

steps:

1. Create a database in Access called **Dragon Designs Database**, click the **Tables tab**, click **New**, click **Design View**, then click **OK**

   You will create a table that lists all the contracts completed by Dragon Designs in June of 1997.

2. As shown in Figure P2-1, enter the field names for the table, then change the Data Type for the Date field to **Date/Time** and the Data Type for the Total Cost field to **Currency**

3. Switch to **Datasheet View**, save the table as **June Contracts**, answer **Yes** to create a Primary Key, then enter the records for the June Contracts table as shown in Figure P2-2

   Enter the dates as shown in Figure P2-2 and Access will display them in the date format. Next, create a query table that lists all the contracts to design homepages.

4. Click the **June Contracts table Close button**, click **Yes**, if necessary, click the **Queries tab**, click **New**, click **Simple Query Wizard**, click **OK**, select all the fields for the query, click **Next**, click **Next**, type **Homepage Contracts** as the query title, click the **Modify the query design option button**, then click **Finish**

5. Click the **Job Category Criteria** cell, type **Homepage**, then click the **Run button** on the toolbar

   Eight of the 14 contracts you completed in June involved the designing of homepages for clients advertising on the World Wide Web. You decide to include this table as part of the company profile you will give to Ms. Dane.

6. Click the **Homepage Contracts query Close button**, click **Yes** to save it, click the **Office Links list arrow** on the toolbar, then click **Analyze It with MS Excel**

7. Click cell **E11**, click the **AutoSum button** on the Standard toolbar, press **[Enter]**, click cell **D11**, then type **Total Earnings**

8. Format the worksheet so that it appears as shown in Figure P2-3, then save it

FIGURE P2-1: Fields and data types for June Contracts table

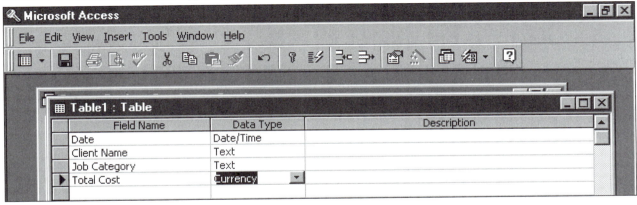

FIGURE P2-2: Records for June Contracts table

Type the dates as written and Access will convert them to a date format

FIGURE P2-3: Completed Homepage Contracts worksheet in Excel

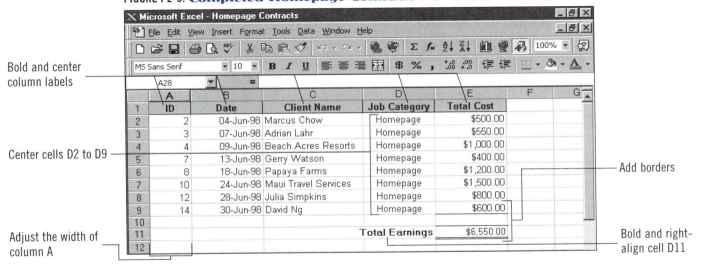

Bold and center column labels

Center cells D2 to D9

Adjust the width of column A

Add borders

Bold and right-align cell D11

COMPANY PROFILE FOR DRAGON DESIGNS

activity:

Create a Pie Chart in Excel

You want to include a pie chart that displays the breakdown of earnings in terms of job category. You will create this chart in Excel from the data entered in the June Contracts table. To simplify the task of creating the pie chart, you will first display the June Contracts table, then sort the Job Category records in alphabetical order.

steps:

1. Display Access, click the **Tables tab**, double-click **June Contracts** to open it, click **Job Category**, then click the **Sort Ascending button** on the toolbar

   Next, display the table in Excel and perform the calculations required to create the pie chart.

2. Click the **June Contracts table Close button**, click **Yes**, click the **Office Links list arrow**, then click **Analyze It with MS Excel**

   The June Contracts table appears in a new worksheet in Excel. To create the pie chart in Excel, you first need to calculate the total earnings for each job category.

3. Click cell **A17**, type **Brochures**, click cell **A18**, enter the formula **=SUM(E2:E5)**, press **[Enter]**, then widen the column

   Your contracts to design brochures total $1,550.00. Next, calculate the totals for homepages and flyers.

The total sales for homepages is $6,550, and the total sales for sales flyers is $500.

4. Click cell **B17**, type **Homepages**, click cell **B18**, enter **=SUM(E6:E13)**, press **[Enter]**, click cell **C17**, type **Sales Flyers**, then click cell **C18**, and calculate the total earnings from sales flyers

   Next, create the pie chart from the data in cells A17 to C18.

5. Click the **Chart Wizard button** on the Standard toolbar, create a **Pie** chart in Step 1 of the Chart Wizard; select cells **A17** to **C18** in Step 2; in Step 3, add the chart title as shown in Figure P2-4 on the **Titles tab**, click the **Show percent option button** on the **Data Labels tab**, click the **Show leader lines check box** to deselect it; then click **Finish** in Step 4

   Now resize the pie chart so it is larger. As you can see, 76% of your contracts involve the designing of homepages. Next, stress the key role that homepages play in your company by "exploding" its slice.

6. Move the pointer just outside of the pie chart so the ToolTip says "Plot Area," click so a selection box appears around the pie chart, then drag the selection handles so the size of the pie chart increases to better fill the space

   Compare your screen to Figure P2-4 and make any adjustments necessary.

7. Click the pie chart to select it, click the **Homepages slice** once, drag the **Homepages slice** down about ¼", click **76%**, click **76%** again, then drag it up and to the left so that it appears as shown in Figure P2-5

   Your pie chart is complete. Next, display a blank Word screen where you will create a Company Profile that includes elements copied from the Dragon Designs database and Excel.

8. Click away from the pie chart to deselect it, then click the **Save button** on the Standard toolbar

   Next, you will enter the text for the Company Profile in Word and then insert elements from Access and Excel.

FIGURE P2-4: Pie chart

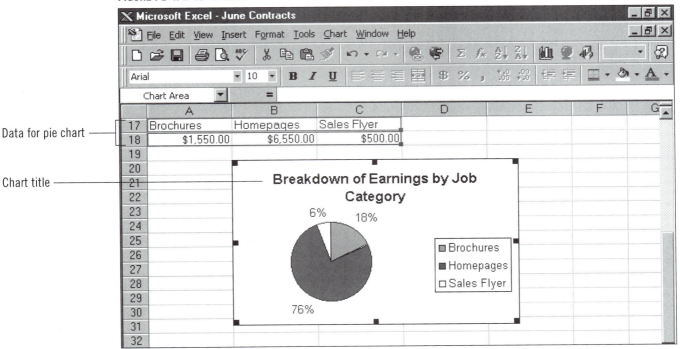

- Data for pie chart
- Chart title

FIGURE P2-5: Exploded Homepage slice

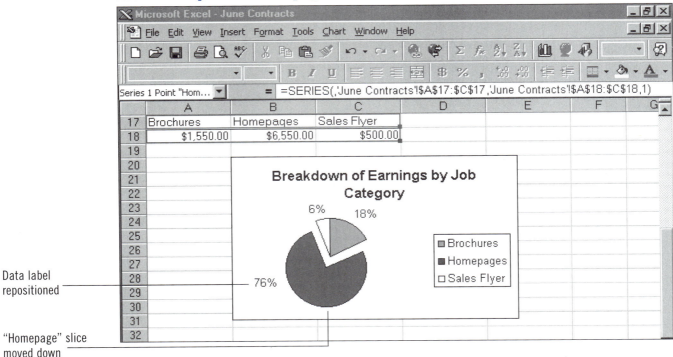

- Data label repositioned
- "Homepage" slice moved down

PROJECT 2

COMPANY PROFILE FOR DRAGON DESIGNS

activity:

Create a Company Profile in Word

The company profile consists of two pages, as shown in Figures P2-6 and P2-7. You will first create the heading and type the text, and then paste the June Contracts table from Access and the pie chart from Excel as links.

Trouble

If the Drawing toolbar is not displayed, click the Drawing button on the Standard toolbar.

steps:

1. Open a new Word document, press **[Enter]** three times, click the first paragraph mark, click the **Insert WordArt button**  on the Drawing toolbar, select the WordArt style in the last row, the fourth column, click **OK**, type **Dragon Designs**, click **OK**, then drag the WordArt object over to the left margin as shown in Figure P2-6, then click away from the object to deselect it

   Next, insert a picture of a dragon.

2. Click away from the WordArt object to deselect it, click **Insert** on the menu bar, point to **Picture**, click **Clip Art**, click **OK** if necessary, click **Animals**, select the **Dragon Powerful** image (or select another image if the Dragon image is not available), then click **Insert**

3. Resize and position the dragon as shown in Figure P2-6, then save the document as **Dragon Designs Company Profile**

Hint

Press [Ctrl][Enter] to insert a hard page break where indicated. Make sure you press [Enter] three times between the paragraphs where the data from Access and Excel will be pasted.

4. Click the last paragraph mark below the WordArt object, type **Company Profile**, enhance it with **bold** and a font size of **16**, center the text, then type the remaining text in **12 pt** and paste the total as a link from Excel **(Edit, Paste Special, Paste Link)** as shown in Figures P2-6 and P2-7

5. Click the **Microsoft Access program button** on the taskbar, click the **Tables tab**, double-click **June Contracts** to open it, click the **Date field**, then click the **Sort Ascending button** on the toolbar

   Next, copy the entire table into Word.

6. Click the **June Contracts table Close button**, click **Yes**, click the **Office Links list arrow** on the toolbar, click **Publish It with MS Word**, when the table appears in Word, click **Table** on the menu bar, click **Select Table**, press **[Ctrl][C]**, click **Window** on the menu bar, click **Dragon Designs Company Profile**, click in the second paragraph mark below the second paragraph, then press **[Ctrl][V]**

   The June Contracts table appears in Word. Note that you use the Publish It option when you do not plan to update the table in Access. When you want any changes you made in the Access table to also appear in the table published in Word, you use the Copy, Paste Special, and Paste Link commands. Next, format the table attractively in Word.

7. Click anywhere in the table, click **Table** on the menu bar, click **Table AutoFormat**, select the **Columns 5** format, click **OK**, click **Table** again, click **Cell Height and Width**, click the **Row tab**, click the **Center option button**, then click **OK**

   Next, insert the pie chart and the worksheet in the June Contracts Query workbook into page 2 of the company profile.

8. Copy the **pie chart** from Excel and paste it as a link after paragraph 1 on the second page of the Company Profile, then copy cells **B1** to **E11** from Homepage Contracts, and paste them as a link into Word

Time To
- ✓ Save
- ✓ Print
- ✓ Close

9. Use your mouse to center the pie chart between the left and right margins; center the table between the left and right margins (**Cell Height and Width**, **Row**, **Center**), click **Insert**, click **Page Numbers**, change the Alignment to **Center**, then click **OK** to insert page numbers

   Refer to Figures P2-6 and P2-7 as you work to complete the profile.

Integration

- Bold titles

FIGURE P2-6: Completed Company Profile: Page 1

Center title and enhance with 16pt bold

Company Profile

Description

Dragon Designs provides desktop-publishing and homepage design services to small business owners in the Honolulu area. At present, few other design services in the Honolulu area offer a homepage design service. *Dragon Designs* focuses primarily on the needs of its clients to advertise effectively on the World Wide Web by offering both writing and design services and ensuring that each homepage is launched successfully on a reputable server. In addition, *Dragon Designs* places the homepage on all the major search engines so that it is easily accessible to millions of Internet subscribers worldwide.

Service Overview

The table displayed below lists all the contracts performed by *Dragon Designs* in June of 1998.

ID	Date	Client Name	Job Category	Total Cost
1	6/1/98	Julia Simpkins	Brochure	$300.00
2	6/4/98	Marcus Chow	Homepage	$500.00
3	6/7/98	Adrian Lahr	Homepage	$550.00
4	6/9/98	Beach Acres Resorts	Homepage	$1,000.00
5	6/12/98	Sally Yamaguchi	Brochure	$400.00
6	6/13/98	Gerry Watson	Homepage	$400.00
7	6/13/98	Joel Adams	Sales Flyer	$200.00
8	6/18/98	Papaya Farms	Homepage	$1,200.00
9	6/21/98	Lanai Motel	Sales Flyer	$300.00
10	6/24/98	Maui Travel Services	Homepage	$1,500.00
11	6/25/98	Peggy Tan	Brochure	$350.00
12	6/28/98	Julia Simpkins	Homepage	$800.00
13	6/29/98	Beach Acres Resort	Brochure	$500.00
14	6/30/98	David Ng	Homepage	$600.00

On average, *Dragon Designs* completes three contracts a week. In June, *Dragon Designs* received orders for ten additional contracts. At present, all the contracts accepted by *Dragon Designs* are completed by its owner. As a result, additional contracts cannot be accepted until new personnel are hired to assist the owner.

Insert page break here

FIGURE P2-7: Completed Company Profile: Page 2

Service Breakdown

The pie chart below shows the breakdown of contracts in terms of the income generated in June of 1997. The Homepages "slice" represents 76% of this income.

Breakdown of Earnings by Job Category

- Brochures
- Homepages
- Sales Flyer

6%
18%
76%

Since January of 1997, the designing of homepages has become the number one concern of *Dragon Designs*. The table below lists all the clients who required homepages in June 1997. A total income of $6,550.00 was earned from designing homepages.

Date	Client Name	Job Category	Total Cost
04-Jun-98	Marcus Chow	Homepage	$500.00
07-Jun-98	Adrian Lahr	Homepage	$550.00
09-Jun-98	Beach Acres Resorts	Homepage	$1,000.00
13-Jun-98	Gerry Watson	Homepage	$400.00
18-Jun-98	Papaya Farms	Homepage	$1,200.00
24-Jun-98	Maui Travel Services	Homepage	$1,500.00
28-Jun-98	Julia Simpkins	Homepage	$800.00
30-Jun-98	David Ng	Homepage	$600.00

Total Earnings $6,550.00

Dragon Designs has outgrown its home-base operation. In September 1997, *Dragon Designs* will move to a commercial office space and hire two homepage design assistants.

Copy from cell E11 in the Excel workbook "Homepage Contracts" and paste as a link

PROJECT 3

OVERVIEW

Video Catalogue for Home Library

Your television set is surrounded by stacks of videos containing all the movies and documentary programs you have taped over the past six months. You have decided that you need to organize these videos into a database that you can then use to produce labels for the videotape spines and create a chart showing the breakdown of videos by category. First, you will **Create the Video Database**, then you will **Create the Labels and Chart**.

activity:

Create the Video Database

You will create the video database in Access.

steps:

1. Create a new database called **Personal Video Library**, click the **Tables tab**, click **New**, click **OK** to accept Datasheet View, then enter only the field names shown in Figure P3-1

2. Switch to **Design View**, name the table **Video List**, answer **No** to create a Primary Key, change the Data Type for Video ID to **AutoNumber**, click **Video ID**, click **Edit** on the menu bar, then click **Primary Key**

3. Switch to **Datasheet View**, enter the 18 records as shown in Figure P3-1, then close and save the table
   Next create a query table that will include only the Video Title and Length fields in alphabetical order by video title.

4. Click the **Queries tab**, click **New**, click **Simple Query Wizard**, click **OK**, insert the **Video Title** and **Length** fields in the table, click **Next**, name the query **Videotape Labels**, then click **Finish**

5. Click the **View list arrow**, click **Design View**, click the **Video Title Sort cell**, select **Ascending**, click the **Run button** on the toolbar, then close and save the query
   Suppose you want to list all the videos that conform to your favorite genres. You are interested in seeing just how many of these types of videos you have in your collection. Next, create a query table that lists only those records that contain Drama or Movie in the Genre 1 field and Literary in the Genre 2 field.

6. Click **New**, click **Simple Query Wizard**, click **OK**, click the **Tables/Queries list arrow**, click **Table: Video List**, insert all the fields into the table, click **Next**, name the query **Literary Videos**, click the **Modify the query design option button**, then click **Finish**

7. Complete the design grid so that it appears as shown in Figure P3-2, then click
   Your screen appears as shown in Figure P3-3.

8. Close and save the query
   Next, create videotape labels in Word and a chart in Excel.

FIGURE P3-1: **Fields and records for Video List table**

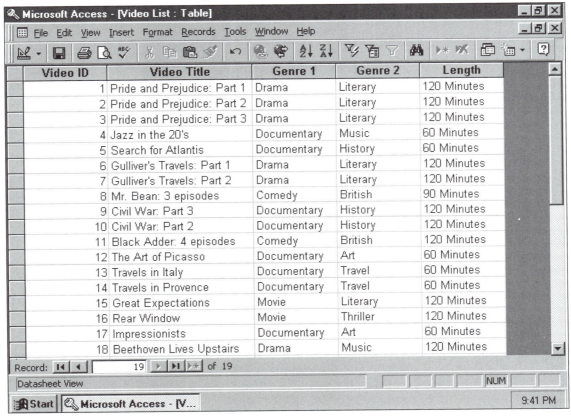

FIGURE P3-2: **Design view for Literary Videos query**

Field:	Video ID	Video Title	Genre 1	Genre 2	Length
Table:	Video List	Video List	Video List	Video List	Video List
Sort:					
Show:	☑	☑	☑	☑	☑
Criteria:			"Drama"	"Literary"	
or:			"Movie"	"Literary"	

Criteria for Genre 1 field

Criteria for Genre 2 field

FIGURE P3-3: **Completed query table**

Video ID	Video Title	Genre 1	Genre 2	Length
1	Pride and Prejudice: Part 1	Drama	Literary	120 Minutes
2	Pride and Prejudice: Part 2	Drama	Literary	120 Minutes
3	Pride and Prejudice: Part 3	Drama	Literary	120 Minutes
6	Gulliver's Travels: Part 1	Drama	Literary	120 Minutes
7	Gulliver's Travels: Part 2	Drama	Literary	120 Minutes
15	Great Expectations	Movie	Literary	120 Minutes
(AutoNumber)				

Integration

PROJECT 3

VIDEO CATALOGUE FOR HOME LIBRARY

activity:

Create Labels and Chart

You will merge the records in the Videotape Labels query table with Word to create a sheet of videotape labels, and then you will display the Video List table in Excel so that you can create a chart that shows the breakdown of videos by genre.

steps:

1. Click **Videotape Labels** on the Queries tab, click the **Office Links list arrow** on the toolbar, click **Merge It with MS Word**, click the **Create a new document and then link the data to it option button**, then click **OK**
   You will need to wait a few minutes while Word is loaded.

2. Maximize the Word window, click **Tools** on the menu bar, click **Mail Merge**, click **Create**, click **Mailing Labels**, click **Change Document Type**, then click **Setup**
   The Labels Options dialog box appears. You need to select the label type for a videotape spine.

3. Select **5199-S - Video Spine** in the Product number list, then click **OK**
   The Create Labels dialog box appears. You need to insert the two fields from the Videotape Labels query table into the label form.

4. Click **Insert Merge Field**, click **Video_blue underscore Title**, press **[Enter]**, click **Insert Merge Field**, then click **Length**
   Next, enhance the Video Title field so that the video titles will appear in Arial, Bold Italic, and 16 pt.

5. Triple-click the **Video_Title** field to select it, click the **right mouse button**, click **Font**, select the **Arial** font, **Bold Italic**, and **16 pt**, then click **OK**
   Next, perform the merge.

6. Click **OK** to close the Create Labels dialog box, click **Merge**, then click **Merge** again
   In a few seconds a sheet of videotape labels appears. Figure P3-4 shows the first four labels that should appear on your screen after you complete the merge.

7. Print a copy of the videotape labels, close the document without saving it, save the label main document as **Videotape Labels**, then close Word
   Next, create a doughnut chart in Excel.

8. In Access sort the **Genre 1** records in the **Video List table** in ascending order, analyze the table in Excel, create the category labels in row 21 as shown in Figure 3-5, then, to count the movies in each category, click **A22**, click the **Paste Function button** on the Standard toolbar, click **All**, select **COUNTA**, click **OK**, select the **Comedy** cells, click **OK**, then repeat the process for the remaining genres

9. Create a doughnut chart that displays the breakdown of genres as shown in Figure P3-5, save and print the worksheet, then close all files and exit all programs
   Note that the data for the doughnut chart appears in cells A21 to D22.

▶ IN B-18 MICROSOFT ACCESS, WORD, AND EXCEL PROJECTS

FIGURE P3-4: **First three videotape labels in Word**

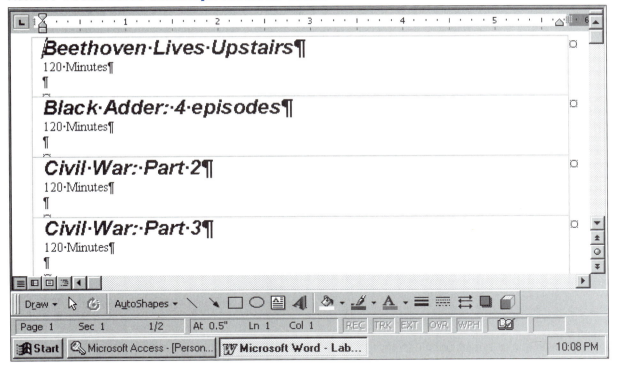

FIGURE P3-5: **Video data and doughnut chart in Excel**

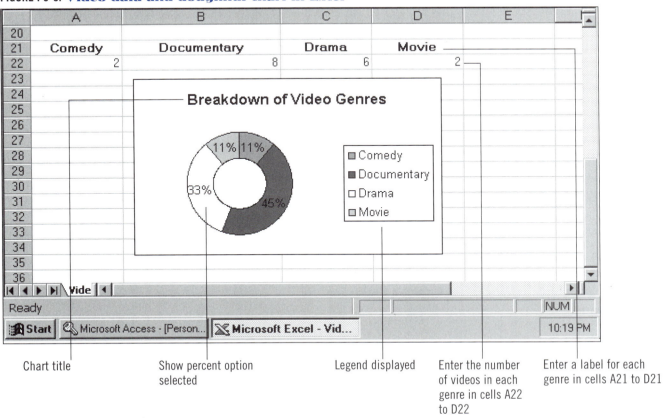

Chart title

Show percent option selected

Legend displayed

Enter the number of videos in each genre in cells A22 to D22

Enter a label for each genre in cells A21 to D21

Independent Challenges

INDEPENDENT CHALLENGE 1

Create a Job Search database similar to the database you created for Project 1 to track your own job search efforts. Even if you are not currently seeking employment, create a "practice" database and accompanying form letter. You can then modify these files when you are ready to seek employment. Follow the steps provided to create the database, merge it with a form letter you create in Word, and then create a chart in Excel that graphically displays your ratings of the companies that responded positively to your form letter.

1. Your first task is to determine the type of job position you are seeking and the type of company or organization you would like to work for. For example, you could seek a job as an office manager at real estate or architectural companies. In the box below, write the job position you are seeking and the types of companies you would like to work for.

   Job Position: ....
   Companies: ....

2. You need at least ten employers for your job search database. Look through the employment advertisements in your local paper to find potential employers, or, if you can't find advertisements for the specific job you require, look through the Yellow Pages to find the names and addresses of at least ten companies that you think you would like to work for and that may be interested in an applicant with your qualifications. Try to include as many realistic records in your job search database as possible.
3. Create a database called "My Job Search Database."
4. Create a Contacts table. Use the Table Wizard to create a table similar to the First Contacts table you created for Project 1. Include at least eight fields, including the position you wish to apply for and the name and date of the newspaper advertising the position (if appropriate). Direct Access to create the primary key.
5. Switch to Word and set up an application form letter. Use the form letter you created in Project 1 to help you determine the information to include. Make sure you fully describe your qualifications and experience. Select the records in the Contacts table as the data source for the form letter, and include the appropriate fields.
6. Merge the data source with the form letter, then print two or three of the letters.
7. Switch back to Access and create a Response table similar to the Search Results table you created in Project 1. Enter positive responses for at least five of the employers.
8. Create a query that lists only the companies that responded positively to your form letter.
9. Copy the Company Name and Position records from the query to a new table called Ratings Table, then enter your ratings for each company in terms of four criteria: Location, Pay, Benefits, and Advancement.
10. Analyze the Ratings table in Excel, then create a pie chart that shows the breakdown of companies according to your ratings. Remember that you will need to add the ratings for each company, then use the Chart Wizard to create a pie chart that includes only the company names and the total ratings.
11. Print the Excel chart then close all the files and applications.

INDEPENDENT CHALLENGE 2

Create a two-page company profile for a company of your choice. You choose the company for the profile. For example, you could create a company profile for a small computer store or a bookkeeping business that you run from your own home. Follow the steps provided to create the data for your company profile, and then publish it in Word, along with a chart you create in Excel.

1. Create a database called "[Company Name] Profile" that contains information about all the sales made in the past month by your company. Create a table called "[Month] Sales" (for example, December Sales). Assign a category to each sale. Direct Access to create the primary key. For example, the categories for items sold in a computer store could be PCs, Laptops, Accessories, and Software. For ideas refer to the June Contracts table you created in Project 2 for Dragon Designs. Make sure you also include the price of each item.
2. Determine the most popular category of items sold, then create a query table that lists all the sales of items in that category.
3. Analyze the query table in Excel to determine the total amount of sales in the most popular category. Format the Excel worksheet attractively for inclusion in the company profile.
4. Analyze the [Month] Sales table in Excel. Create a pie chart that shows the total sales of items in each category. Refer to the pie chart you created in Project 2 for ideas.
5. Switch to Word, create an attractive heading (use WordArt and insert a picture, if you wish), then write text for your company profile, similar to the text included in the company profile in Project 2.
6. Publish the [Month] Sales table in the Word summary, then copy the pie chart and worksheet from Excel, and paste them as links into the Word summary.
7. Save the Word summary as "[Company Name] Profile."
8. Format your company profile attractively, then print a copy.

INDEPENDENT CHALLENGE 3

Create a database that contains information about your personal collection of CDs, records, tapes, videos, photographs, or a collection of your choice. Plan and then create the database as follows:

1. Create a database called "My Collection of [Items]." For example, a database for a vintage comic book collection could be called "My Collection of Vintage Comic Books."
2. Set up a table for your list. Include fields that will differentiate the various records in terms of genre, category, or type, as appropriate. If your table lists all your CDs, for example, you could include fields for Music Genre, Artist, and even Price.
3. Switch to Word and create labels for each item in your collection. Look through the list of labels available in the Labels Options dialog box. You will probably find a label appropriate for the items in your collection. Print your labels.
4. Select the Access table as the data source to merge with your labels, enter the appropriate fields in the label, then run the merge and print a sheet of labels.
5. Switch back to Access, sort one of the genres in the table alphabetically, then analyze it in Excel, and create a chart that shows the breakdown of items by genre. Print the Excel chart and worksheet.

INDEPENDENT CHALLENGE 4

You own a small software company that creates imaginative computer games for children and adults. You've decided to analyze the types of customers who have bought your games in the past month in terms of age, occupation, and geographical location. Follow the instructions provided to create a table in Access, analyze it in Excel, publish it in Word, and then update the table in Access so that the data is also updated in Word and Excel.

1. Create a database called "Software Quest Customer Database," then create a table called "Customer List," as shown in Figure IC-1. Make ID the primary key.

FIGURE IC-1: **Customer List table**

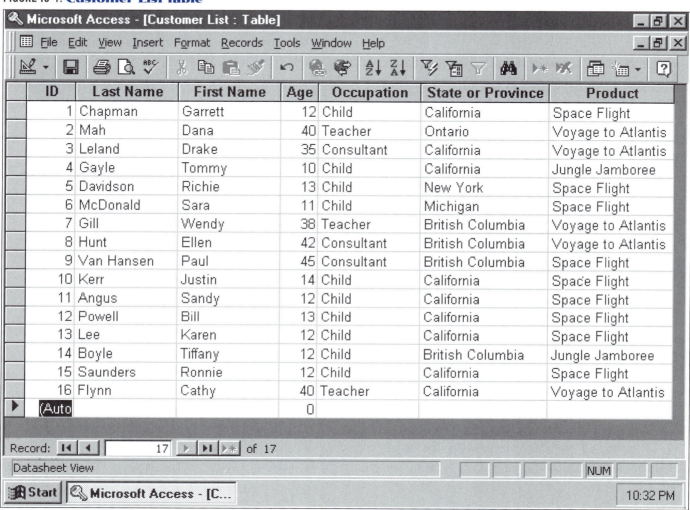

2. Sort the Occupation records in ascending order.
3. Analyze the Customer List in Excel, then create a doughnut chart that shows the breakdown of customers by occupation. You will need to count the number of records in each category in order to create the doughnut chart.
4. Switch back to Access, create a query table called Children that lists only those products bought by children, sort the Age field in ascending order, analyze the query table in Excel, then create a bar chart that shows the breakdown of children by age. Here's how to create the bar chart in Excel:
   a. Enter labels and values in cells A13 to B18, as shown in Figure IC-2.

FIGURE IC-2: Labels and values for bar chart

	A	B
12		
13	Age	Number
14	10	1
15	11	1
16	12	5
17	13	2
18	14	1

   b. Select cells B14 to B18, click the ChartWizard button, click Bar, then click Next.
   c. Click the Series tab, click the Collapse Dialog button to the right of Category (X) axis labels, select cells A14 to A18, click the Restore Dialog button, then click Next.
   d. On the Titles tab, enter "Number of Children by Age Group" as the chart title and "Age Group" as the X-axis title. On the Legend tab, click the Show Legend check box to deselect it, then click Finish.
   e. Right-click the x-axis, click Format Axis, click the Font tab, change the font size to 8 point, click OK, right-click the y-axis, click Format Axis, change the font size to 8 point, click OK, then change the font size of the chart title to 10 point.
5. Switch to Word, create "Software Quest" as a WordArt object, then insert a picture.
6. Type a paragraph of text to introduce the Customer List table, then save the document as Software Quest Customer Analysis.
7. Use the Copy and Paste Link method to copy the Customer List table from Access to Word so that when you update the records in Access, the table in Word will also be updated. Copy and paste the Customer List from Access to Word as follows:
   a. Switch to Access, click the Tables tab, then click Customer List.
   b. Click the right mouse button, then click Copy.
   c. Switch to Word, click below the paragraph of text, then click Edit, Paste Special, Paste Link, and OK.
8. Format the Access table attractively in Word. Use one of the Table AutoFormats if you wish.
9. Switch to Excel then copy both charts and paste them as links into Word. Type short explanatory paragraphs before each chart. Format the pages attractively in Word and print a copy.

Visual Workshop

Create a database called "Westcoast Computers," create a table called "Western Sales" in datasheet view, as shown in Figure VW-1, close the table, answer Yes to create a Primary Key, copy the table, switch to Excel, then paste the copied table as a link. You will need to display the dollar amounts in the Currency style. Create a bar chart in Excel, as shown in Figure VW-2. You will need to resize the chart and format the labels. Return to Access, change the CD-ROM sales for Arizona from $3,000 to $8,000, close the table, then return to Excel. In a few seconds the bar chart will change to reflect the increased amount of Arizona's CD-ROM sales. Print the Excel worksheet.

FIGURE VW-1: Western Sales table

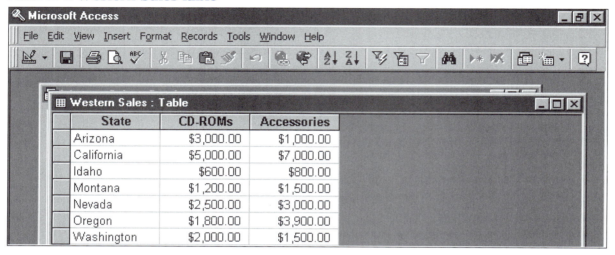

FIGURE VW-2: Western Sales by State bar chart

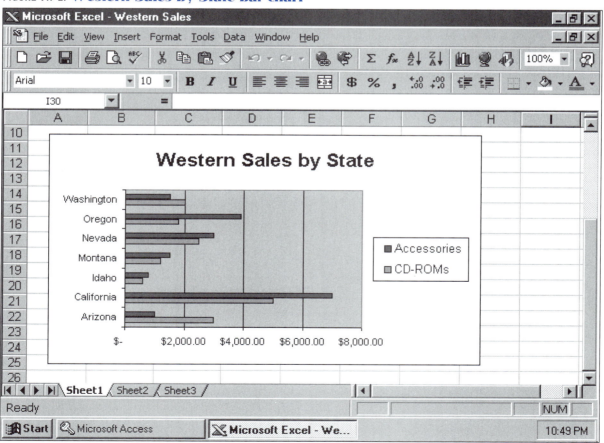

Microsoft ▶ PowerPoint Projects

Presentation Graphics

In This Unit You Will Create:

▶ **Training Presentation**

▶ **Event Poster**

▶ **Lecture Presentation**

You use PowerPoint to create attractively formatted presentations, posters, and flyers that communicate important information to an audience. Suppose you have been asked to present a lecture to your co-workers to describe what you learned at a seminar on how to use Microsoft Access. Your audience will apply the information you give them to develop their own databases. You could, of course, just talk to your audience and perhaps hand out a sheet or two of notes. But imagine how much more compelling your lecture would be if you accompanied it with colorful slides or overheads that provided your audience with a visual backup to your words. People learn best when they can see, hear, and then write down information. You supply the words, and PowerPoint supplies the visual information that your audience can then write down in note form. ▶ In this unit you will learn how to use PowerPoint to create and run presentations and how to use the graphics capabilities of PowerPoint to create posters and flyers.

OVERVIEW

Training Presentation on Oral Presentation Skills

You have been asked to teach a group of your co-workers how to give an oral presentation. To help emphasize the points you plan to make, you will accompany your lecture with an on-screen presentation that you create in PowerPoint. Four activities are required to complete the training presentation for Project 1:

Project Activities

Choose a Presentation Design and Create the Presentation Outline

A presentation consists of a series of slides. Each slide contains a title and a series of points—often in bullet form. Your first task is to enter the information you would like to display on each slide. You enter this information in Outline view. Figure P1-1 shows the Outline view of the first three slides for the Oral Presentation Pointers presentation.

Add Transition and Animation Effects to Slides

Once you have entered all the information you wish to include in your presentation, you can make your electronic slide show more visually interesting. You will add a transition effect to all the slides in the presentation, then you will add an animation effect to all slides except the title slide.

Modify Individual Slides

Pictures from the ClipArt gallery and geometric shapes that you draw right on the screen help enliven selected slides and highlight important information. The slide shown in Figure P1-2 includes a clip art image and two geometric shapes.

Edit and Show the Presentation

You will preview the slides in Slide Sorter view so that you can switch the order of selected slides and then preview the presentation in Slide Show view, where you will learn how to annotate a slide during a slide show.

FIGURE P1-1: **Outline view of Slides 1 to 4**

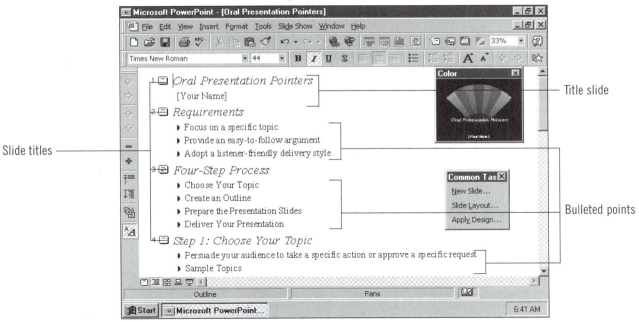

FIGURE P1-2: **Slide with clip art image and two Autoshapes**

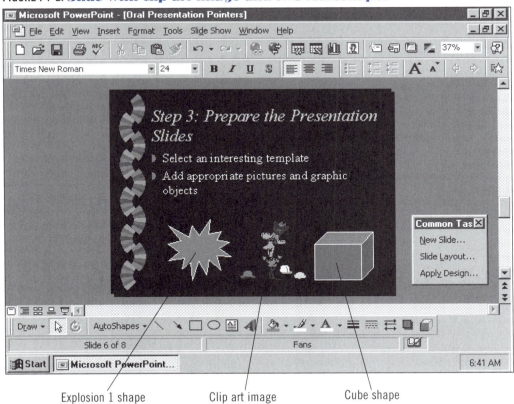

Training Presentation on Oral Presentation Skills

activity:

Choose a Presentation Design and Create the Presentation Outline

You need to access PowerPoint, create a new presentation using a Presentation Design template, then display Outline view so that you can enter the information you wish to display on each of the eight slides in the Oral Presentation Pointers presentation.

steps:

Hint

You can also click the New Office Document button on the Office Shortcut bar.

1. Start PowerPoint, **click the Template option button**, click **OK**, click **FANS** in the New Presentation dialog box, then click **OK**.
   The New Slide dialog box appears.

2. Click **OK** to accept the **Title Slide** AutoLayout, then click the **Outline View button**, in the lower-left corner of the PowerPoint screen (second button from the left)
   You are now ready to enter the titles and other information you wish to include in your presentation.

3. Type **Oral Presentation Pointers**, press **[Enter]**, press **[Tab]**, type your name, as shown in Figure P1-3, then save the presentation as **Oral Presentation Pointers** on the disk where you plan to store all files for this book
   You have entered the information that will be displayed on the first slide in your presentation. Next, enter the information for the second slide.

4. Press **[Enter]**, press **[Shift][Tab]** to start a new slide, type **Four-Step Process**, press **[Enter]**, press **[Tab]**, then type **Choose Your Topic**
   The text you just typed will appear as the first bulleted item on the slide titled "Four-Step Process." You need to enter three more items for this slide.

5. Press **[Enter]**, type **Create an Outline**, press **[Enter]**, type **Prepare the Presentation Slides**, press **[Enter]**, type **Deliver Your Presentation**, then press **[Enter]**
   Another bullet appears. To return the insertion point to the left margin so you can start a new slide, you press [Shift][Tab].

6. Press **[Shift][Tab]**, type **Requirements**, press **[Enter]**, press **[Tab]**, then type the three points as shown for Slide 3 in Figure P1-3
   Remember to press [Enter] after each entry. PowerPoint automatically displays a bullet for the next entry. Next, create the remaining slides for your presentation.

7. Press **[Enter]** after the third point in Slide 3, press **[Shift][Tab]**, type **Step 1: Choose Your Topic**, press **[Enter]**, press **[Tab]**, type **Persuade your audience to take a specific action or approve a specific request**, press **[Enter]**, type **Sample Topics**, then press **[Enter]**
   You want to enter three sub-items under Sample Topics. To move one level to the right, you press [Tab].

Hint

You can also click the Demote (Indent More) button or the Promote (Indent Less) button to move the insertion point to the right or left.

8. Press **[Tab]**, enter the three items under Sample Topics, as shown in Figure P1-3, press **[Enter]**, then press **[Shift][Tab]** twice to return to the left margin
   Next, enter the information for the remaining slides.

9. Enter the information for Slides 5, 6, 7, and 8, as shown in Figure P1-3, click the **Spelling button** and make any corrections required, then save the presentation
   Remember to press [Tab] to move the insertion point to the right and [Shift][Tab] to move the insertion point to the left. Next, go on to apply and then modify a presentation template.

FIGURE P1-3: **Outline view of Oral Presentation Pointers**

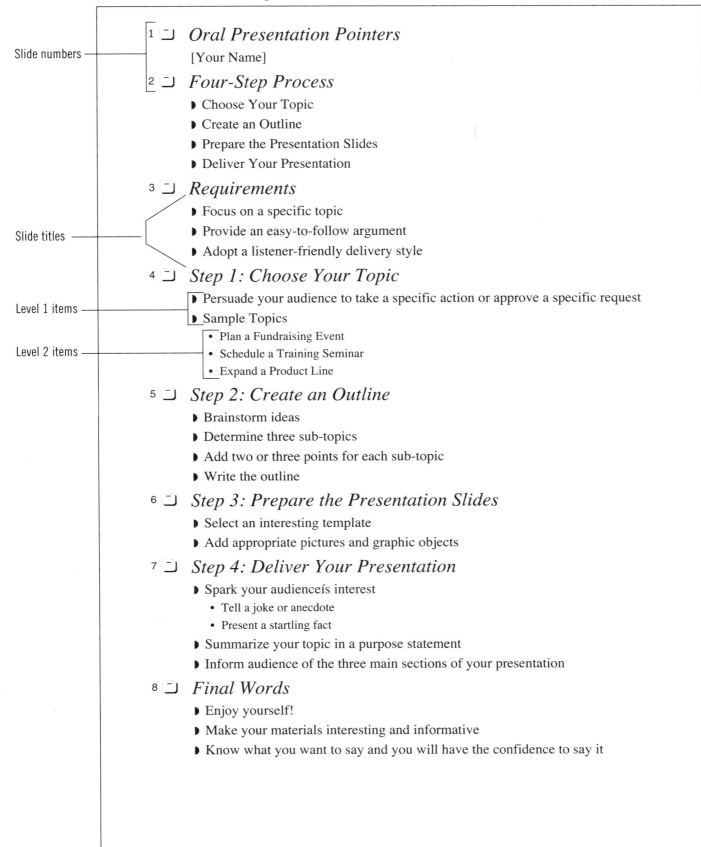

TRAINING PRESENTATION ON ORAL PRESENTATION SKILLS

activity:

Add Transition and Animation Effects to Slides

Next, you need to add transition and animation effects to the slides. Switch to Slide Show view, then select the slides to which you want to add the transition and animation effects.

steps:

1. Click the **Slide Sorter View button**

   You want to add transition and animation effects to all the slides in the presentation.

2. Click **Edit** on the menu bar, then click **Select All**

   First add a transition effect.

3. Click the **Slide Transition Effect list arrow** on the Slide Sorter toolbar, then scroll down and click **Split Vertical In**.

   To see what your transition effect looks like, click the transition effects icon under one of the slides as shown in Figure P1-4.

4. Click the **transition effects icon** under one of the slides.

   Watch the slide to see the effect. Next, add a preset animation to the slides.

Hint

To apply custom animation effects to a specific slide, switch to Slide view, click the Animation Effects button or click Slide Show on the menu bar, then click Custom Animation.

5. Select all the slides again, click the **Text Preset Animation list arrow** on the Slide Sorter toolbar, then click **Appear**.

   To see the animation effect, you need to run the slide show.

6. Click anywhere in the Presentation window to deselect all the slides, click **Slide 1**, click the **Slide Show button**, then press **[Spacebar]** or click the **left mouse button** to scroll through the presentation

   The transition effect works nicely, and the animation effect of having each bullet appear as you press [Spacebar] is effective for controlling the rate at which your audience sees the content of your presentation. However, you don't want your name on Slide 1 to appear after the slide title, so remove the animation effect from this slide.

7. With Slide 1 selected, click the **Text Preset Animation list arrow**, then click **No Effect**

   Check Slide 1 in Slide Show view.

Time To
✓ Save

8. Click , click **[Spacebar]** once to move to Slide 2, then press **[Esc]** to end the slide show

   Your screen appears similar to Figure P1-5.

▶ PPT A-6   MICROSOFT POWERPOINT PROJECTS

FIGURE P1-4: **Transition effect added in Slide Sorter view**

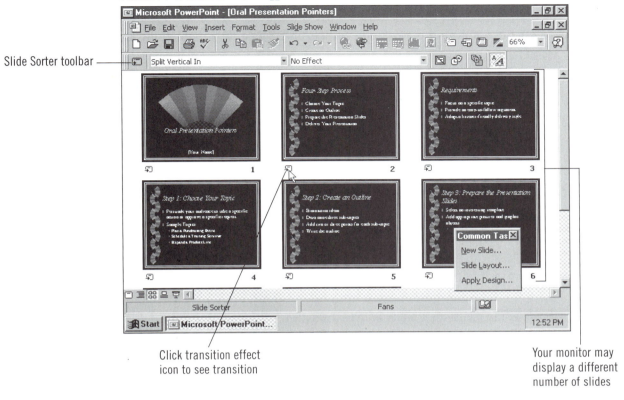

FIGURE P1-5: **Animation effects added to Slides 2 through 8**

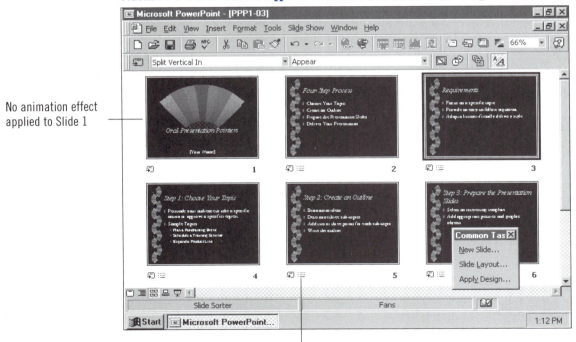

TRAINING PRESENTATION ON ORAL PRESENTATION SKILLS

activity:

Modify Individual Slides

You need to add some clip art and geometric objects to selected slides to emphasize important points and add interest to your presentation. Start by inserting a clip art object on Slide 2.

steps:

1. Double-click **Slide2** to switch to SlideView, click the **Insert Clip Art button**, select **Shapes** in the category list (you will need to scroll down), select the **check box shape** (you will need to scroll down), as shown in Figure P1-6, then click **Insert**

   The check box object is a bit large. You need to resize and position it.

If the Picture toolbar is in the way, drag it by its title bar.

2. Drag the sizing handles to resize the object and position it as shown in Figure P1-7

   Next, draw two objects and insert another clip art object on Slide 6.

3. Click the **Next Slide button** until Slide 6 appears, then click the **AutoShapes menu button** on the Drawing toolbar, point to **Stars and Banners**, then click the **Explosion 1 shape** (first row, first column)

4. Position the mouse in a blank area of the screen, click and drag the mouse to draw the shape, as shown in Figure P1-8, then drag it to position the shape as shown in the figure

   If your shape is a slightly different size, drag the sizing handles to modify it. Next, fill the shape with magenta.

5. Click the **Fill Color list arrow** on the Drawing toolbar, then click the **magenta box**

   Next, draw a cube.

6. Use the Basic Shapes command on the AutoShapes menu to draw a cube similar to the cube shown in Figure P1-8, then fill it with dark purple

   Don't worry yet about positioning your objects exactly as shown in Figure P1-8. Just move the objects to their approximate locations. You will position them exactly in Step 8. Finally, insert a clip art object between the two geometric objects.

7. Insert the clip art object from the **Cartoons category** shown in Figure P1-8, then slightly reduce its size

   Next, you need to position the three objects on the slide.

You can move all three objects at the same time only when they are all selected. Always use the [Shift] key to select multiple objects.

8. Click the **explosion shape** to select it, press and hold **[Shift]**, click the **clip art object**, then click the **cube**

   All three objects are selected. Next, align the objects.

9. Click the **Draw menu button** on the Drawing toolbar, point to **Align or Distribute**, click **Align Bottom**, then drag the three selected objects down so that they are positioned as shown in Figure P1-8, then save the presentation

   To close the AutoShapes dialog box, just click the Close button.

FIGURE P1-6: **Clip Art Gallery**

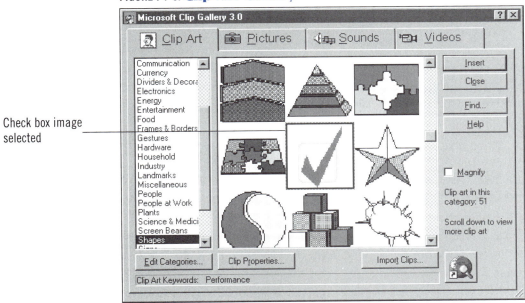

Check box image selected

FIGURE P1-7: **Clip art sized and positioned on Slide 2**

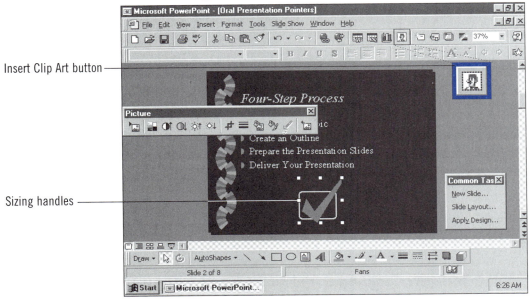

Insert Clip Art button

Sizing handles

FIGURE P1-8: **Completed objects for Slide 6**

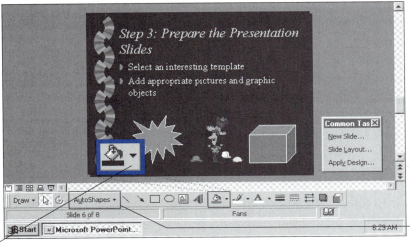

AutoShapes menu button

Fill Color list arrow

TRAINING PRESENTATION ON ORAL PRESENTATION SKILLS

activity:

Edit and Show the Presentation

You need to add a clip art object to Slide 8, modify the title slide, switch the order of Slides 2 and 3 in Slide Sorter view, and then run the presentation in Slide Show view. Start by adding a large clip art object to Slide 9 that you will display under the text.

steps:

Trouble
If you do not have this Clip Art image, choose another one.

1. Click the **Next Slide button** until you reach Slide 8, click the **Insert Clip Art button**, select the **People at Work** category, select the **Speakers Speeches** picture, then click **Insert**

    The image is almost impossible to see because it is black on the black background. You want to change the color of the Speakers Speeches picture and then increase its size so that it appears as a watermark behind the text. To modify a clip art object with the drawing tools on the Drawing toolbar, you first need to ungroup it.

Trouble
If the image becomes unselected while you are executing Step 2, click the Undo button as many times as necessary, then try the step again.

2. Click the **Draw menu button** on the Drawing toolbar, click **Ungroup**, click **Yes** to convert the clip art object to a PowerPoint drawing, click **Draw** again on the menu bar, then click **Group**

    You first converted the speaker picture into numerous objects and then grouped the picture into one object. Next, apply a gray fill.

3. Click the **Fill Color list arrow**, click the **gray box**, then drag the sizing handles to increase the size of the picture, as shown in Figure P1-9

    At present, the speaker picture appears in front of the text. You need to send the picture behind the text.

Hint
If the Drawing toolbar is not visible, click the Drawing button on the Standard toolbar.

4. Click the **Draw menu button**, point to **Order**, then click **Send to Back**

    Slide 8 looks quite striking! Now ungroup the check box image on Slide 2 and change the color of the checkmark. Next, preview the presentation in Slide Sorter view so that you can change the order of Slides 2 and 3.

5. Move to **Slide 2**, select the **check box image**, click **Draw**, **Ungroup**, **Yes**, click away from the image to deselect it, then click only the **checkmark**, click the **Fill Color list arrow**, then click the **magenta box**

6. Press **[Ctrl][Home]**, click the **Slide Sorter View button**, click **Slide 2**, then drag it to the right of Slide 3, as shown in Figure P1-10

    Next, view your presentation in Slide Show view so you can annotate Slide 2.

7. Click **Slide 1**, click the **Slide Show button**, then press **[Spacebar]** to scroll through the presentation until you return to Slide Sorter view

    During the presentation, you've decided that you want to emphasize the first bulleted point on Slide 2. You can use the annotation tools to draw right on the slide show screen during a presentation. Next, return to the Slide Show view, display Slide 2, then draw a line around a portion of the text.

Hint
If your line is a bit too wobbly, click the right mouse button, click Screen, then click Erase Pen and try again.

8. Click **Slide 2**, click , click the **left mouse button** three times to display all three bullets, click the **right mouse button**, click **Pen**, then use to draw a line around the text, as shown in Figure P1-11

    Next, print the presentation as a handout that displays all eight slides on two pages.

9. Click the **right mouse button**, click **End Show**, click **File** on the menu bar, click **Print**, click the **Print what list arrow**, click **Handouts (6 slides per page)**, click **OK**, then save and close the presentation

FIGURE P1-9: **Modified Speakers Speeches image for Slide 8**

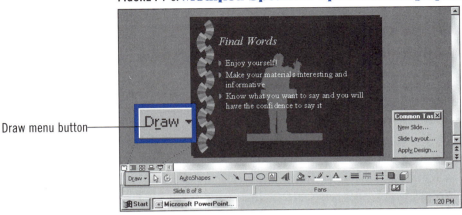

Draw menu button

FIGURE P1-10: **Slides 2 and 3 reversed**

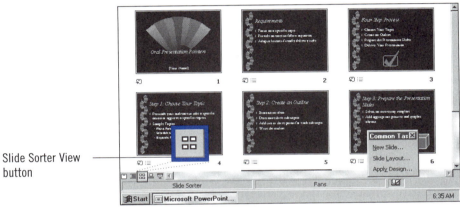

Slide Sorter View button

FIGURE P1-11: **Slide 2 annotated in Slide Show view**

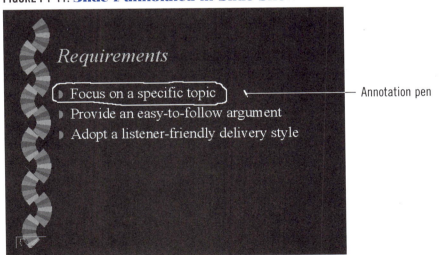

Annotation pen

Grouping and Ungrouping

You can modify any clip art image or graphic on the Slide Master by first "ungrouping" it to separate it into its component elements. You can then modify individual elements or "regroup" the object and then modify all the elements at once.

OVERVIEW

Event Poster for First Night Celebration

On New Year's Eve, your community will sponsor a First Night Celebration at various venues in the town center. Family-oriented concerts and entertainment will be performed throughout the evening, culminating in a spectacular fireworks display at midnight. As a volunteer on your community's local council, you have been asked to produce an attractive poster to advertise the event. You will **Insert WordArt and Clip Art Objects**, **Insert Text Objects**, and then **Format the Poster for Printing**.

activity:

Insert WordArt and Clip Art Objects

steps:

Hint
If PowerPoint is not running, start PowerPoint, then click the Blank presentation option button.

1. From a blank PowerPoint screen, click the **New button** on the Standard toolbar, click the **Blank AutoLayout** in the lower right corner, then click **OK**
   Next, create a WordArt object for "First Night 1999!".

2. Click the **Insert WordArt button** on the Drawing toolbar, select the third WordArt style in the first row, click **OK**, type **First Night 1999!**, select the **Garamond** font, click **OK**, click the **WordArt Shape button** on the WordArt toolbar, then choose the **Deflate Bottom shape** as shown in Figure P2-1.
   Now drag the WordArt object into position and resize it.

3. Drag the object up to the top of the slide, then resize the object so it appears as shown in Figure P2-2.
   Next, insert and modify two clip art objects—a champagne bottle and musical notes.

Trouble
If you do not have this ClipArt image, choose another one.

4. Click the **Insert Clip Art button**, click the **Entertainment** category, click the **champagne bottle** (called **Success Victory Champagne Bottle**), click **Insert**, then save the poster as **First Night 1999**
   You need to modify the champagne bottle so that the cap and bubbles are disconnected.

5. Click the **Draw menu button** on the Drawing toolbar, click **Ungroup**, click **Yes**, click away from the selected objects, click just the bubbles, click **Draw**, then click **Ungroup**
   The champagne bottle now consists of four objects—the bottle, the bubbles, the spray, and the cap.

6. Use your mouse to drag each of the four elements so they are positioned as shown in Figure P2-2
   Take your time. Moving objects with the mouse requires practice and a steady hand! Now that the four objects in the champagne bottle image are separated, you will regroup the image and reduce its size.

7. Press and hold **[Shift]**, click the **bottle**, click the **bubbles**, click the **spray**, then click the **cap** so that all four objects are selected, click **Draw**, click **Group**, drag the **lower-right sizing handle** to reduce the size of the image, then position it in the center of the screen, as shown in Figure P2-3
   Next, insert the notes image.

8. Click, click the **Notes** image (called **Harmony Music**) in the Entertainment category, click **Insert**, then click **Draw**, **Ungroup**, and **Yes**

Trouble
If you select the grouped champagne bottle object when you try to select a note, press [Alt] while you click a note.

9. Drag the dark blue note down to the bottom right corner, resize it slightly larger, delete three of the remaining notes, position the notes around the champagne bottle so that your screen appears similar to Figure P2-3, then save your changes
   Use your own judgment to position the notes. You don't need to copy the illustration in Figure P2-3 exactly. Next, go on to create four text objects for your poster.

▶ PPT A-12   MICROSOFT POWERPOINT PROJECTS

FIGURE P2-1: WordArt Shape dialog box

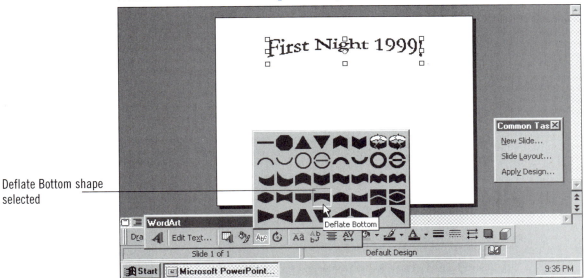

Deflate Bottom shape selected

FIGURE P2-2: WordArt object and ungrouped champagne bottle

Completed WordArt object

Spray

Bottle

Cap

Bubbles

FIGURE P2-3: Champagne bottle and notes images

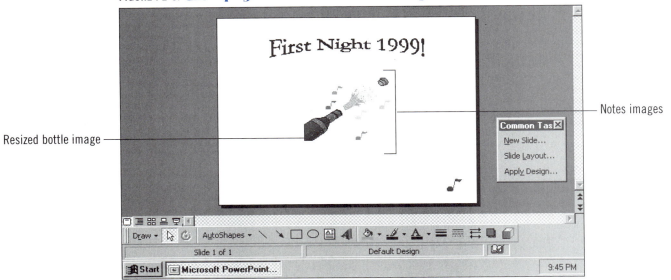

Resized bottle image

Notes images

EVENT POSTER FOR FIRST NIGHT CELEBRATION

activity:

Insert Text Objects

You need to insert four of the seven text objects required for the poster. Start by entering the text object for the subtitle: "Celebrate a Family-Style New Year's Eve."

steps:

Hint
You need to select the slanted-line border so that any changes you make will be applied to all the text in the box.

1. Click the **Text Box button** on the Drawing toolbar, position your mouse under and to the left of the WordArt object, draw a box across the screen, then type **Celebrate a Family-Style New Year's Eve**

   Next, increase the font size of the text object and position it.

2. Click the slanted-line border surrounding the text object, click the **Increase Font Size button**, click the **Bold button**, then drag the shaded border to position the object attractively under the WordArt object, as shown in Figure P2-4

   If the text wraps or if the box extends too far to the right, drag the corner handles to adjust the size of the text object so that all the text appears on one line and you can easily center it under the WordArt object. If necessary, move the WordArt object up a bit so that the text object does not overlap the champagne bottle and notes images. Next, enter the text object that describes the performances.

3. Click away from the text object to deselect it, click, then draw a box starting at the left edge of the page about 1" under "Celebrate"

4. Enter the text, as shown in Figure P2-5

   The box will grow as you press [Enter] after each line. Don't worry if the box extends off the screen or if the first line wraps. Next, decrease the font size of the text object.

5. Click the slanted-line border surrounding the text object, click the **Font Size list arrow**, then click **16**

   Next, adjust the line spacing of the text and center it.

6. Click **Format** on the menu bar, click **Line Spacing**, reduce the **Before Paragraph Spacing** to **0**, click **OK**, click the **Center button**, then position the object, as shown in Figure P2-6

   The text object may overlap the champagne bottle picture. You'll reduce the size of the picture later. Next, enter the two text objects for the "small print" at the bottom of the poster.

Hint
Move the note up so it is above the text object.

7. Click the, draw a box about 4" wide starting at the bottom left corner of the page, type **Sponsored by: [Your Town] Community Council**, click the slanted-line border, reduce the font size to **12**, then position the text object at the bottom left corner of the screen

8. Create another text object that contains **For more information and a complete concert schedule, call 962-4491**, reduce the font size to **12**, then position the text object at the bottom right corner of the screen, as shown in Figure P2-6

   You may need to decrease the size of the second text object in order to position it at the bottom right corner. Next, align the two text objects at the bottom of the screen.

Time To
✓ Save

9. Press and hold **[Shift]**, click both text objects at the bottom of the screen, click the **Draw menu button**, click **Align or Distribute**, then click **Align Bottom**

   Compare your screen with Figure P2-6. Next, go on to add three rotated text objects and then format the poster for printing.

FIGURE P2-4: **Subtitle enhanced and positioned**

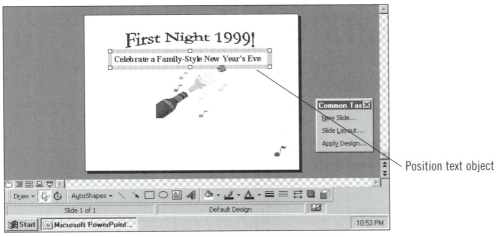

Position text object

FIGURE P2-5: **Text for description of performances**

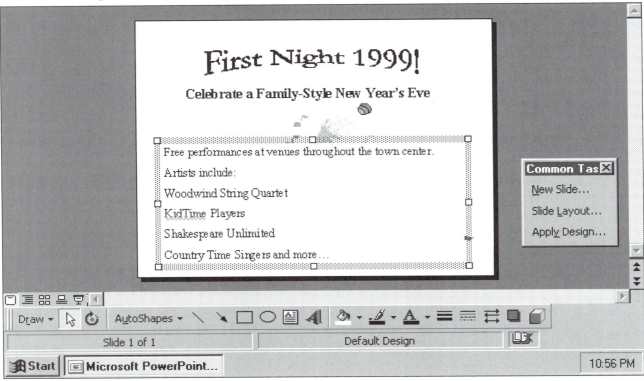

FIGURE P2-6: **Text objects completed**

PRESENTATION GRAPHICS PPT A-15

EVENT POSTER FOR FIRST NIGHT CELEBRATION

activity:

Format the Poster for Printing

You will first create the three rotated text objects, and then you will size and position all the objects on the page so that they appear as shown in Figure P2-7. If you do not like a change you make to an object, just click the Undo button, and try again. Sizing and positioning a large number of objects requires time and patience. Experiment with different looks as you work so that your poster appears similar to the completed poster shown in Figure P2-7.

steps:

1. Create a text object for **Non-alcoholic Refreshments!**

2. Select the text box (click the slanted-line border), reduce the font size to **16**, resize the text object so that the text wraps to two lines, then click the **Free Rotate button** on the Drawing toolbar
   Green dots appear at the four corners of the text object. You need to drag the bottom right dot up to rotate the object.

3. Point the mouse over the lower right green dot (the mouse pointer changes to), then click and drag the dot up to rotate the object, as shown in Figure P2-7

4. Create the rotated text objects for **Outdoor Barbecue!** and **Midnight Fireworks Display!**, as shown in Figure P2-7
   You have created all the elements required for your poster. Next, adjust the size and position of all the objects.

5. Position the rotated text objects on either side of the champagne bottle, as shown in Figure P2-7

6. Drag the text that describes the performances below the champagne bottle so that it is clearly visible

7. Press and hold **[Shift]**, click the WordArt object, the subheading, and the list of performances to select all of them, click **Draw**, **Align or Distribute**, and **Align Center**, then move and size all three objects at once so that they appear centered in relation to the left and right edges of the page

8. Work until you are satisfied with the appearance of your poster, print a copy, then save and close the presentation

FIGURE P2-7: **Completed poster for First Night 1999**

OVERVIEW

Lecture Presentation on Time Management

To give a presentation on time management to your classmates in a business course, you have decided to use PowerPoint to create black and white slides in the portrait format that you can then photocopy onto overhead transparencies to display on an overhead projector as you progress through your presentation. You will **Create Black and White Slides**.

activity:

Create Black and White Slides

steps:

1. Open a new, blank PowerPoint presentation, and select the Title Slide AutoLayout, click **File** on the menu bar, click **Page Setup**, click the **Portrait option button** in the Slides section, then click **OK**
   Next, enter the text for the presentation.
2. Click the **Outline View button** , enter the text for the six slides in the presentation, as shown in Figure P3-1, check the spelling, then save the presentation as **Time Management Presentation**
3. Switch to Slide view, apply the **Meadow template**, then click the **Black and White View button** on the Standard toolbar
   Now you can see how the slides will appear when printed in black and white. You first need to display the Slide Master so you can change the font style.
4. Click **View** on the menu bar, point to **Master**, then click **Slide Master**
5. Click the **Master title style placeholder**, change the font to **Arial** and select **Bold**, then click the **Master text styles placeholder**, and select **Bold** as shown in Figure P3-2
   Next, add clip art to selected slides.
6. Switch to Slide view, then add and modify the clip art objects, as described below:

Slide #	Clip Art Category	Clip Art Object Keywords	Modification
3	Cartoons	Worried Confusion Risk	Size and position
5	Screen Beans	People Happy Joy	Size, Ungroup, fill objects with light gray, regroup, send backward, then flip horizontal
6	Screen Beans	People Adjustment Realignment Schedule Timeline	Size and position

   Finally, view your presentation in Slide Sorter view.
7. Switch to Slide Sorter view, move the Stress Control slide next to the Strategies slide, as shown in Figure P3-3, switch to Outline view, modify Slide 2 so that **Stress Control** comes before **Time Management Techniques**, then click **File** on the menu bar, click **Print**, click the **Print what list arrow**, click **Handouts (6 slides per Page)**, click **OK**, then save and close the presentation

Trouble
Make sure the dotted line selection box appears around the Master text styles placeholder to apply Bold to all of the Master text styles.

FIGURE P3-1: **Outline view of Time Management presentation**

1. Time Management
   [Your Name]
   Business Management 101
2. Time Management Topics
   - Strategies
   - Time Management Techniques
   - Stress Control
3. Strategies
   - Use your time effectively
   - Make responsible decisions
   - Control your stress
4. Time Management Techniques
   - Prepare daily to-do lists
   - Handle paperwork as few times as possible
   - Simplify repetitive work
   - Perform work correctly the first time
5. Stress Control
   - Control your food intake
   - Exercise regularly
   - Visualize non-stress situations
   - Clarify work roles
   - Avoid over-scheduling
6. Time Management Goal
   - Control your workday rather than allowing your workday to control you!

FIGURE P3-2: **Modified Slide Master**

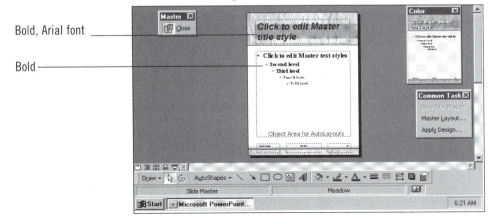

Bold, Arial font

Bold

FIGURE P3-3: **Completed presentation in Slide Sorter view**

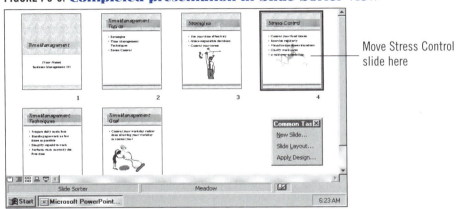

Move Stress Control slide here

Independent Challenges

INDEPENDENT CHALLENGE 1

Create a 6- to 10-slide presentation in portrait format that you could use to help teach a specific concept or task. For example, your presentation could present guidelines for purchasing a computer system, buying a used car, taking effective vacation photographs, planning an event such as a class party or a wedding, seeing the major sites in your home town, etc. Follow the steps provided to create the presentation in PowerPoint.

1. Your first task is to determine the topic of your presentation. Think about an activity or task that you know well and that you can present in short, easy-to-understand steps. Start with the words "How to ...," followed by a verb and then the activity. For example, your presentation topic could be "How to Create a Balcony Garden," or "How to Plan a Backpacking Trip." In the box below, write the topic of your presentation.

    Presentation Topic:

2. You need to determine three main sections for your presentation. Each of these sections will cover a specific activity related to your topic. For example, the three sections for a presentation titled "How to Find a Job" could be 1. Personal Profile, 2. Employment Sources, and 3. Interview Techniques. You will present each of these sections on one slide along with three or four bulleted points that describe it. Write the three sections of your presentation in the box below.

    Section 1:

    Section 2:

    Section 3:

3. Open PowerPoint and create an outline of your presentation. Here's a suggested format:

Slide #	Slide Title	Text
1	Presentation Topic	Your Name
2	Overview	List the three sections in your presentation
3	Section 1 Title	List three or four bulleted points related to Section 1
4	Section 2 Title	List three or four bulleted points related to Section 2
5	Section 3 Title	List three or four bulleted points related to Section 3
6	Conclusion	Create a "motivational" slide to summarize your presentation

    If you wish, you can add more slides for each of the three sections. You may discover that you have enough information in a section to require two or even three slides in order to present it effectively.

4. Switch to Slide view, change the page orientation to Portrait, then apply a Presentation Design template.
5. Switch to Slide Master view, and modify the appearance of the text in the placeholders. You may wish, for example, to change the font size and style of the text in the Master Title Style placeholder. If you wish to change the bullet style, click to the right of the bullet, then click Format on the menu bar, select Bullet, and select the bullet style you prefer from the Bullet dialog box.
6. In Slide view add clip art pictures to selected slides. Remember that you can use the Drawing tools to modify a clip art image after you have ungrouped it.
7. Add one or two geometric objects to selected slides. If you wish to include a geometric object or a clip art on every slide, insert them in Slide Master view.
8. When you are satisfied with the appearance of your slides, switch to Slide Sorter view, add transition effects to all the slides, then switch to Slide Show view, and run the presentation. During the presentation use the pen to highlight important points.
9. Save, print, and close the presentation.

INDEPENDENT CHALLENGE 2

Create a poster that announces some kind of event, such as a concert series, sports tournament, or club meeting.

1. Determine the type of event your poster will announce. Think of your own interests. What type of event would you most likely participate in? If you are involved in sports, you could create a poster to advertise an upcoming game or tournament. If you belong to a club, you could create a poster to advertise a special event such as a fund-raising bake sale or craft fair.
2. Think of an interesting title for your event. For example, a poster that announces a celebrity golf tournament could be called "Stars on Par," or a poster that advertises running events for cash prizes could be called "Dash for Cash."
3. Determine the details that readers of your poster will need to know in order to participate in the event advertised. You need to specify *where* the event will be held, *when* it will be held (date and time), *what* activities will occur at the event, and *who* readers should contact for more information.
4. On a blank piece of paper, create a rough draft of your poster. Determine where you will place the various blocks of text and one or two clip art images.
5. Create the poster on a blank PowerPoint slide. Add at least one clip art image that you have altered in some way. Remember that you need to ungroup the image before you can modify it with the drawing tools. Experiment with the various tools available. You will soon discover numerous ways in which you can modify the available clip art images to create exciting images of your own. For ideas refer to the poster you created for Project 2.
6. Rotate some of the text objects and create a WordArt object for the poster title.
7. Save your poster frequently as you work. Creating an interesting and informative poster takes time and patience. Experiment and remember that you can always click the Undo button if you make a change that you don't like.
8. Print a copy of your poster.

INDEPENDENT CHALLENGE 3

1. Create a sales flyer that advertises a special sale, promotion, or event sponsored by a company of your choice. For example, you could advertise a fall clearance sale at a local furniture store or a two-for-one deal at a local restaurant.
2. Determine the following information for your poster:
   a. Name, address, and phone number of the company
   b. Sales information; for example, special discounts, items on sale, promotional deal, etc.
   c. Price information
3. On a blank piece of paper, create a rough draft of your sales flyer. Determine where you will place the various blocks of text and one or two clip art images.
4. Create the sales flyer on a blank PowerPoint slide. Add at least one clip art image that you have altered in some way.
5. Rotate some of the text objects, and create a WordArt object for the company name.
6. Save the sales flyer frequently as you work.
7. Print a copy of your sales flyer.

INDEPENDENT CHALLENGE 4

You have helped to organize a three-day convention for home-based entrepreneurs in your state or province. This convention will include seminars, booths for the entrepreneurs to promote their products or services, a keynote speech by your state governor or provincial premier, and plenty of opportunities for entrepreneurs to network. A few months prior to the convention, you will hold a meeting for local entrepreneurs to inform them about the conference and encourage them to participate. Follow the instructions provided to create and then modify the presentation that you plan to give at this meeting.

1. Display Outline view of a blank presentation, then enter the slide titles and text for the presentation as shown below:

Slide #	Slide Title	Level 1 Text	Level 2 Text
1	Home-Based Entrepreneurs Convention	[Your town and state/province]	[Your name]
2	Convention Details	Location	[Enter an appropriate location in your hometown, e.g., "Westside Convention Center, San Diego"]
		Dates	May 3 to May 5, 1998
		Time	8 a.m. to 6 p.m.
			Banquet on May 4 at 8 p.m.
3	Convention Activities	Seminars	
		Booth Rentals	
		Networking	
		Keynote Speech	
4	Seminars	Selected Seminars:	Business on the Internet
			Marketing Your Service Business
			Basic Accounting for Small Businesses
			Organizing Your Home Office

Slide #	Slide Title	Level 1 Text	Level 2 Text
5	Booth Rentals	50 square feet: $1000 100 square feet: $2000	
6	Networking	Contact hundreds of local and national distributors Form new business alliances Trade success stories	
7	Keynote Speech	[Name of your governor, premier, or other leader] will present a keynote speech on:	Government Support for the Home-Based Businessperson
8	Home Is Where the Business Is!	[Create a "motivational" slide to encourage attendance at the convention]	

2. Switch to Slide view, change the page orientation to Portrait, then apply a Presentation Design template.
3. Switch to Slide Master view, and modify the appearance of the text in the placeholders. Remember that you can also change the bullet styles for Levels 1 and 2 (Format, Bullet).
4. In Slide view, add clip art pictures to selected slides. Remember that you can use the Drawing tools to modify a clip art image after you have ungrouped it.
5. Add one or two geometric objects to selected slides. If you wish to include a geometric object or a clip art on every slide, insert them in Slide Master view.
6. When you are satisfied with the appearance of your slides, print them in black and white. If possible, copy the printed pages onto overhead transparencies, and give your presentation in class.
7. Save, print, and close the presentation.

Visual Workshop

As part of a presentation on Saving Endangered Species that you are giving at a meeting of a local environmental group, you need to create the two slides shown in figures VW-1 and VW-2. Enter the slide titles in Outline view, select the Contemporary template, remove the "Enter text here" box from Slide 2, add text blocks and clip art to Slide 2, then modify the master title style on the slide master so that the title of Slide 2 appears as shown below. Save the presentation as Saving Endangered Species, print, and close the presentation.

FIGURE VW-1: Title Slide

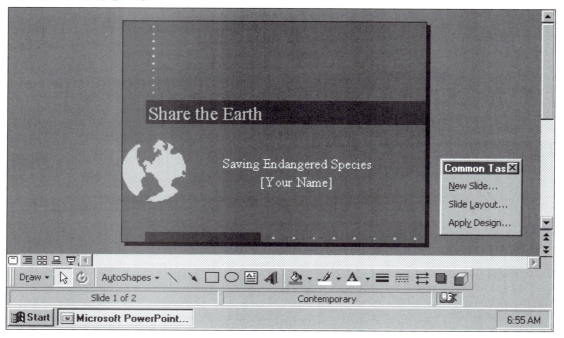

FIGURE VW-2: Slide 2

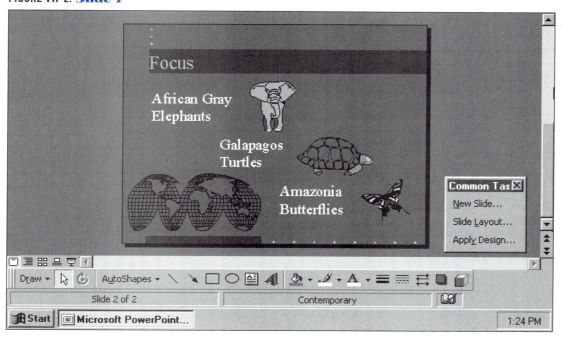

Microsoft ► PowerPoint, Word, Excel, and Access Projects

Integrated Presentations

In This Unit You Will Create:

- ► **Sales Presentation**
- ► **Career Options Presentation**
- ► **Class Party Presentation**

You can integrate all four Office programs to produce PowerPoint presentations that reflect a broad spectrum of company activities. For example, suppose you own a small company that sells gourmet snack products. A group of potential investors has asked you to make a sales presentation. You already have information about your customers and products stored in an Access database, financial information stored in Excel workbooks, and sales literature stored in Word. Now you want to take elements from each of these sources and present them in a format that your investors can quickly and easily understand. The PowerPoint onscreen slide presentation provides you with a flexible medium in which to bring together information from a variety of sources. By creating links between PowerPoint and the source programs, you can also keep the presentation up-to-date and ready to go at a moment's notice. ► In this unit, you will integrate Access, Excel, and Word with PowerPoint to produce exciting on-screen presentations that incorporate slide transitions and animation effects.

OVERVIEW

Sales Presentation for On the Edge Travel

On the Edge Travel organizes guided tours to "adventure" destinations around the world. From canoeing trips into the depths of the Amazon rain forest to survival adventures on a remote Pacific island, On the Edge Travel provides each client with a uniquely exciting travel experience. As a sales manager for On the Edge Travel, you will produce an on-screen presentation for your co-workers that highlights the most popular tours and communicates your new marketing plan to further increase sales. Four activities are required to complete the sales presentation for On the Edge Travel:

Project Activities

Create Source Materials

Much of the data you need for your sales presentation is stored in the Tours database. This database contains the Tours table that lists the sales from On the Edge Travel's last 10 tours. The first three records in this table are shown in Figure P1-1. Once you have created the table in Access, you will copy it into Excel and create the two charts you plan to use in your presentation.

Create the Presentation and Add Charts

You will first access Outline view in PowerPoint, then enter the text required for each slide. All slides will contain a title, and some slides will also contain bulleted points. Once you have entered the text, you will apply a PowerPoint template to the slide show, copy the charts from Excel into selected slides, then modify the charts in PowerPoint.

Modify the Presentation and Create a Word Booklet

First you will adjust the appearance of the slide show in Slide Master view. You then decide that you want your audience to have printed copies of all the slides in the presentation. As the audience listens to your presentation, they can write notes in the spaces next to each slide. You will use the Send To option in PowerPoint to publish the slides in a Word document as shown in Figure P1-2. The slides in the Word document (called a booklet) will be linked to the PowerPoint presentation so that when you update the presentation, the slides in the Word document will also be updated.

Update the Presentation

A few weeks after you give your presentation, new sales figures are entered into the Access database. You decide to give the presentation again to a different group of co-workers, but you want the new presentation to contain the new data entered in the Access database. Fortunately, you linked the table in Access with the charts in Excel, which you then linked to the slides in PowerPoint and the booklet in Word! You will change some of the figures in the Access table, then apply some transition effects and animation effects to produce a whole new slide show. Figures P1-3 and P1-4 show the original and revised versions of one of the slides in the presentation.

FIGURE P1-1: First three records in the Tours table

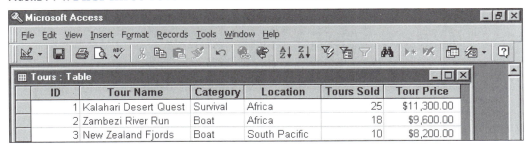

FIGURE P1-2: Pages 1 and 2 of Word booklet

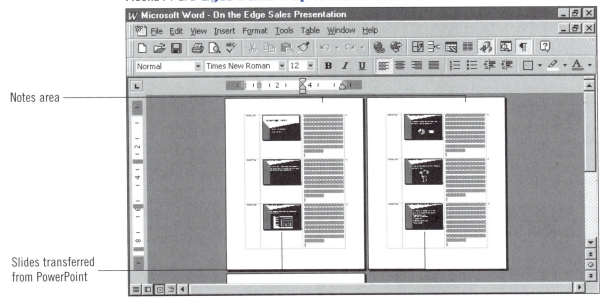

Notes area

Slides transferred from PowerPoint

FIGURE P1-3: Version 1 of Slide 4

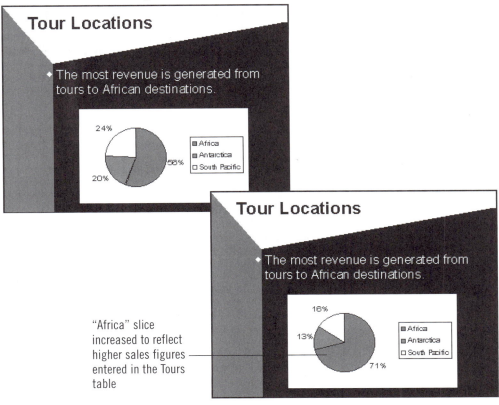

"Africa" slice increased to reflect higher sales figures entered in the Tours table

FIGURE P1-4: Version 2 of Slide 4

PROJECT 1 — SALES PRESENTATION FOR ON THE EDGE TRAVEL

activity:

Create Source Materials

You need to create the Tours table in Access, then copy the table to Excel and create two charts required for your presentation. Before you create the Tours table in Access, you need to activate all four of the Office programs so that you can move quickly between them as your presentation begins to grow.

Hint

You can also click the New Office Document button on the Office Shortcut bar to open new documents in each of the programs.

Hint

To change the data type for the Tours Sold and Tour Price fields, click the Data Type cell next to the field name, then click the Data Type list arrow, and select Number for the Tours Sold field and Currency for the Tour Price field.

steps:

1. Start Excel, start Word, and then start PowerPoint, click the **Blank Presentation option button**, click **OK**, then click **OK** to accept the Title Slide AutoLayout

   The program buttons for Word, Excel, and PowerPoint appear along the bottom of your screen. To display one of the programs, you just click the appropriate program button. Next, create the database that will contain much of the data required for the presentation.

2. Start Access, open a blank database, access the drive where you plan to store all your files for this book, double-click the **File name text box**, type **On the Edge Travel Database**, then click **Create**

   Next, create the Tours table. You will start in Design View, where you will enter the field names and select new data types where required.

3. Click **New**, click **Design View**, click **OK**, then enter the five field names, and select the appropriate data types as shown in Figure P1-5

   Next, enter the data for each record in the Tours table.

4. Click the **View list arrow**, click **Datasheet View**, click **Yes**, name the table **Tours**, click **OK**, click **Yes** to create a Primary Key, then enter the records for the Tours table as shown in Figure P1-6

   Your Access table is complete. Next, you need to create two charts in Excel.

5. Close and save the Tours table, click the **Copy button** on the Database toolbar, click the **Microsoft Excel program button** in the Taskbar, click **Edit** on the menu bar, click **Paste Special**, click the **Paste link option button**, click **OK**, then save the worksheet as **On the Edge Travel Sales Presentation**

   The Tours table appears in Excel. Next, calculate the total amount of money made from each tour.

6. Click cell **G2**, enter the formula to multiply the Tours Sold by the Tour Price **(=E2*F2)**, copy the formula down the column to cell **G11**, click the **Currency Style button** $, then modify the widths of the other columns, as necessary, so you can easily see the cell contents

   Next, create a column chart that shows the breakdown of sales by tour category.

7. Click cell **B13**, type **Survival**, press **[Tab]**, type **Boat** in cell **C13**, press **[Tab]**, type **Land** in cell **D13**, then click cell **B14**, and enter the formula that adds the total tour sales for each Survival tour as shown in Figure P1-7

8. Enter the formulas required to calculate the total tour sales for the Boat tours and the Land tours, then use the Chart Wizard to create a column chart from cells **B13** to **D14** as shown in Figure P1-7

   Note that you must enter formulas to calculate the values in cells B14 to D14 so that the chart will automatically be updated when you change selected values in the Tours table.

Time To
✓ Save

9. Create a pie chart that shows the breakdown of tours by location as shown in Figure P1-7, then save the workbook

   The values in cells F14 to H14 must be formulas that calculate the total sales for each location. For example, the formula in cell F14 is =G2+G3+G7+G8+G11, which calculates the total sales of tours to Africa.

FIGURE P1-5: **Design view of Tours table**

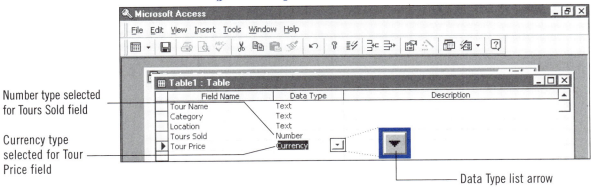

Number type selected for Tours Sold field

Currency type selected for Tour Price field

Data Type list arrow

FIGURE P1-6: **Records for Tours table**

ID	Tour Name	Category	Location	Tours Sold	Tour Price
1	Kalahari Desert Quest	Survival	Africa	25	$11,300.00
2	Zambezi River Run	Boat	Africa	18	$9,600.00
3	New Zealand Fjords	Boat	South Pacific	10	$8,200.00
4	Penguin Cruise	Boat	Antarctica	12	$9,500.00
5	Outback Exploration	Survival	South Pacific	20	$9,500.00
6	Photo Safari	Land	Africa	15	$8,600.00
7	Nile Source Exploration	Land	Africa	12	$9,600.00
8	Island Survival	Survival	South Pacific	20	$5,800.00
9	Antarctic Explorer	Land	Antarctica	15	$13,500.00
10	Congo Jungle	Survival	Africa	25	$7,500.00
(AutoN)				0	$0.00

FIGURE P1-7: **Completed column and pie charts**

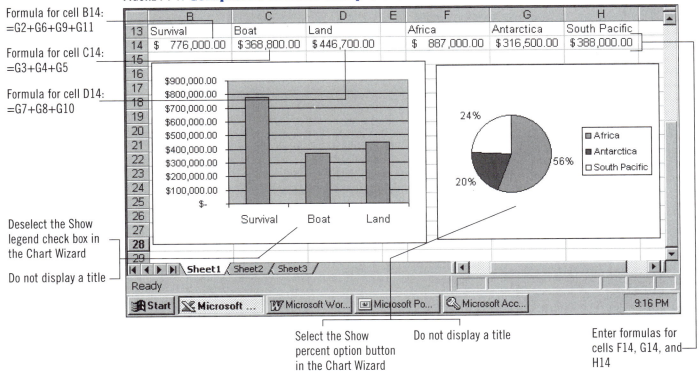

Formula for cell B14: =G2+G6+G9+G11

Formula for cell C14: =G3+G4+G5

Formula for cell D14: =G7+G8+G10

Deselect the Show legend check box in the Chart Wizard

Do not display a title

Select the Show percent option button in the Chart Wizard

Do not display a title

Enter formulas for cells F14, G14, and H14

PROJECT 1 — SALES PRESENTATION FOR ON THE EDGE TRAVEL

activity:

Create the Presentation and Add Charts

You've created the source materials required for your presentation. Now you need to display PowerPoint so that you can enter the slide titles and text in Outline view. You will then format the presentation with a PowerPoint template and add the two charts you created in Excel.

steps:

1. Switch to PowerPoint, then click the **Outline View button**

   Next, enter the text for the title slide.

2. Type **On the Edge Travel**, press **[Enter]**, press **[Tab]**, type **Sales Presentation**, press **[Enter]**, type your name, press **[Enter]**, then save the presentation as **On The Edge Travel Sales Presentation**

   You are ready to enter the text for Slide 2. You first need to return the cursor to the left margin.

3. Press **[Shift][Tab]**, type **Sales Mission**, press **[Enter]**, press **[Tab]**, type the text for the remaining slides, as shown in Figure P1-8, then check the spelling

   Next, apply a PowerPoint template to the entire presentation.

   Hint: Remember to press [Tab] to move the cursor to the right and [Shift][Tab] to move the cursor to the left.

4. Press **[Ctrl][Home]** to move to Slide 1, click the **Slide View button**, click **Apply Design** on the Common Tasks toolbar, select **Angles**, then click **Apply**

   Next, copy the charts from Excel and paste them as links into PowerPoint.

5. Click the **Microsoft Excel program button** on the taskbar, click the **Column chart**, click the **Copy button** on the Standard toolbar, click the **PowerPoint program button** on the taskbar, drag the scroll box down the vertical scroll bar to **Slide 3: Tour Categories**, click **Edit** on the menu bar, click **Paste Special**, click the **Paste link option button**, then click **OK**

6. Drag the sizing handles and reposition the chart so that it appears as shown in Figure P1-9

   The text of the chart is difficult to read, and the gray chart background interferes with the slide background. You need to recolor the chart so it appears attractively on the slide.

7. Click the **Recolor Picture button** on the Picture toolbar, click **OK** if you get an alert message about the number of colors, click the **Fills option button**, click the **list arrow** next to the blue color, click the **red square**, then click **OK**

   Trouble: If the Picture toolbar is not displayed, click View on the menu bar, point to Toolbars, then click Picture.

8. Copy the pie chart from Excel, paste it as a link into Slide 4, use your own judgment to select appropriate colors for the pie chart from the Recolor dialog box, resize and position the pie chart so that it fills the slide attractively as shown in Figure P1-10, then save the presentation

► IN C-6   MICROSOFT POWERPOINT, WORD, EXCEL, AND ACCESS PROJECTS

FIGURE P1-8: *Outline view of On the Edge Travel Sales Presentation*

1. **On the Edge Travel**
   Sales Presentation
   [Your Name]

2. **Sales Mission**
   - On the Edge Travel needs to develop a marketing plan to promote the tours that have attracted the most clients.

3. **Tour Categories**
   - Survival tours is currently the most popular tour category.

4. **Tour Locations**
   - The most revenue is generated from tours to African destinations.

5. **African Tours**
   - Focus our marketing plan on promoting tours to Africa!

6. **Revenue: African Tours**
   - The following five tours to Africa generated a total of $887,000.00:
     – Zambezi River Run
     – Nile Source Exploration
     – Photo Safari
     – Kalahari Desert Quest
     – Congo Jungle

7. **Marketing Plan**
   - Develop an African Tours slide show
   - Produce an African Tours brochure
   - Offer discounts to repeat customers

8. **To the Top!**
   - The marketing plan for African tours aims to increase revenues by 40% over the next year.

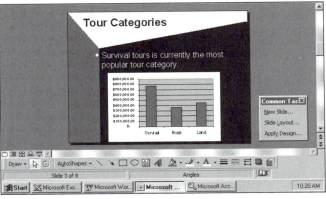

FIGURE P1-9: *Sized and positioned column chart on Slide 3*

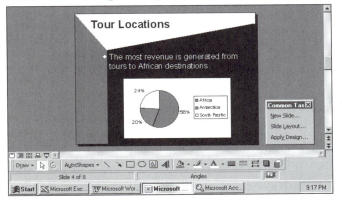

FIGURE P1-10: *Completed pie chart on Slide 4*

SALES PRESENTATION FOR ON THE EDGE TRAVEL

activity:

Modify the Presentation and Create a Word Booklet

You need to do some fine-tuning of the presentation, add clip art to selected slides, and then create a booklet in Word that is linked to the PowerPoint presentation.

steps:

1. Click **View** on the menu bar, point to **Master**, then click **Slide Master**

   The Slide Master view appears. Next, modify the text styles in the Master Title Style placeholder and the Master Text Styles placeholder.

2. Click the **Master title style placeholder**, change the font to **Arial**, then click the **Bold button**

3. Click the **Master Text Styles placeholder**, change the font to **Arial** for both Levels 1 and 2, click **Format** on the menu bar, click **Bullet**, change the font to **Wingdings**, choose the fourth symbol in the fourth row, click **OK**, click the **Slide View button**, then click the **Next Slide button** to scroll through the presentation

   As you can see, Slides 5 and 8 look particularly bare. Next, add two clip art pictures to these slides.

Trouble
If you don't have the elephant image, insert another piece of clip art.

4. Drag the scroll box to **Slide 5**, click the **Insert Clip Art button** on the Standard toolbar, click **Animals**, select the picture of the **gray elephant** (called **Elephant Strong Large**), insert it, then resize and position it as shown in Figure P1-11

   Next, add a picture to Slide 8.

5. Drag the scroll box to **Slide 8**, insert the **Climbing the Mountain** (may be called **Opportunity Challenge Difficult**) picture from the **Cartoons category**, then resize and position it as shown in Figure P1-12

   Next, create a Word booklet that is linked to the PowerPoint presentation.

6. Click **File** on the menu bar, point to **Send To**, click **Microsoft Word**, click the **Blank lines next to slides option button**, click the **Paste link option button**, then click **OK**

   You will need to wait for a few minutes while PowerPoint transfers the slide presentation to Word.

7. When the transfer is complete, press **[Ctrl][Home]** to move to the top of the Word document

   Your screen appears as shown in Figure P1-13

8. Save the Word document as **On the Edge Sales Presentation**, print a copy, then return to PowerPoint

FIGURE P1-11: **Clip art for Slide 5**

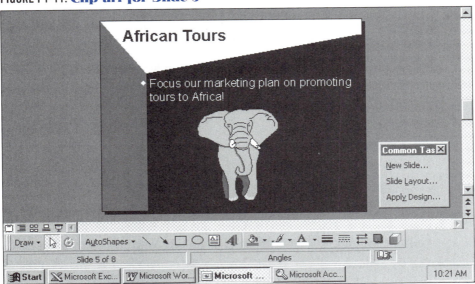

FIGURE P1-12: **Clip art for Slide 8**

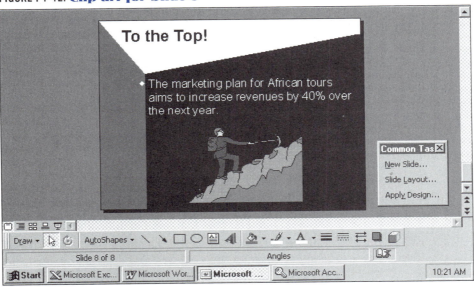

FIGURE P1-13: **PowerPoint presentation in Word**

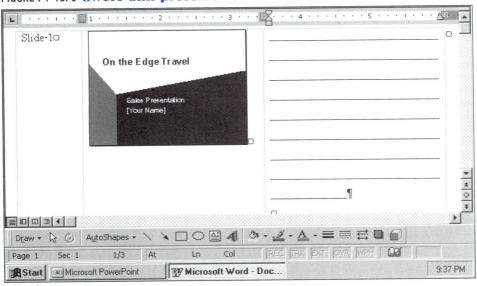

SALES PRESENTATION FOR ON THE EDGE TRAVEL

activity:

Update the Presentation

After you give the sales presentation, the number of tours sold increases. You will display the Tours table in Access, change the number of tours sold, then update the links to the charts in both PowerPoint and the slide booklet in Word.

steps:

1. Click the **Microsoft Access program button**, open the **Tours table**, then enter new values for the Tours Sold column as shown in Table P1-1

2. Close the Tours table, switch to PowerPoint, click **Edit** on the menu bar, click **Links**, press and hold **[Shift]**, click the two links entered, click **Update Now**, then click **Close**
   Display Slides 3 and 4 to see how the two charts have changed to reflect the new data you entered in the Tours table. Next, change the total sales revenue for the African tours entered in Slide 6. You will change this amount by hand, because PowerPoint does not update numbers or text copied from other applications.

Hint
Word automatically updates the links, but using Update Now is faster.

3. Display Excel, click the cell containing the total revenue from African tours, click the **Copy button** on the Standard toolbar, switch to PowerPoint, display Slide 6, select the current amount entered (**$887,000**), delete this amount, click the **Paste button** on the Standard toolbar, then delete any extra spaces

4. Switch to Word, click **Edit** on the menu bar, click **Links**, select all the slides displayed (use **[Shift]**), click **Update Now**, click **Close**, display Slide 6, then check that the new amount ($1,738,200.00) appears in the document
   Next, add some transition effects to your slide show presentation.

5. Switch to PowerPoint, click the **Slide Sorter View button**, click **Slide Show** on the menu bar, click **Slide Transition**, click the **Effects list arrow**, click **Random Transition** (bottom selection) as shown in Figure P1-14, then click **Apply to All**
   When you select Random Transition effects, PowerPoint applies a different effect to each slide.

6. Click the **Text Preset Animation list arrow** on the Slide Sorter toolbar, then click **Random Effects** (bottom selection) as shown in Figure P1-15
   Next, preview the slide show.

7. Click the **Slide Show button**, then click the left mouse button to move from slide to slide
   You can select different slide transitions and build effects for each slide in Slide Sorter view.

8. Save and close your presentation, then save and close the files in Access, Excel, and Word
   Next, open the files again so you can practice reestablishing links. You will start with the application that does not contain links and then open the remaining files in the order in which they are linked. For this presentation, the order of files is Access, Excel, PowerPoint, and Word.

Time To
✓ Save
✓ Print
✓ Close all files
✓ Exit all programs

9. Click the **Access program button** on the taskbar, click the **Open button** on the toolbar, open **On the Edge Travel Database**, click the **Excel program button**, open **On the Edge Travel Sales Presentation**, click **Yes** to reestablish links, click the **PowerPoint program button**, open **On the Edge Travel Sales Presentation**, click **OK** then click **Yes** to reestablish links, switch to Word, then open **On the Edge Travel Sales Presentation**
   You have reestablished all the links between the files. Note that your computer may not have enough memory to do this step.

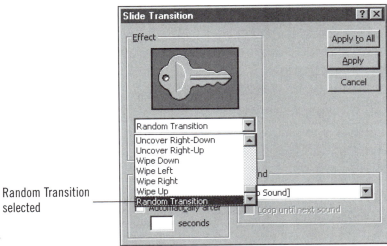

FIGURE P1-14: **Transition effect selected**

Random Transition selected

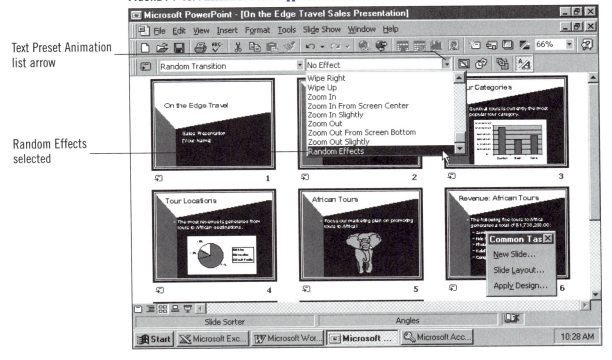

FIGURE P1-15: **Animation effect selected**

Text Preset Animation list arrow

Random Effects selected

TABLE P1-1

TOUR NAME	TOURS SOLD
Kalahari Desert Quest	55
Zambezi River Run	40
Photo Safari	50

OVERVIEW

Career Options Presentation

As the marketing coordinator at Alma Business College, you will prepare a presentation to inform potential students of the courses offered and the career options they can expect after graduating from the college. For this project you will **Create the Source Materials and the Presentation**, **Add Charts**, and **Add a Word Table and Animation Effects**.

activity:

Create the Source Materials and the Presentation

You plan to include two charts that display the employment success of former students. The statistics you need for your charts are entered in an Access table. First create the Access table, then create the charts, and finally enter the slide titles and text required for the presentation.

Hint
Remember to select Paste Special from the Edit menu.

steps:

1. Create an Access database called **Alma Business College**, create a new table, enter the fields and records in Datasheet View as shown in Figure P2-1, close the table, name it **Employment Table**, then answer **Yes** to create a Primary Key

2. Copy the Employment Table, paste it as a link into a blank Excel worksheet, then save the workbook as **Career Options Presentation**
   You need to create two charts in Excel. Start by creating a column chart that shows the employment statistics for each of the four programs.

3. Select cells **B1** to **E5**, create a column chart in the third Chart Wizard dialog box, click the **Legend tab**, click the **Bottom option button**, then complete the Chart Wizard steps
   Next, calculate the total employment figures and create a pie chart that shows the employment statistics for all four programs.

4. Select cells **C2** to **F6**, click the **AutoSum button** Σ on the Standard toolbar, click the **Chart Wizard button** on the Standard toolbar, create a **Pie chart**, in the second Chart Wizard dialog box click the **Collapse Dialog Box button**, select cells **C1** to **E1**, type a **comma**, select cells **C6** to **E6**, click the **Restore Dialog Box button**, then complete the Chart Wizard
   Next, switch to PowerPoint and enter the slide titles and text required for the Career Options presentation.

5. Open a blank presentation in PowerPoint, click the **Outline View button**, enter the slide titles and text required for the presentation as shown in Figure P2-2, check the spelling, then save the presentation as **Career Options Presentation**
   Next, enhance the presentation with a template, then add the charts.

▶ IN C-12 MICROSOFT POWERPOINT, WORD, EXCEL, AND ACCESS PROJECTS

FIGURE P2-1: Employment table

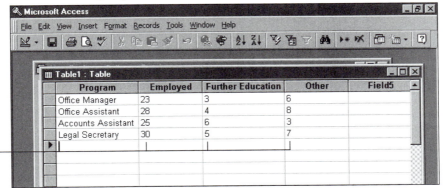

Change the Data Type to Number for the Employed, Further Education, and Other fields

FIGURE P2-2: Career Options Presentation outline

1. Career Choices
   Alma Business College
   [Your Name]

2. Program Objectives
   - Develop marketable skills
   - Achieve computer expertise
   - Qualify for employment
   - Build a solid foundation for further education

3. Marketable Skills
   - Document and Word Processing
   - Accounting Procedures and Spreadsheet Analysis
   - Office Management
   - Small Business Development
   - Business Writing
   - Desktop Publishing
   - Internet Communications

4. Employment Opportunities
   - Administrative and Executive Assistants
   - Accounting Assistants
   - Office Managers
   - Legal Secretaries

5. Special Features
   - Intensive hands-on training
   - Three-week employment practicum
   - Career counseling

6. Employment Statistics

7. Graduate Profile

8. Program Overview

9. Core Courses

10. Alma Business College

CAREER OPTIONS PRESENTATION

activity:

Add Charts

You need to apply a presentation template, copy and modify the two Excel charts, then create an organizational chart for Slide 8.

steps:

To remove the "Click to add text" box, click it, click the shaded border, then press [Delete].

1. Switch to Slide view, click **Apply Design** on the Common Tasks toolbar, select **Dads Tie**, then click **Apply**

   Next, copy the charts from Excel and paste them as links into Slides 6 and 7.

2. Switch to Excel, click the **Column chart**, click the **Copy button**, switch to PowerPoint, display **Slide 6: Employment Statistics**, delete the "Click to add text" box, click **Edit** on the menu bar, click **Paste Special**, click the **Paste link option button**, then click **OK**

   Next, modify the chart color scheme.

3. Size and position the chart attractively on the slide, display the Picture toolbar, if necessary, click the **Recolor Picture button** on the Picture toolbar, click **OK** if you get an alert message about the number of colors, click the **Fills option button**, click the **list arrow** next to the blue color, click the **turquoise square** (the fifth square) as shown in Figure P2-3, then click **OK**

   Next, copy the pie chart from Excel and paste it as a link into Slide 7

Remember to delete the "Click to add text" box before pasting the pie chart in Slide 7.

4. Copy the pie chart from Excel, paste it as a link into Slide 7, then modify the colors, size, and position of the chart so it appears attractive on the slide

   Use your own judgment to determine the best colors to use. You will need to experiment! Next, create an organizational chart in Slide 8.

5. Drag the scroll box to Slide 8, delete the "Click to add text" box, click **Slide Layout** on the Common Tasks toolbar, click the **Organization Chart layout**, click **Apply**, then double-click the **org chart icon**

   Next, enter text in each of the four boxes that appear on the screen.

6. Type **Core Program**, click the **far left box**, type **Office Manager**, click the **middle box**, type **Office Assistant**, click the **far right box**, then type **Accounts Assistant**

   You need to add one more box to the right of the Accounts Assistant box.

7. Click the **Right co-worker button** [Co-worker], click the **Accounts Assistant** box, type **Legal Secretary**, click away from the boxes, then delete the "Type title here" text in each box

   Next, delete "Chart Title," then rearrange the boxes in a vertical format.

8. Drag your mouse across **Chart Title** to select it, press **[Delete]**, press **[Ctrl][A]** to select all the boxes in the chart, click **Styles** on the menu bar, then click the middle selection in the top row as shown in Figure P2-4

   Next, display the organizational chart on Slide 8 of your presentation.

9. Click **File** on the menu bar, click **Exit and Return to Career Options Presentation**, click **Yes**, then use your mouse to resize and position the organizational chart so it appears as shown in Figure P2-5, then save the presentation

FIGURE P2-3: Recolor dialog box

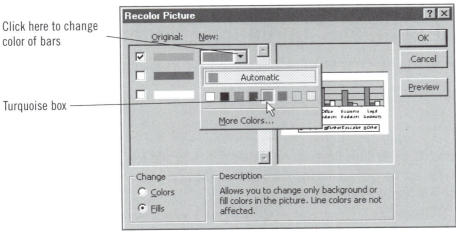

FIGURE P2-4: Groups dialog box

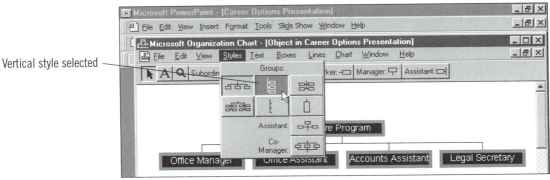

FIGURE P2-5: Completed organizational chart on Slide 8

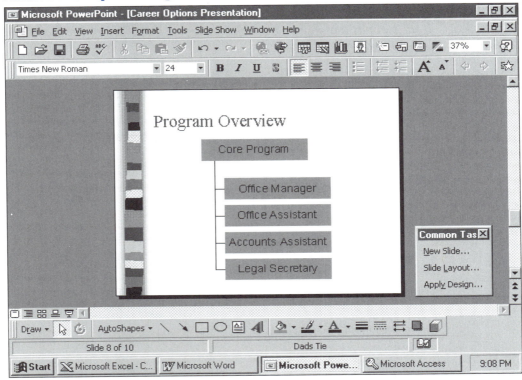

CAREER OPTIONS PRESENTATION

activity:

Add a Word Table and Animation Effects

You will add a Word table to Slide 9 and a WordArt object to Slide 10, then apply animation effects to selected slides.

steps:

1. Drag the scroll box to **Slide 9: Core Courses**, delete the "Click to add text" box, click the **Insert Microsoft Word Table button** on the Standard toolbar, then drag the mouse across the table grid to create a table of four rows and two columns

   In a few seconds a blank table form will appear on the slide. You need to enter the text for the table.

2. Enter the text for the table as shown in Figure P2-6

   You can modify a Word table inserted in PowerPoint just as you would a normal Word table. You need to reduce the size of column 1, then add a Table AutoFormat.

Trouble
If "Course #" moves to two lines, enlarge the entire table object, then drag the left column divider to the left.

3. Drag the column divider to the left to reduce the size of column 1 so that "Accounting Procedures" fits on one line, click **Table** on the menu bar, click **Table AutoFormat**, select the **Colorful 1** format, then click **OK**

4. Click away from the table, then position it attractively on the slide

   Next, enhance Slide 10 with a WordArt object.

5. Click the **Next Slide button** to move to Slide 10, delete the "Click to add text" box, click the **Insert WordArt button** on the Drawing toolbar, then create a WordArt object as shown in Figure P2-7

   You need to select the second WordArt style in the fourth row, then click the Fill Color list arrow on the Drawing toolbar and select the yellow box.

6. Insert and modify the two clip art images from the **People at Work** category so that they appear as shown in Figure P2-7

   If the two pictures are not available, make your own choices. Next, add some animation effects to selected slides.

7. Drag the scroll box to **Slide 3: Marketable Skills**, select the bulleted text (make sure handles appear in the shaded border), click the **Animation Effects button** on the Formatting toolbar, then click the **Camera Effect button** on the Animation Effects toolbar

   To see the animation effect, you need to switch to Slide Show view.

8. Click the **Slide Show button**, click the left mouse button to see the animation effect, click the **right mouse button**, then click **End Show** on the pop-up menu to return to Slide view

   You can add a wide variety of animation and build effects to selected slides by either selecting one of the preset animation effects or creating your own animation effect.

Hint
You can add Animation Effects only in Slide view.

9. Press **[Ctrl][Home]**, add animation effects to selected slides, preview the effect in Slide Show view, switch to Slide Sorter view, add transition and build effects to selected slides, run the slide show, print a copy of the presentation in black and white, then save and close all files

   The completed presentation appears as shown in Figure P2-8. Experiment with a variety of transition, animation, and build effects.

Drag the column divider to the left to adjust the column width

FIGURE P2-6: **Text for Word table**

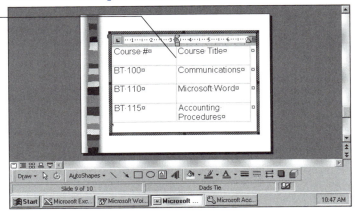

FIGURE P2-7: **Slide 10 completed**

WordArt object

Yellow fill color selected

FIGURE P2-8: **Completed presentation in Slide Sorter view**

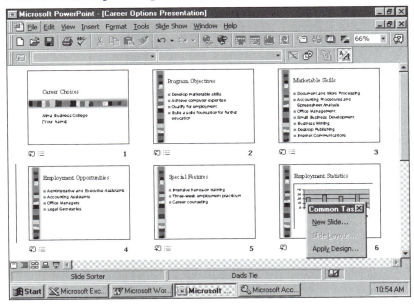

Creating Animation Effects

To create your own animation effect, display a slide, select the bulleted text (animation effects do not work on charts and tables), click Slide Show on the menu bar, click Custom Animation, then select the animation and sound effects you require. Click Preview in the dialog box to see the effects you selected.

OVERVIEW

Class Party Presentation

You are on a committee formed to organize a class party to celebrate the end of a year-long business administration course at Mariposa Community College in Louisville, Kentucky. Your job is to create a slide show presentation that will inform your classmates about the party and encourage them to attend. As you create the presentation in PowerPoint, you will enter some of the data in Word and Excel and then copy it into PowerPoint. Often you will find that you need to retrieve data from other applications for inclusion in a PowerPoint presentation.

steps:

1. Open a new presentation, create an outline as shown in Figure P3-1, check the spelling, then save the presentation as **Class Party Presentation**

   Instead of selecting one of the PowerPoint templates, you will add a custom background to your presentation.

2. Switch to Slide view, click **Format** on the menu bar, click **Background**, click the **Background fill list arrow**, then click **Fill effects**

   Next, select a custom Shaded Fill for your presentation background.

3. Click the **Preset option button**, click the **Preset colors list arrow**, select **Late Sunset**, click **OK**, then click **Apply to all**

   As you can see, most of the text on the slide is not visible. You need to change the slide color scheme.

4. Click **Format** on the menu bar, click **Slide Color Scheme**, click the middle scheme in the top row, then click **Apply to All**

   Next, switch to Word and enter the data you wish to include in the Party Details slide.

5. Switch to a blank Word document, type **Date:**, press **[Tab]**, type **June 10**, press **[Enter]**, type **Time:**, press **[Tab]**, type **6 pm to ?**, press **[Enter]**, type **Place:**, press **[Tab]**, then type **Le Figaro Restaurant**

   Next, select the text and copy it as unformatted text into Slide 3 of your presentation.

6. Press **[Ctrl][A]** to select all the text, click the **Copy button** on the Standard toolbar, switch to PowerPoint, display **Slide 3: Party Details**, delete the "Click to add text" box, click **Edit** on the menu bar, click **Paste Special**, click **Unformatted Text**, click **OK**, increase the font size to **40**, then position the text attractively on the slide

7. Switch to a blank Excel worksheet, enter the data shown in Figure P3-2 in cells A1 to D2, select cells **A1** to **D2**, click, switch to PowerPoint, display **Slide 4: Cost Breakdown**, delete the "Click to add text" box, click the **Insert Chart button** on the Standard toolbar, click the **Chart Type list arrow** on the Standard toolbar, click the **Pie Chart**, select columns **A** to **D**, click the **Paste button**, then delete rows 2 and 3 in the datasheet as shown in Figure P3-2

8. Click away from the datasheet to place the pie chart on the slide, position the pie chart attractively on the slide, double-click the pie chart, move the legend to the bottom right corner, delete the white line around the pie chart, then click away from the pie chart to deselect it

9. Add a WordArt object and some clip art to Slide 5 to encourage your audience to attend the party, add animation effects to selected slides in Slide view, add slide transitions and builds in Slide Sorter view, compare your screen with Figure P3-3, run your slide show in Slide Show view, print it, close the Word and Excel documents without saving them, then save and close the presentation

   Ideas for Slide 5 include "We Deserve a Break!" or "Let's Celebrate!" as a WordArt object, accompanied by an appropriate clip art picture. Use your imagination to create an interesting and motivating slide.

Hint

Select Unformatted Text in the Paste Special dialog box to copy text from Word into PowerPoint.

FIGURE P3-1: Outline view of Class Party Presentation

FIGURE P3-2: Datasheet and pie chart for Slide 4

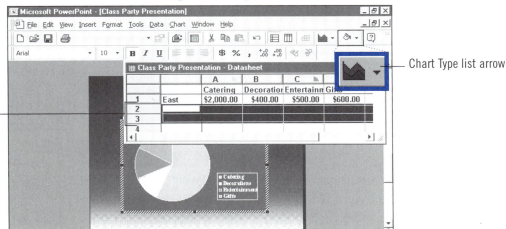

FIGURE P3-3: Class Party Presentation in Slide Sorter view

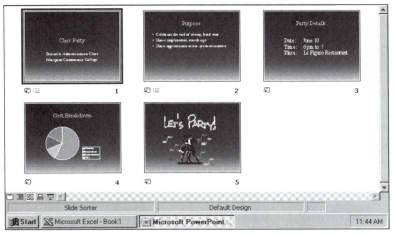

Clues to Use

Enhancing the Look of a Slide Presentation

You can achieve an almost limitless variety of looks by working with the options available in the Custom Background and Slide Color Schemes dialog boxes. You can display a textured or patterned background, select your own colors for each element on a slide, and modify any of the preset shading patterns.

Independent Challenges

INDEPENDENT CHALLENGE 1

Create an on-screen presentation of 8 to 10 slides that highlights sales information and recommends marketing strategies for a company of your choice. You could create a presentation for a movie production company that presents the revenues from the last 10 movies produced and recommends producing movies in the most popular category. Alternatively, you could create a presentation for a theme park that displays the revenues from 10 rides and then offers marketing suggestions for attracting more customers to the two most popular rides. For ideas, check the business section of your local newspaper, surf the World Wide Web, or browse through the clip art categories. For example, the roller coaster clip art image in the Entertainment category may inspire you to create a presentation involving a theme park. Follow the steps provided to create a table in Access, charts in Excel, the presentation in PowerPoint, and a presentation booklet in Word.

1. You need to know the name of your company and the type of products or services that it sells. For example, you could call your company Vitamin Vigor and describe it as a retail operation that sells vitamins, herbal teas, and other health products. Write the name and a brief description of your company in the box below:

   Company Name: ....
   Description: ....
   ....

2. Open Access, create a database called [Company Name] Sales Presentation, and create a table consisting of at least 10 records. Call the table [Product] table (e.g., Rides table). Include fields in the table that you will be able to use in charts. For example, a table for the theme park presentation could include the following fields: Ride Name, Category (e.g., Kiddie, Moderate, and Hair-raising), Number of Riders, and Ride Price.
3. Copy the table and paste it as a link into Excel. Create two charts that display sales information about your company. For example, you could create a pie chart that shows the breakdown of ride sales by category and a column or bar chart that displays the revenue from each of the 10 rides listed in the Access table.
4. Switch to PowerPoint, create an outline of your presentation, then save it as [Company Name] Sales Presentation.

Slide #	Slide Title	Text
1	[Company Name]	Sales Presentation
		[Your Name]
2	Mission	Write a one- or two-sentence description of your company's goals. For ideas, refer to Slide 2 of the On the Edge Travel sales presentation you created for Project 1.
3	[Product] Categories	Write one sentence describing a chart that displays the breakdown of sales by category.
4	[Product] Sales or Location	Write one sentence describing a chart that displays the breakdown of sales by location or overall sales, depending on the type of chart you have created.
5	[Most Popular Product/Category]	Write a sentence describing your marketing plan, e.g., to focus on a specific product category.
6	Revenue: [Most Popular Product/Category]	List the products that generated the most income in the category you've chosen to focus on, then copy the total revenue from the category from Excel into PowerPoint.
7	Marketing Plan	Write two or three points describing your marketing plan.
8	Conclusion	Create an interesting "motivational" slide to conclude your presentation.

Add additional slides to your presentation, if you wish.

5. Switch to Slide view and apply a presentation template or a custom background. Spend some time experimenting with the wide variety of looks you can achieve by working with the options available in the Custom Background dialog boxes. Don't forget to check out the preset backgrounds!
6. Switch to Slide Master view and modify the appearance of the text in the placeholders. You may wish, for example, to change the font size and style of the text in the Master Title Style placeholder. Add a clip art image to the Slide Master, if you wish.
7. In Slide view, copy the charts to the appropriate slides (paste them as links) and add clip art pictures to selected slides. Remember that you can use the Drawing tools to modify a clip art image after you have ungrouped it. You may need to recolor the charts so that they are clear and easy to read on the slide background or template you have chosen.
8. When you are satisfied with the appearance of your slides, switch to Slide Sorter view and add some slide transitions and build effects. You can also add animation effects to selected slides in Slide view.
9. Preview your slide show and make any formatting adjustments required.
10. Create a Word booklet from the slides in the PowerPoint presentation, then save the Word booklet as [Company Name] Sales Presentation.
11. Change some of the values in the Access table, then update the charts in PowerPoint and the booklet in Word.
12. Print a copy of the Word booklet.

INDEPENDENT CHALLENGE 2

Create a presentation that informs an audience about a specific college program or organization. Imagine that your audience will be people interested in attending the program or joining the organization. Your presentation needs to inform them about the program or organization and encourage them to enroll or join. If you wish, adapt the presentation you created for Project 2 to suit the needs of a program or organization of your choice.

1. Determine the program or organization about which you will present information. For example, you could present information about a charity organization, such as M.A.D.D. (Mothers Against Drunk Driving), the Cancer Foundation, or a Community Arts Group. Create meaningful names for each of your files.
2. Think of an interesting slant regarding the program or organization. The presentation you created for Project 2 was called "Career Choices" because it focused on how the business program at Alma Business College helps students obtain employment in office management and administrative positions. A presentation to encourage people to join a Children's Hospital Association could be called "Caring for Kids."
3. Create a table in Access that lists certain statistics regarding the program or organization. For example, you could list three or four of the activities funded by the Children's Hospital Association and then display three categories of funding (for example, Corporate, Private, and Government). For ideas, refer to the Access table you created for Project 2.
4. Copy the Access table to Excel and create one or two charts from the data.
5. Create the presentation outline in PowerPoint. Include at least eight slides in your presentation. The information you present should inform your audience about your program or organization and encourage their participation. Allow at least one slide for a Word table and one slide for an organization chart.
6. Copy the charts from Excel into PowerPoint.
7. Create an organization chart on one of the slides. For example, you could create a chart that shows the various activities funded by your organization or the electives students can take after completing the required courses.
8. Switch to Slide view and apply a presentation template or a custom background.
9. Switch to Slide Master view and modify the appearance of the text in the placeholders.
10. Add clip art images to selected slides. Modify the clip art images to suit the message you are trying to communicate.
11. Add slide transitions, build effects, and animation effects to your slides, then preview your slide show in Slide Show view.
12. Change some of the values in the Access table, update the charts in PowerPoint, then print a copy of your presentation in black and white.

INDEPENDENT CHALLENGE 3

Create a presentation that proposes a special event, entertainment, or party to a group of your choice. For example, you can create your own class party presentation similar to the presentation you created for Project 3. Alternatively, you can create a presentation that proposes a class reunion, a company picnic, or a weekend seminar. Create meaningful names for each of your files.

1. Create an outline in PowerPoint that includes the following information:
    a. Type of party or event
    b. Purpose of the party or event
    c. Location, time, and cost
    d. Chart showing the cost breakdown
    e. "Motivational" slide
2. Use as many slides as you wish. For ideas, refer to the presentation you created for Project 3.
3. Enter the party details in Word, then copy them, and paste them as unformatted text into PowerPoint.
4. Create a worksheet in Excel that shows the cost breakdown for the party, copy the data into a datasheet that you create in PowerPoint, then create a pie chart.
5. Modify the presentation—use custom backgrounds, templates, slide transitions, slide builds, and animation effects—then print a copy.

INDEPENDENT CHALLENGE 4

Your supervisor has asked you to create a presentation that will convince the executives of your company to launch a homepage on the World Wide Web. The company is called Balloon Magic and sells all kinds of balloons and novelties for parties, conventions, and special events. You and your supervisor feel that a presence on the World Wide Web would greatly assist the company's recent decision to expand its mail order department. Follow the instructions provided to create and then modify the presentation that you plan to give to the executives. Save all the files you create as Balloon Magic.

1. Display a blank presentation in Outline view, then enter the slide titles and text for the presentation as shown below:

Slide #	Slide Title	Level 1 Text
1	Balloon Magic	Publishing on the World Wide Web
2	Purpose	Publish a homepage on the World Wide Web to promote Balloon Magic's products
		Provide online ordering to Web customers
		Connect with other balloon and novelty businesses
3	Web Overview	The World Wide Web has grown at an incredible pace over the past three years, nearly doubling its users every year.
4	Web Users Profile	65% of Web users are in their mid-thirties and make over $65,000 per year.
5	Business on the Web	40% of businesses advertising on the Web over the past year report a 30% increase in revenues
		20% report more than a 50% increase in revenues
6	Web Launch Strategy	Create a homepage
		Establish links with related businesses
		Launch the homepage on the Internet Access server
7	First-Year Costs	Web page costs for the first year break down as shown in the table below.
8	Goals	Increase mail order revenues by 30% in year 1
		Increase mail order revenues by 40% in year 2
		Hire an in-house "webmaster" to service the page at the end of year 1

2. Switch to Slide view and apply the Daybreak preset background to all the slides.
3. Switch to Slide Master view, change the font in the Master Title Style placeholder to Britannic Bold, increase the font size to 48, insert the Prism image from the Science and Medicine clip art category, then size and position the image in the lower right corner of the slide master.
4. Switch to Slide view, display Slide 3, display a blank worksheet in Excel, complete the worksheet shown below, copy it, paste it into a PowerPoint datasheet, then create a column chart.

FIGURE IC-1: Excel worksheet data for column chart on Slide 3

	A	B	C	D	E
1		1996	1997	1998	1999
2		20	40	65	120
3					
4					
5					

5. Display Slide 7, switch to Word, type the text as shown below, then copy it to PowerPoint, and paste it as unformatted text.

Web Page Design	$300
Server Space for One Year	$1,200
Web Page Maintenance	$300

6. Add clip art pictures to selected slides. Remember that you can use the Drawing tools to modify a clip art image after you have ungrouped it.

7. In Slide view add preset animation effects as listed below to the bulleted text in the slides specified.

    Slide 2: Drive-in Effect

    Slide 4: Camera Effect

    Slide 5: Typewriter Text Effect

8. In Slide Sorter view, add slide transition and build effects to selected slides, preview the slide show, make different choices as required, then print the slides in your presentation.

Visual Workshop

For a course on tourism in Hawaii, you have decided to create a presentation that focuses on popular hotels on the Hawaiian islands. One of the slides will display a pie chart that shows the breakdown of hotel guests by location. Create the Hotels table in Access as shown in Figure VW-1, answer Yes to create a Primary Key, copy the table and paste it as a link into Excel, create a pie chart that shows the number of guests on each island, open PowerPoint, select the Title Only slide layout, then copy the pie chart and paste it as a link into the slide. Add the title, apply the Rainbow preset background, and insert the butterfly clip art image. Double-click the chart, right-click the chart again, click Format Chart Area, choose no border and no fill, click just outside the pie chart to select the Plot area, then drag a Plot area sizing handle to increase the size of the pie chart. Switch to Access, change the number of guests who stayed at the Waikiki Sands Resort on Oahu to 500, switch back to PowerPoint, update the link so that the Oahu slice increases to 35% as shown in Figure VW-2, then print a copy of the slide. Save all documents as "Hawaii Tourism."

FIGURE VW-1: *Hotels table*

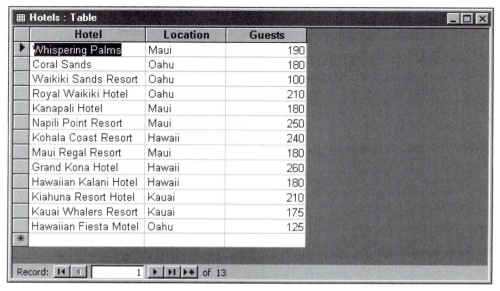

FIGURE VW-2: *Completed slide*

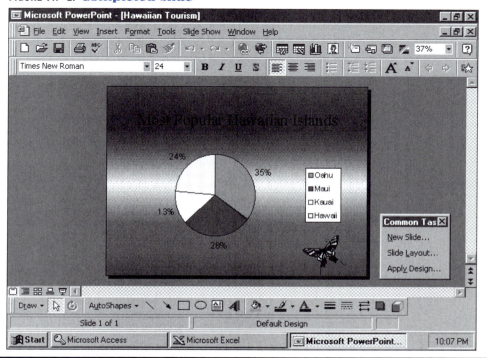

▶ World Wide Web Projects

College and Job Search

In This Unit You Will Create:

 ▶ **College Programs for Studying Abroad**

 ▶ **Summer Job Opportunities**

 ▶ **Resume Posting**

You can use the World Wide Web to find information about colleges and universities all over the world. Many college sites consist of hundreds of pages containing information about courses, prerequisites, professors, student groups, and even dormitory accommodations. Some pages even allow you to register online. Another fast-growing area of the World Wide Web concerns job opportunities. Companies and organizations around the world post job vacancies, and individuals post their resumes. For specialized jobs, in particular, the World Wide Web's employment resources provide valuable opportunities for job seekers. ▶ In this unit, you will explore some college sites that offer overseas study programs, look for a summer job, and post your own resume on the World Wide Web.

OVERVIEW

College Programs for Studying Abroad

You've decided that you would like to investigate the possibility of studying in a foreign country for an academic term or even a full year. From the hundreds of programs offered, you need to select one that suits your academic interests and is located in a country to which you want to travel. To help you choose the best program, you will search the World Wide Web for information about programs for studying abroad and then create a table in your word processing program that compares five of the programs that most interest you. Four activities are required to complete this project.

Project Activities

Search for Study Abroad Programs

Several sites exist that contain databases of Study Abroad programs. A **database** contains information related to a specific subject, project, enterprise, or business. For example, a database can contain all the names and addresses of a company's clients or a list of all the universities that sponsor Study Abroad programs. Often databases are organized both by subject and by location. You can search a database for a program on a specific subject, such as Physics, or for a program in a specific country, such as Mexico. Some of the sites that list Study Abroad programs are maintained by a particular university and provide information only on programs sponsored by that university. Other sites provide information on programs sponsored by universities all over the world. You will start your search for one of these databases by first displaying the Infoseek search page and then selecting the Infoseek College topic. Often, you can find information faster by selecting a topic listed on a search page than by entering search terms. Table P1-1 describes the five major search tools. As you develop your Web-surfing skills, you will learn to identify the search tool best suited to finding the type of information you require.

Identify a Program

You will display the Studying Abroad page in the Peterson's Education Center site and explore its links to an Archaeology program in Belize. You will then display the site of the college that sponsors the program.

Set up a Comparison Table

Next, you will set up a comparison table in your word processing program that includes headings for the type of information you need to gather about five Study Abroad programs.

Gather Information and Print the Comparison Table

Finally, you need to choose the type of program and location that interest you, gather information about each program, then copy it into the table. You will find the required information at a variety of college sites. The sample table in Figure P1-1 lists information about three Study Abroad programs. The table you produce will include information about five programs that interest you.

TABLE P1-1: **Description of major search sites**

SEARCH TOOL	DESCRIPTION	TIPS AND COMMENTS
Excite	• Displays a review of each site found • Searches Usenet discussion groups and classified ads	• Good for keyword searches • Click the Sort by Site button to remove reviews and see more sites on the screen at one time
Infoseek	• Displays a guide that shows Web pages matching search criteria • Provides lists of pages in related categories	• Use to find pages in the categories provided • Good for finding related categories; useful reviews
Lycos	• Catalogs Web pages, rather than entire sites • Provides an outline and abstract for each page that matches search criteria	• Use the Top 5% Sites and Sites by Subject links • Excellent reviews; good source for commercial sites
Magellan	• Reviews and rates sites	• Click Magellan in the complete list of search tools to display a comprehensive list of topics • Good for academic research topics
Yahoo	• Organizes sites by catogory • Displays both a summary and a link to the related category	• Use for finding sites in specific categories • Great source for sites related to geographical location (e.g., Regional)

FIGURE P1-1: **Comparison table of Study Abroad programs**

Studying Abroad Programs

University	**Boston University**
Program	The Belize Program
Field of Study	Archaeology
Field Trips	Scheduled travel to Copan, Tikal; field trips to Lamanai, Cerros
Requirements	Coursework in archaeology, anthropology; 3.0 GPA
Cost	Tuition $10,285 per semester and Fees $3,525 per semester
University URL	http://web.bu.edu/abroad/english/belize.html
University	**American University in Cairo**
Program	Study Abroad Program
Field of Study	Anthropology, Arabic, art, economics, Egyptian studies, Middle Eastern studies, political science and government, sociology
Field Trips	Field trips to Luxor, Abu Simbel, Red Sea; optional travel to oasis in Western Desert, Greece, Turkey, Cyprus at an extra cost
Requirements	2.0 GPA; interest in Middle Eastern studies
Cost	Not Available
University URL	http://auc-acs.eun.eg/#uni
University	**Duke University**
Program	Duke in the Andes, La Paz, Bolivia
Field of Study	Latin American studies, Spanish language and literature
Field Trips	Scheduled travel to Lake Titicaca, Isla del Sol; field trips to Chulumani, Potosi, Sucre
Requirements	Coursework in Spanish (2 years or equivalent); 3.0 GPA
Cost	$11,140
University URL	http://www.mis.duke.edu/study_abroad/andes.html

PROJECT 1 — COLLEGE PROGRAMS FOR STUDYING ABROAD

activity:

Search for Programs

You will use Infoseek to display the Colleges topic and then explore a site that includes a large Study Abroad database.

Internet Explorer 3 Users

Refer here for steps 1, 2, 4, and 6.

1. Substitute Internet Explorer for all references to Netscape, and click the Search button to display the search page throughout this unit.
2. Click the **Infoseek radio button**, click **Search**, click **InfoSeek home**, then click **colleges** in the **Education** section.
4. Click the Address box instead of the Location box throughout this unit.
6. To Bookmark a site, click **Favorites**, click **Add To Favorites**, then click **OK**.

steps:

1. Connect to the Internet, launch Netscape, then click the **Net Search button** [Net Search] to display the Netscape Navigator search page

2. Click **Infoseek**, click **Click here** as shown in Figure P1-2, then click **colleges** in the **Education** section

3. Scroll down the Infoseek Colleges page to view the college topics, then click **Studying Abroad**, as shown in Figure P1-3

4. When the list of Web sites appears, scroll down the list and click **Peterson's Education Center— Studying Abroad** or, if it does not appear, click the **Location box**, type http://www.course.com press **[Enter]**, click **Course Technology Student Online Companions**, click **World Wide Web Illustrated Projects**, then click **College and Job Search: Project 1**

   The Peterson's Studying Abroad page appears.

5. Click **Academic year programs around the world for U.S. students**

   If you are not a U.S. student, follow the Peterson link for now, and then try the College and Job Search: Project 1 Additional link on the Course Technology Student Online Companion to check out the WorldWide Classroom. You can choose to search by Fields of Study or Countries. Next, bookmark the page that appears, then search for programs about a specific subject—archaeology.

6. Click **Bookmarks** on the menu bar, then click **Add Bookmark**

7. Click **Fields of Study**, scroll down the list of subjects that appears, click **Archaeology**, then click the **Submit Selection button**

   A list of universities that offer programs in Archaeology appears as shown in Figure P1-4. Next, go on to check one of the universities listed.

FIGURE P1-2: **Infoseek search page**

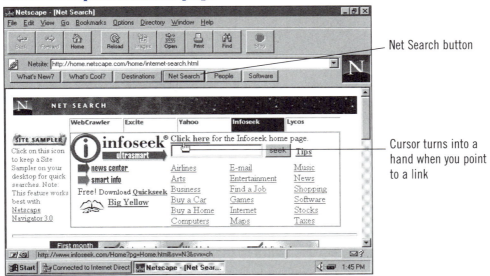

Net Search button

Cursor turns into a hand when you point to a link

FIGURE P1-3: **Infoseek directory page**

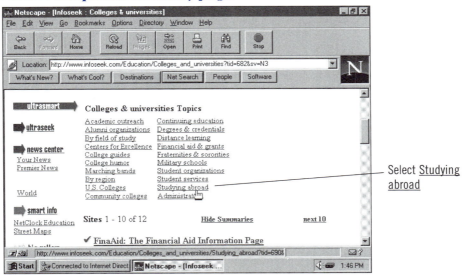

Select Studying abroad

FIGURE P1-4: **List of programs**

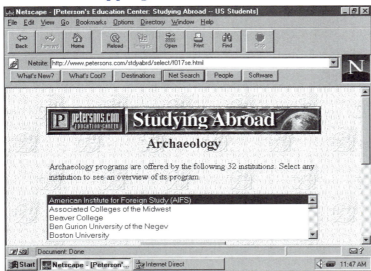

PROJECT 1: COLLEGE PROGRAMS FOR STUDYING ABROAD

activity:

Identify a Program

You will first take a look at the listing on the Peterson's page for Boston University and then access the Boston University Web site to find more detailed information about their Studying Abroad program in Belize.

steps:

1. Select **Boston University** from the list of universities displayed, click the **Submit Selection button**, then, when the next page appears, click **Archaeological Field School in Belize**

   A brief description of the Archaeological Field School in Belize appears as shown in Figure P1-5. As you can see, the page provides only general information about the program and directs you to consult one of Peterson's publications for more information. Instead, you will bookmark this page, then go to the Web site maintained by Boston University to find more information about the Belize program.

2. Click **Bookmarks** on the menu bar, then click **Add Bookmark**

3. Select the text **Boston University**, click **Edit** on the menu bar, click **Copy**, click the **Net Search button**, then, when the Net Search page appears, click **Infoseek**, if necessary

4. Right-click the **Infoseek Search box**, click **Paste**, then click **seek**

   You save time by copying and pasting the search words instead of typing them. Next, find information about Boston University from the list of sites displayed.

5. Scroll down the list of search results, click **About Boston University** or a similar site that will lead you to information about Boston University, scroll down the page that appears, then click **Home** at the bottom of the page, if necessary

   The Web site for Boston University appears. You want to find information about the Studying Abroad program in Belize, so now you need to find the required link.

6. Scroll down the page until you come to a listing of Other Academic Programs, click **Division of International Programs**, scroll down the page to display the selection of international flags, then click **Belize**

   A detailed description of the Belize program appears as shown in Figure P1-6.

7. Scroll down the page to read about the program, then bookmark the page

   You will return to this page later. Next, return to the Peterson's Studying Abroad page and try searching for programs by Country.

8. Click **Bookmarks**, click **More Bookmarks**, if necessary, to display the Peterson's site, double-click the entry for **Peterson's Education Center: Studying Abroad**, then click **Countries**

   Now that you've discovered an archaeological program in Belize, you've decided to look for programs in other Central American countries.

9. Scroll down the list of countries displayed, click **Costa Rica**, then click the **Submit Selection button**

   A list of universities that offer Study Abroad programs in Costa Rica appears, as shown in Figure P1-7. Next, you will go on to set up a table in your word processing program and then to gather information about five programs in an academic area and location of your choice.

Internet Explorer 3 Users

Right-click the **Internet Searches box**, click **Paste**, then click **Search**.

FIGURE P1-5: Description of Archaeological Field School in Belize

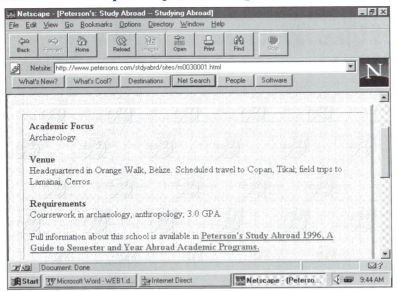

FIGURE P1-6: Information about The Belize Program

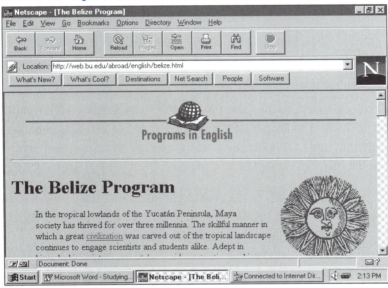

FIGURE P1-7: List of programs in Costa Rica

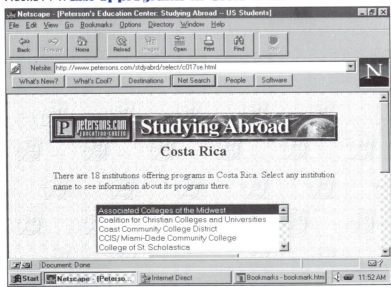

COLLEGE PROGRAMS FOR STUDYING ABROAD

activity:

Set Up a Comparison Table

You need to develop a system to gather information and display it in a table you create in your word processing program. First, you will set up the table, and then you will copy selected information from the Belize program into the table. Once you have completed these steps, you can go on to gather information about other programs and locations of your choice.

steps:

1. Display your word processing program, open a blank document, create a table consisting of 30 rows and two columns, then reduce the width of column 1 to 1½"

   Next, enter the labels required for the table.

2. Type the labels in rows 1 to 7 as shown in Figure P1-8, then save the document as **Studying Abroad Programs**

   The words "Boston University" are still on your clipboard from when you copied them earlier. Next, paste these words into the appropriate cell in your table.

3. Right-click the cell next to University, click **Paste**, then switch to Netscape

   Next, you need to enter the field of study. You will display the Peterson's description of the Belize program to copy the required information.

4. Click **Bookmarks**, double-click **Peterson's: Study Abroad—Studying Abroad** to display the description of the field study program in Belize, select the text **Archaeological Field School in Belize**, as shown in Figure P1-9, click **Edit** on the menu bar, click **Copy**, switch to your word processing program, click the cell next to Program, click **Edit** on the menu bar, then click **Paste**

5. Switch to Netscape, select the field of study ("Archaeology" under Academic Focus), press **[Ctrl][C]** to copy the selection, display your word processing program, click the cell next to Field of Study, then press **[Ctrl][V]** to paste the selection into your document

   Note that you can use the [Ctrl][C] and [Ctrl][V] keystroke commands to speed up the copy/paste process. Next, you will copy the information about field trips and requirements.

6. Display Netscape, select the sentence that begins "**Scheduled travel to…**," press **[Ctrl][C]**, display your word processing program, click the cell next to Field Trips, press **[Ctrl][V]**, display Netscape, copy the sentence that describes the requirements, paste it into the appropriate cell in your table, then delete any extra spaces and hard returns

   Next, display the description of the Belize program in the Boston University site, then copy the cost information.

7. Display Netscape, display your list of bookmarks, double-click **The Belize Program**, scroll down the screen until you see the information about the program costs, select the two lines of information about costs, copy the information, then paste it into the appropriate cell of your table

   Finally, you need to copy the URL for the Belize program page into your table.

8. Display Netscape, click the URL entered in the Location box to select it, press **[Ctrl][C]**, display your word processing program, click the cell next to University URL, press **[Ctrl][V]**, delete any extra hard returns and spaces in the copied entries, compare your table to Figure P1-10, then save your document

   Next, go on to gather information about four more programs that interest you.

FIGURE P1-8: Table setup

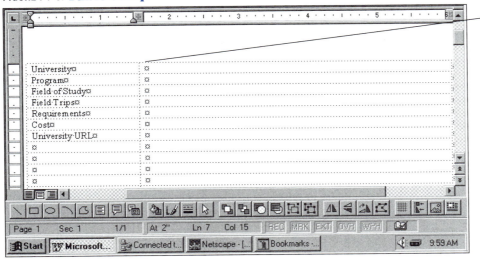

Column 1 reduced to 1½"

FIGURE P1-9: Archaeological Field School in Belize selected

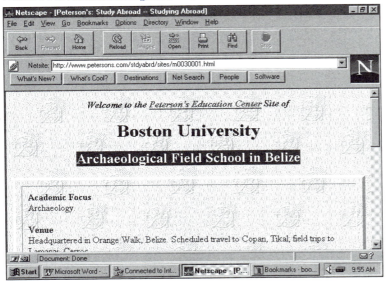

FIGURE P1-10: Information about the Belize program

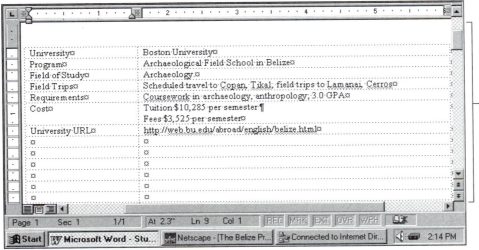

The information you copy may be slightly different

COLLEGE PROGRAMS FOR STUDYING ABROAD

activity:

Gather Information and Print the Comparison Table

You need to gather the information required for your table from a variety of sites and then format the table attractively for printing. Figure P1-11 displays the formatted table with information about the Belize program along with information about four additional programs in a variety of fields. Your table will display information about the Belize program and four different programs.

Hint

Use Copy and Paste to copy the row headings down the table.

steps:

1. Decide what field of study and location you prefer, apply the techniques you have learned to identify four programs that interest you, then gather the information required for your table

   Remember to bookmark pages that you will need to display again and to try searching for both Fields of Study and Countries from the Peterson's site. Note also that you will need to find additional information from individual university sites about the programs you have selected. You may need to try two or three searches and use a variety of search tools (e.g., Excite, Yahoo!, and so on) to find the university sites. Finding the information in the university sites will take the most time. If you cannot find a university's Web site after searching for several minutes, select a different program. If a university has a Web site but no information about the program costs, enter Not Available in the Costs row, and copy the URL for the university site.

2. Close Netscape, disconnect from the Internet, display your word processing program, move to the top of the document, press **[Enter]** twice to move down the table, turn on centering, type **Studying Abroad Programs**, press **[Enter]**, then enhance the text with **20 point** and **Bold** as shown in Figure P1-11

3. Select the first row of your table, then enhance the text with **14 point** and **Bold** as shown in Figure P1-11

4. Enhance each of the remaining four university names with **14 point** and **Bold** as shown in Figure P1-11

5. Enhance the table form attractively

   You can choose to add border lines, shading, and additional text formatting. In the sample table in Figure P1-11, the row labels were right-aligned and bolded, border lines were added, the rows containing the university names were shaded, the cost information was bolded, and the URLs were italicized. You decide how best to display the information you have gathered.

6. View your document in Whole Page or Full Page view, make any spacing adjustments required so that the table appears attractively spaced over one or two pages, print a copy of your table, then save and close the document

FIGURE P1-11: Sample list of Studying Abroad programs

Studying Abroad Programs

University	**Boston University**
Program	The Belize Program
Field of Study	Archaeology
Field Trips	Scheduled travel to Copan, Tikal; field trips to Lamanai, Cerros
Requirements	Coursework in archaeology, anthropology; 3.0 GPA
Cost	**Tuition $10,285 per semester and Fees $3,525 per semester**
University URL	http://web.bu.edu/abroad/english/belize.html
University	**American University in Cairo**
Program	Study Abroad Program
Field of Study	Anthropology, Arabic, art, economics, Egyptian studies, Middle Eastern studies, political science and government, sociology
Field Trips	Field trips to Luxor, Abu Simbel, Red Sea; optional travel to oasis in Western Desert, Greece, Turkey, Cyprus at an extra cost
Requirements	2.0 GPA; interest in Middle Eastern studies
Cost	**Not Available**
University URL	http://auc-acs.eun.eg/#uni
University	**Duke University**
Program	Duke in the Andes, La Paz, Bolivia
Field of Study	Latin American studies, Spanish language and literature
Field Trips	Scheduled travel to Lake Titicaca, Isla del Sol; field trips to Chulumani, Potosi, Sucre
Requirements	Coursework in Spanish (2 years or equivalent); 3.0 GPA
Cost	**$11,140**
University URL	http://www.mis.duke.edu/study_abroad/andes.html
University	**University of Delaware**
Program	Spring Semester in Costa Rica
Field of Study	History, intercultural studies, international affairs, political science and government, Spanish language and literature
Field Trips	Field trips to Gold Museum, National Museum, National Theater, Cahuita National Park, volcanoes Poas and Irazu
Requirements	2.0 GPA; application, letters of recommendation
Cost	**$2500 for a semester and $1800 for a session**
University URL	http://www.udel.edu/IntlProg/studyabroad/sanjose.htm
University	**Augsburg College, Center for Global Education**
Program	Sustainable Development and Social Change in Central America: Race, Class and Ethnicity
Field of Study	Economics, interdisciplinary studies, religious studies, Spanish language and literature
Field Trips	Scheduled travel to Guatemala, El Salvador, Nicaragua; field trips
Requirements	Coursework in Spanish (1 semester); 2.5 GPA
Cost	**The overall cost covers tuition, room and board, travel within Central America, and all other program costs. Actual cost not available.**
University URL	http://www.augsburg.edu/global/camsem.html

OVERVIEW

Summer Job Opportunities

You could spend days—weeks even—surfing the hundreds of job search databases on the World Wide Web. To make your search as efficient as possible, you need to focus on a specific job category and location. For Project 2, you will compile postings for summer job opportunities. To complete this project, you will **Explore National Park Jobs** and then **Compile Five Additional Postings**

activity:

Explore National Park Jobs

To begin your search for summer job opportunities, you will display a site that lists jobs available in various national parks throughout the United States.

steps:

1. In Netscape, click the **Net Search button**, click **Excite**, enter **Summer Employment Opportunities** in the Search box, then click **Search**

2. Bookmark the site

   You will return to this list to explore sites related to job opportunities that interest you. Next, display an employment site related to summer employment and seasonal work.

3. Scroll down the list of search results, click **Summer Employment Opportunities**, then click **Coolworks** or, if these links do not appear, display the World Wide Web Illustrated Projects Student Online Companion, then click **College and Job Search: Project 2**

   Next, explore some of the job opportunities in national parks.

4. Click **Jobs in National Parks, Preserves, Monuments and Recreational Areas**

5. Click **Bryce Canyon National Park**, scroll down the page, then click **Positions Available**

6. Scroll down the page to read the various positions available

7. Select one of the positions in the Food and Beverage Department as shown in Figure P2-1, copy it, display a blank document in your word processing program, then paste the description

8. Return to Netscape, scroll to the top of the page, select the text **Grand Canyon - Zion - Bryce Canyon National Park Lodges**, then copy it above the job description in your word processing program

9. Return to Netscape, click the **Back button** ⇐, click **Application Forms**, select the address listed as shown in Figure P2-2, copy it below the job description in your word processing program, then save your document as **Summer Job Opportunities**

   Next, go on to compile your own list of summer jobs.

FIGURE P2-1: Position selected

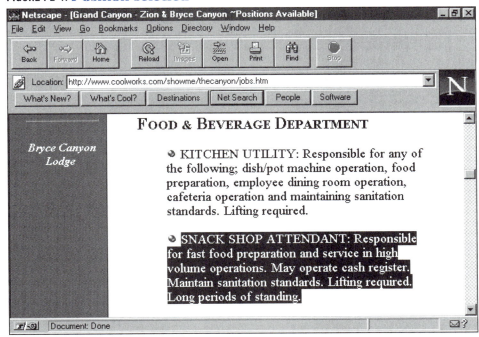

FIGURE P2-2: Address selected

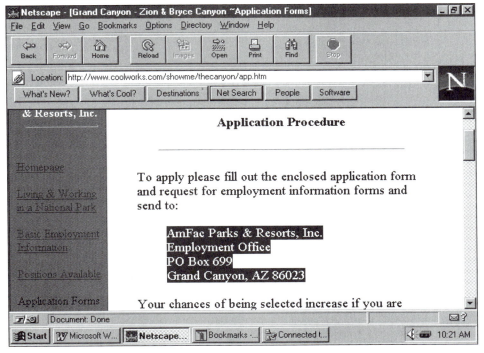

SUMMER JOB OPPORTUNITIES

activity:

Compile Five Additional Postings

You need to find information about five positions for a summer job that interests you and then copy the information to your word processing document.

steps:

1. Return to Netscape, click the URL in the Location box, then copy it below the contact address in your word processing program

2. Move to the top of your word processing program, then type and format **Summer Job Opportunities** as shown in Figure P2-3

3. Format the National Park job posting so that it appears similar to Figure P2-3
   Note that you will need to remove extra spaces and hard returns, add Bold to selected headings, and increase the font size of the company/organization name.

4. Determine the type of summer job you might enjoy

5. Return to Netscape, then explore the Coolworks Summer Jobs Resources site and other sites listed in the Excite search results

6. Identify five summer jobs that interest you, then copy and paste the information into your word processing document so that the completed document lists six summer job postings (including the posting for Bryce Canyon National Park)
   Try to gather information from at least three different sites. Once you have identified a job that interests you, you need to copy the name of the company or organization, the job description, the contact information, and the URL to your word processing program. Note that the contact information may be an e-mail address.

7. Format the document attractively over two pages, then print a copy
   A sample Summer Job Opportunities document appears in Figure P2-4. This sample document includes jobs from a variety of fields. Your Summer Job Opportunities document should list postings that interest you and for which you are qualified.

FIGURE P2-3: **National Park job position formatted**

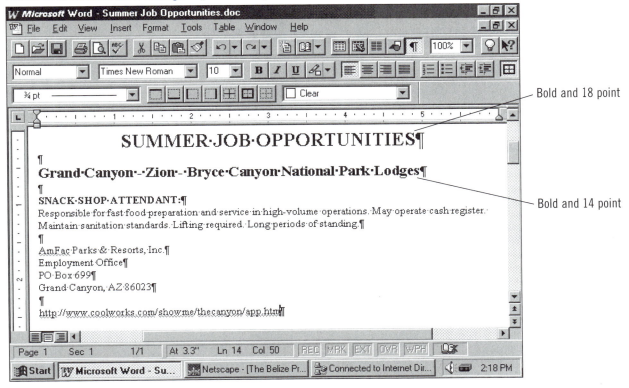

FIGURE P2-4: **Sample list of summer job opportunities**

SUMMER JOB OPPORTUNITIES

Grand Canyon - Zion - Bryce Canyon National Park Lodges

SNACK SHOP ATTENDANT:
Responsible for fast food preparation and service in high-volume operations. May operate cash register. Maintain sanitation standards. Lifting required. Long periods of standing.

AmFac Parks & Resorts, Inc.
Employment Office
PO Box 699
Grand Canyon, AZ 86023

http://www.coolworks.com/showme/thecanyon/app.htm

Denali Park Resorts

TOUR DESK STAFF
Assist park visitors with booking tour and activity reservations. Answer guest questions. Strong people and sales skills helpful. Extensive public contact.

Human Resources
Denali Park Resorts
P.O. Box 87 - Dept CW
Denali Park, Alaska 99755

http://www.coolworks.com/showme/denaliak/apply.htm

Alaska Sightseeing Cruise West

CRUISE COORDINATOR
Cruise Coordinators organize all guest programs and activities. This includes providing on-deck narrative, formal lectures, safety and schedule information, announcements, informal entertainment programs, selling/arranging/expediting shore excursions, escorting included tours, and providing guests with whatever day-to-day information and assistance they need to best enjoy their vacation. 12-to 16-hour days are the norm. Cruise Coordinators must be extremely organized, flexible, able to judge a variety of tasks and time demands, act quickly, and maintain a pleasant demeanor to both crew and guests even when under pressure and/or fatigued. Public speaking experience, preferably in interpretation, is essential.

Alaska Sightseeing/Cruise West
4th & Battery Building, Suite #700
Seattle, WA 98121
Attn: Department I

http://www.coolworks.com/showme/akcruise/apply.htm

YMCA Camp Duncan

ASSISTANT PROGRAM DIRECTOR
Responsibilities: Works with Program Director with daily planning, implementation of programs. Responsible for camper discipline. Requirements: Minimum age: 21; CPR and First Aid, good driving record.

Ms. Rona Roffey, Program Director
Phone: 847-546-8086 Fax: 847-546-3550
E-mail: duncan@inhomeprof.com

http://www.inhomeprof.com/ymcacamp/duncan.htm

Camp High Rocks, Cedar Mountain, NC

MOUNTAINEERING INSTRUCTORS
Camp High Rocks, a private boys camp in Western North Carolina, has instructor openings for its summer mountaineering program. Instructors should have experience with backpacking, camping, and related outdoor skills. A majority of our backpacking trips utilize the trails in Pisgah National Forest, though we do also venture into the Nantahala National Forest and Linville Gorge Area.

Responsibilities: Instruct outdoor skills, environmental ethics. Lead hiking and backpacking trips up to five days in length. Cabin counselor for group of 6 boys.

Qualifications: At least 19 years of age or rising college sophomore, hiking and backpacking experience.

Camp High Rocks, Inc.
PO Box 127 Cedar Mountain NC 28718
(704) 885-2153 hwbirdsong@aol.com

http://members.gnn.com/highrocks/hrp8.htm#Position

Maria Mitchell Observatory

RESEARCH ASSISTANT
Do astronomical research at historic island observatory. For students having at least one year of physics; can be majors in physical sciences, math, or CS; cannot graduate before September. $1000/month plus housing, some travel.

Dr. Eileen D. Friel c/o
CTIO Liaison Office, P.O. Box 26730
Tucson, AZ 85726.

http://yorty.sonoma.edu/people/faculty/tenn/SummerScienceAvailNow.html

OVERVIEW

Resume Posting

New resume-posting services are hitting the World Wide Web almost daily. While many of these services charge a fee for posting your resume, you can still find some services that will post your resume for free. Employers seeking job candidates can search for key words to access resumes of candidates that may suit the offered position. Once you have posted your resume, you can update it and check whether any employers have accessed it. In Project 3, you will **Create Your Resume** and then **Post Your Resume**.

activity

Create Your Resume

To post your resume on one of the free services, you copy it from your word processing program and paste it into the space allocated on the Web site. Any formatting included in your resume, such as bolding and font sizes, will be lost. Your first step, therefore, is to create an unformatted text version of your resume. If you already have a resume on file, you can save it as a new file, then remove all the formatting.

steps

1. If you have your resume on file, open it in your word processing program, or create a one-page resume similar to the sample resume displayed in Figure P3-1

    If you need to create your resume, make sure you include an objective along with information about your education and work experience. The objective states the type of position you are looking for and usually the location that interests you. For example, if you are seeking employment as an accountant, you could enter "To obtain employment as a Cost Accountant for a service-oriented business in the Little Rock area" as your objective. Use the resume displayed in Figure P3-1 as your guide. If you have already created your resume, make sure you include an objective. Next, you need to save the resume as a new file.

2. Save your formatted resume as **My Resume**, then save the resume again as **Resume for Posting on the Web**

    You now have two copies of your resume. Next, remove the formatting from the "Resume for Posting on the Web" version.

3. Remove all text formatting (e.g., bold, italics, and font sizes) and enhancements such as border lines, then display all the entries starting from the left margin as shown in the sample resume in Figure P3-2

    Your goal is to display the information as clear and easy-to-read text. Use semicolons to separate information originally included over several lines and format headings in all capital letters.

4. Save your unformatted resume

    Next, display Netscape and access a site where you can post your resume.

5. Connect to the Internet, display the Netscape Navigator search page, then click **Excite**

6. Enter **Resume Posting** in the Excite search box, then click **Search**

7. When the list of sites appears, bookmark the page, click **Sort by Site**, then click **www.careercenter.com** or, if the link does not appear, display the **World Wide Web Illustrated Projects Student Online Companion**, then click **College and Job Search: Project 3**

    The Career Center site appears as shown in Figure P3-3. Next, go on to learn how to post your resume on the selected site.

FIGURE P3-1: Sample resume: formatted

MARY McDONALD
2131 Dollarton Hwy.
North Vancouver, BC V7H 1A8
Phone/Fax: (604) 929-4431
e-mail: marym@commerce.ca

Objective
To apply my organizational and computer skills as an Administrative Assistant in a service-based company or organization.

Education

1995-1996: **Capilano College**, North Vancouver, BC
Administrative Assistant Certificate
- Computer Skills: Microsoft Office, WordPerfect 6.0, Lotus 1-2-3
- Business Communications and Organizational Behavior
- Basic Accounting and Bookkeeping
- Administrative Procedures
- Internet Communications

1990-1995: **Point Gray Senior Secondary School**
Grade 12 Graduation

Work Experience

1995-1996: **Best Bookkeeping**, 3095 West George Street, Vancouver
Office Assistant (part-time)
Responsibilities included:
- Maintaining company records
- Formatting documents in Word 7.0
- Organizing company database with Access 7.0

1991-1994: **Camp Haida**, Gambier Island, British Columbia
Camp Counselor (summers)
Responsibilities included:
- Supervising groups of 10 campers aged 9 to 11
- Organizing craft and sports activities
- Assisting with general office duties

Volunteer Experience

1993-1995: **Mothers' March**, North Vancouver Chapter
General Office Duties (part-time: January to April)

1995-1996: **Capilano College Applied Business Technology Department**
Student Activities Coordinator

References
Available on request

FIGURE P3-2: Sample resume: formatting removed

MARY MCDONALD
2131 Dollarton Hwy.
North Vancouver, BC V7H 1A8
Phone/Fax: (604) 929-4431
e-mail: marym@commerce.ca

OBJECTIVE
To apply my organizational and computer skills as an Administrative Assistant in a service-based company or organization.

EDUCATION

1995-1996:
Capilano College, North Vancouver, BC; Administrative Assistant Certificate
Computer Skills: Microsoft Office, WordPerfect 6.0, Lotus 1-2-3; Business Communications and Organizational Behavior; Basic Accounting and Bookkeeping; Administrative Procedures; Internet Communications
1990-1995:
Point Gray Senior Secondary School; Grade 12 Graduation

WORK EXPERIENCE

1995-1996:
Best Bookkeeping, 3095 West George Street, Vancouver; Office Assistant (part-time)
Responsibilities included:
Maintaining company records; Formatting documents in Word 7.0; Organizing company database with Access 7.0

1991-1994:
Camp Haida, Gambier Island, British Columbia; Camp Counselor (summers)
Responsibilities included:
Supervising groups of 10 campers aged 9 to 11; Organizing craft and sports activities; Assisting with general office duties

VOLUNTEER EXPERIENCE

1993-1995:
Mothers' March, North Vancouver Chapter; General Office Duties (part-time: January to April)

1995-1996:
Capilano College Applied Business Technology Department; Student Activities Coordinator

REFERENCES
Available on request

FIGURE P3-3: Career Center site

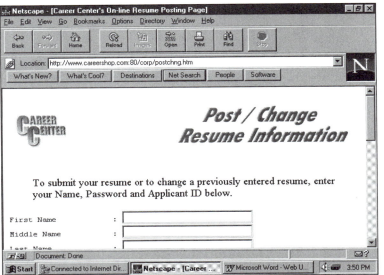

PROJECT 3: RESUME POSTING

activity

Post Your Resume

You will post your resume on one site, as directed below, and then post your resume on two more sites that you find on your own.

Internet Explorer 3 Users

Click **Click Here to Enter**, click **Post/Change Resume**, then scroll down the page to display the login form that appears as shown in Figure P3-4.

steps

1. Scroll down the page to display the login form

2. Enter your full name in the three boxes provided, enter a password consisting of ten or fewer characters, enter **NEW** in the box next to resume ID, then click **Login**

3. Write down the Applicant ID number that appears once you have logged in, then scroll to the section headed Entering resume Information

   Before you can post your resume, you need to enter personal information and job search information in the forms provided.

4. Click **Personal Information**, fill in the form provided with the information requested (if you don't know the information requested, leave the box blank), click the **Submit Your Info button** displayed at the bottom of the form, fill in the Employment Preferences form, then click the **Submit Your Info button**

   A sample Employment Preferences form appears in Figure P3-4. Your form will contain different entries, depending on your own employment preferences. Note that you need to enter your preferred start date (not shown in Figure P3-4) in the month/day/year format. Next, post your resume.

5. Click **Free-form Import Resume**, click in the blank box displayed, display your word processing program, select all the text in your resume, press **[Ctrl][C]**, display Netscape, press **[Ctrl][V]**, then scroll to the top of the box

   Figure P3-5 displays the copied resume for Mary McDonald.

6. Click the **Submit Your Info button**

   Your personal page on the site appears. You can make changes to this page by selecting Back to the Applicant Options Page and then selecting the information you wish to change. For example, if you select Import Resume, the page containing your imported resume will appear. You can then select and delete this resume, replace it with a new resume, then click the Submit Your Info button.

7. Return to the Excite Search Results page, explore some of the other sites listed, then post your resume to at least two more sites

   Note that many of the sites charge a fee to post resumes so you will need to spend some time finding sites that do not charge fees. The process required to post your resume will differ from site to site. Follow the directions provided on each site.

8. After you have posted your resume to a site, copy the site's URL to a blank document in your word processing program, enter a brief description of each site to which you successfully posted your resume, then save the word processing document as **List of Resume Posting Sites**

9. Print a copy of your unformatted resume, print a copy of the list of the sites you accessed to post your resume, save and close the word processing documents, then disconnect from the Internet

   Over the next few weeks, check the sites to which you posted your resume. You may have attracted an employer!

FIGURE P3-4: Sample Employment Preferences form

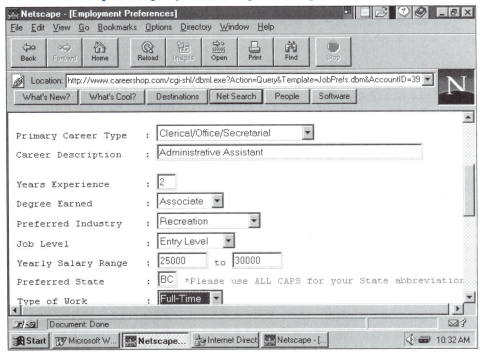

FIGURE P3-5: Sample resume copied to Web site

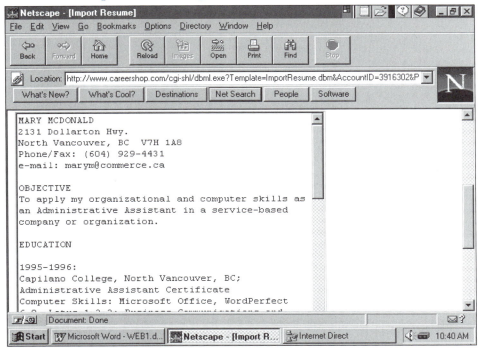

Independent Challenges

INDEPENDENT CHALLENGE 1

Search for three colleges in a location of your choice that offer a two- or four-year program that interests you, and then create a table in your word processing program that displays the results of your search. Follow the steps provided to organize your search and then present your search results.

1. Determine where you would like to attend college and the type of program that interests you. For example, you could decide that you'd like to obtain a four-year degree in Business Administration from a college in Hawaii or a two-year degree in Computer Programming from a college in Ontario. If you wish, you can choose to search for colleges outside your home country. In the box below, write your preferred location and program:

   Location: ....

   Program: ....

   ....

2. Set up a table in your word processing program that lists the information categories displayed below. Once you begin to search for colleges, you will fill in the table with the information required.

College Name	
Location	
Department	
Program Description	
Degree/Certificate	
Yearly Tuition	
Special Features	
Contact Address/e-mail	
College URL	

3. Save the document in your word processing program as "My Search for a College."
4. Connect to the Internet, then use Excite or Yahoo to search for colleges in the location of your choice (for example, enter "Colleges in Ohio" or "College Accounting Programs in New York"). You will need to spend some time narrowing your search.
5. Bookmark the college sites that interest you.
6. Once you have found three colleges that meet your needs, use the Copy and Paste functions to copy the required information to the table in your word processing program. You will need to follow numerous links in the college sites you select in order to find the required information. For the Special Feature section, enter information that you feel makes the college interesting to you. For example, a special feature may be that the college offers reasonable student accommodations or interesting extracurricular programs or is located near an area that you particularly wish to explore.
7. Make sure you include the URL of each of the three college sites you choose.
8. Format the completed table attractively, then print a copy.

INDEPENDENT CHALLENGE 2

Search a variety of employment databases to find five job postings in your area of expertise and preferred location.

1. Determine the type of job for which you are qualified and the location in which you prefer to work.
2. Identify possible titles for the job. For example, you could look for jobs as an Administrative Assistant, an Office Manager, an Elementary School Teacher, an Accounts Manager, and so on. Try to identify at least four or five job title variations so that you have several possibilities for keyword searches.
3. Create a document in your word processing program titled "Job Postings for [Job Title] in [Location]," then save the document as "My Job Postings."
4. Connect to the Internet, then initiate searches for job postings in your area of expertise. You may wish to start with some of the job search databases. The AT&T College Links page includes a searchable database of job titles. To access this site, display the Course Technology Student Online Companions site, click World Wide Web Illustrated Projects, then click College and Job Search: Independent Challenge 2.
5. As you find job postings appropriate to your area of expertise and preferred location, copy the postings to your word processing document. Note that your document should include the name of the company, the job title, the job posting, the contact information (address or e-mail), and the URL of the site on which the posting appeared.
6. Gather information related to five postings.
7. Format the word processing document attractively, then print a copy.

INDEPENDENT CHALLENGE 3

Search a variety of employment databases to find the qualifications for ten jobs that you feel you could apply for once you have received the required training.

1. Identify the job area in which you would like to work. For example, you may decide that you would like to work in the Film industry.
2. Identify the specific job type for which you would like to obtain qualifications. For example, if you are seeking work in the Film industry, you can decide that you want employment as a Key Grip or a Location Manager or a Production Assistant. You may need to check some job databases related to your preferred area to determine the position types that interest you.
3. Search a variety of employment databases to find ten postings for the job you have selected. To increase your chances of success, do not limit your search to a specific geographic location. Your goal is to find out what qualifications you need to apply for the job of your choice.
4. Create a document in your word processing program titled "Qualifications for [Job Title]," then save the document as "Qualifications for [Job Title]." Set up a table in the document that appears as shown below:

Job Title	
Academic Qualifications	
Skills	
Years of Experience	
Other Qualifications	
Posting URL	

5. Copy the required information from the postings you have selected to the table in your word processing document. Note that you need to gather information about qualifications from ten job postings in the area of your choice. Each of the postings should relate to the same type of job.
6. Format the table attractively in your word processing document, then print a copy.

INDEPENDENT CHALLENGE 4

You need to find information about English-teaching jobs in Japan. Follow the instructions provided to perform the searches required.

1. Display the Course Technology Student Online Companions, click World Wide Web Illustrated Projects, then click College and Job Search: Independent Challenge 4. The ELT Job Vacancies page appears. You need to find information about job postings in Japan.
2. Click the Find button located to the left of the Stop button in Netscape, type "Japan," then click Find Next. The first listing for a job in Japan appears. (For Internet Explorer 3 users: Click Edit, then click Find.)
3. Copy the listing to a new document in your word processing program, then save the document as "English Teaching Jobs in Japan."
4. Continue to find and then copy all the jobs listed for Japan.
5. Display the Netscape Navigator search page, select the search engine of your choice, then try a variety of search terms to find listings of jobs teaching English in Japan. Search examples include: Teaching English in Japan, Teaching Jobs in Japan, Japan: Teaching English, English Teaching: Japan, and so on. (For Internet Explorer 3 users: Display the Internet Explorer Find Fast page.)
6. Find additional job postings for teaching English in Japan to bring the total number of job postings copied to your word processing program to 10. If you cannot find enough postings for Japan, find postings for other Asian countries such as Korea, Taiwan, China, Malaysia, or Hong Kong.
7. Copy the postings to your word processing document, then format each posting so that it occupies one paragraph.
8. If your list includes jobs from other Asian countries, sort the postings in alphabetical order by country.
9. Add a title to the document, format it attractively on one page, then print a copy. Figure IC-1 displays a sample list of postings for jobs teaching English in European countries.

FIGURE IC-1: **Sample List of Job Postings**

Jobs Teaching English in European Countries
[Current Date]

FRANCE immediate vacancies in Compiegne, car essential (allowance paid), permanent posts, send cv, handwritten letter, + photo to DRH, Inlingua, BP 156, 76143 Petit Quevilly Cedex, France (GE 17.9.96)

GERMANY Business English teaching, see full listing (GE 8.10.96)

GREECE graduate teacher of English urgently reqd, apply by letter with recent photo to The Director, PO Box 414, Rhodes, Greece 85100 (TES 11.10.96)

ITALY EFL teacher reqd in Belluno, Veneto, Oct-May must have degree + TEFL Cert, exp of Camb exams preferred, send cv to Scuola di Lingue Europa, Via Zupanni, 32100 Belluno, Italy (GE 27.08.96)

ITALY experienced & qualified EFL teachers required for 3 schools in Italy, send cv + photo to: British Institutes Vico II Collemaggio, 4-67035, Pratola Peligna (AQ), Italy; British Institutes PO Box 164, 62012 Civitanova Marche (MC), Italy; British Institutes, via Ravenna 22/3, 67100 Pescara, Italy (GE 27.08.96)

ITALY experienced qualified teacher required, send cv + photo to LTC, via Medaglio d'Oro 130, Taranto, Italy (GE 10.9.96)

POLAND Teachers of Business and General English, CVs to Aidan Chalk (DOS), English Unlimited, Podmylnska 10, 80-885 Gdansk, Poland (GE 22.10.96)

PORTUGAL Qual teachers for primary cses, CV+2 refs+photo to Communicate Lang. Inst., Praceta Joao Villaret 12-B, 2675 Povoa de St Adriao, Portugal (GE 22.10.96)

SPAIN EFL teaching staff for Centro Britanico schools, see full listing (TES 20.09.96)

UK qual. & exp. EFL teachers reqd, contact Jayney Hamilton, English Language Inst, Royal Waterloo House, 51-55 Waterloo Road, London SE1 8TX (GE 15.10.96)

UKRAINE experienced and qualified ESL teachers of ESP, particularly Business English, see full listing (TES 25.10.96)

Hot Spots

You need to find two new Web sites related to jobs or colleges around the world. To find new sites, you will explore the What's New and What's Cool pages in Netscape. First, click the What's New button in Netscape, then scan the list that appears for sites related to either employment or colleges. (If you are using Internet Explorer, click Go on the main menu, then click Best of the Web.) If you find a site, go to it, then print its home page. To print a home page, click File, then click Print. Next, click the What's Cool button in Netscape, scan the list that appears, explore any sites related to employment or colleges, then print a copy of the appropriate home pages. If you can't find any new or cool sites related to employment or colleges, use the search engine of your choice to find one site that contains useful links to college resources and one site that contains useful links to employment resources, then print one page from each site. Figure HS-1 illustrates a new employment site, and Figure HS-2 illustrates a new college site.

FIGURE HS-1: Sample employment site

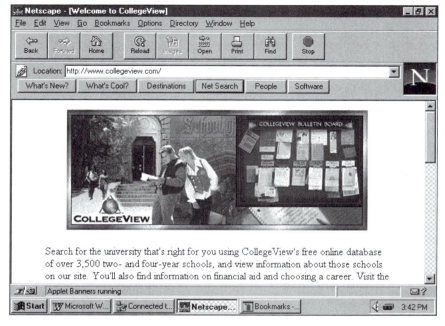

FIGURE HS-2: Sample college site

Index

► Special Characters

$ (dollar sign), *EX A-7*
¶ (end of paragraph mark), *WD A-4*

► A

absolute cell references, *EX A-7*
accelerated depreciation, *EX A-14*
Access. *See also* databases
   creating tables, *IN C-4*
aligning
   clip art objects, *PPT A-8*
   labels, *EX A-16*
Align Left button, *IN B-6*
Alignment tab, Format Cells dialog box, *EX A-5*
Align Right button, *IN A-8*
animation effects, *IN C-16*, *PPT A-6*, *PPT A-7*
Animation Effects button, *IN C-16*, *PPT A-6*
annotation tools, *PPT A-10*, *PPT A-11*
AutoComplete feature, *IN A-17*
AutoFit check box, *IN A-18*
AutoShapes menu, *PPT A-8*
AutoShapes menu button, *IN A-12*, *IN A-13*, *PPT A-8*, *PPT A-9*
AutoSum button, *IN A-4*, *IN B-8*, *IN B-10*, *IN C-12*
axis titles, entering, *IN A-10*, *IN A-11*

► B

Back button, *WWW A-12*
backgrounds, presentations, customizing, *IN C-19*
Black and White View button, *PPT A-18*
Blank Database option button, *AC A-4*
Blank presentation option button, *PPT A-12*
Bold button, *IN A-4*, *IN A-8*, *IN A-12*, *PPT A-14*, *WD A-18*
bookmarking, *WWW A-4*, *WWW A-6*
borders
   displaying, *EX A-10*
   heading styles, *WD A-6*
   letters, *IN A-6*
   removing from charts, *IN A-10*
   text objects, *PPT A-14*
Borders and Shading dialog box, *WD A-7*
budgets, *EX A-2–11*, *EX A-16–19*
   calculating totals, *EX A-6–7*
   formatting and printing, *EX A-10–11*
   planning, *EX A-16–17*
   reducing costs, *EX A-18–19*
   "what if?" questions, *EX A-8–9*
   worksheet labels, *EX A-4–5*
build effects, *IN C-10*
bulleted items, *PPT A-4*
Bullets button, *WD A-8*, *WD A-9*
business cards, *WD A-10–15*
   creating labels, *WD A-10*, *WD A-11*
   entering text, *WD A-10*, *WD A-11*
   formatting label sheet, *WD A-14–15*
   WordArt logos, *WD A-12–13*

► C

calculating
   percentages, *EX A-8*
   totals, *EX A-6–7*
Camera Effect button, *IN C-16*
cards. *See* business cards
career options presentations, *IN C-12–17*
   adding charts, *IN C-14–15*
   adding Word tables and animation effects, *IN C-16–17*
   creating source materials and presentation, *IN C-12–13*
cell contents, replacing existing values, *EX A-8*
cell references
   absolute. *See* absolute cell references
   relative, *EX A-7*
cells, merging, *EX A-5*
Center button, *AC A-16*, *IN A-4*, *IN A-12*, *PPT A-14*, *WD A-8*, *WD A-10*
centering text, *AC A-16*, *WD A-10*, *WD A-11*, *WD A-14*

charts
  adding to presentations, *IN C-14–15*
  colors, *IN C-6, IN C-14*
  copying, *IN C-14*
  creating, *IN A-10–11, IN B-18, IN B-19, IN C-4, IN C-12*
  displaying, *IN C-14*
  entering titles, *IN A-10, IN A-11*
  linking with summaries, *IN A-14–15*
  moving, *IN A-10, IN C-18*
  organizational, creating, *IN C-14, IN C-15*
  pasting as links in PowerPoint, *IN C-6*
  pie charts. *See* pie charts
  removing borders, *IN A-10*
  sizing, *IN A-10*
Chart Wizard button, *IN A-10, IN A-11, IN B-12, IN C-12*
Chart Wizard dialog box, moving, *IN A-10*
class party presentations, *IN C-18–19*
Clip Art Gallery, *IN A-14, PPT A-9*
clip art objects
  adding to slides, *IN C-8*
  aligning, *PPT A-8*
  color, *PPT A-10*
  fill, *PPT A-10*
  folders on networks, *AC A-16*
  grouping and ungrouping, *PPT A-10, PPT A-11*
  inserting in presentations, *IN C-18, PPT A-8, PPT A-9, PPT A-12–13, PPT A-18*
  moving, *PPT A-8, PPT A-9*
  multiple, selecting, *PPT A-8, PPT A-9*
  sizing, *AC A-16, PPT A-8, PPT A-9*
Close button, *AC A-4*
Collapse Dialog Box button, *IN C-12*
Collapse dialog box button, *IN A-10, IN A-11*
Collapse Dialog button, *IN B-8*
college study abroad programs. *See* study abroad programs
colors
  charts, *IN C-6, IN C-14*
  clip art objects, *PPT A-10*
Column Break option button, *IN A-12*
column charts, creating, *IN A-10*
columns, adjusting, *IN A-14*
common fields, *AC A-6*
company profile databases, *IN B-10–15*
  creating, *IN B-10–11*
  creating pie charts in Excel, *IN B-12–13*
  Word documents, *IN B-14–15*
comparison tables, *WWW A-8–11*
  gathering information and printing, *WWW A-10–11*
  setting up, *WWW A-8–9*

Copy button, *AC A-12, IN A-10, IN A-14, IN B-4, IN B-8, IN C-4, IN C-6, IN C-10, IN C-18, WD A-4, WD A-5, WD A-12*
Copy command, *IN A-18*
copying
  charts, *IN C-14*
  formats, *WD A-9*
  formulas, *IN A-10, IN A-16*
  labels in tables, *WWW A-8*
  records, *AC A-12*
  row headings in tables, *WWW A-10*
  tables, *IN B-14*
  text from Word to PowerPoint, *IN C-19*
  URLs, *WWW A-8*
  WordArt, *WD A-12, WD A-13*
Create Labels dialog box, *IN B-18*
Currency Style button, *IN A-4*
currency symbols, *WD A-18*
customizing presentation backgrounds, *IN C-19*

D

databases, *AC A-1–24*
  company profile. *See* company profile databases
  creating, *AC A-18, AC A-19*
  creating tables, *AC A-4–7, AC A-12–13*
  data types. *See* data types
  design, *AC A-3*
  formatting and printing reports, *AC A-10–11, AC A-16–17, AC A-18, AC A-19*
  incorrect data type, *AC A-4*
  job search. *See* job search databases
  queries. *See* queries
  video catalogue. *See* video database
Datasheet View, *AC A-4, AC A-18*
Datasheet view, *AC A-8, AC A-9, IN B-10*
Data Type list arrow, *AC A-4, AC A-5*
data types
  changing, *IN C-4*
  databases, *AC A-4, AC A-12, AC A-18*
dates
  entering as fields in form letters, *IN B-6*
  entering in letters, *IN A-6*
Deflate Bottom shape, *PPT A-12, PPT A-13*
deleting. *See also* removing
  records, *AC A-12*
Demote (Indent More) button, *PPT A-4*
depreciation
  accelerated, *EX A-14*
  straight line, *EX A-14*
Design View, *AC A-10*
Design view, *AC A-8, AC A-18*

displaying
  borders, *EX A-10*
  charts, *IN C-14*
  documents in page width, *IN A-18*
  Picture toolbar, *IN C-6*
  presentations, *PPT A-10, PPT A-11, PPT A-18*
  programs, *IN C-4*
documents
  formatting. *See* formatting documents
  inserting WordArt objects, *IN B-14*
  linking. *See* linking documents
  main, creating, *IN B-6–7*
  modifying style, *IN A-6*
  printing, *WD A-14*
  viewing in page width, *IN A-18*
dollar sign ($), absolute cell references, *EX A-7*
Drawing button, *IN A-12, IN A-13, IN B-14, PPT A-10*
duplicate information, entering, *AC A-18, IN B-4*

► E

editing presentations, *PPT A-10, PPT A-11*
end of paragraph mark (¶), *WD A-4*
entering. *See also* inserting; inserting WordArt objects
  axis titles, *IN A-10, IN A-11*
  chart titles, *IN A-10, IN A-11*
  data. *See* entering data; entering data in databases
  dates in letters. *See* dates
  duplicate information, *IN B-4*
  fields in form letters, *IN B-6*
  formulas, *IN C-4*
  labels. *See* entering labels
  text. *See* entering text
entering data
  databases. *See* entering data in databases
  presentations, *PPT A-4*
  tables, *IN C-4*
  worksheets, *IN A-16*
entering data in databases, *AC A-18*
  duplicate information, *AC A-18*
  records, *AC A-12*
entering labels, *EX A-4-5*
  tables, *WWW A-8–9*
  values in workbooks, *IN A-4, IN A-5*
  workbooks, *IN A-4, IN A-5*
entering text
  business cards, *WD A-10, WD A-11*
  letters, *IN A-6*
  resumes, *WD A-4–5*
  sales letters, *WD A-18, WD A-19*

summaries, *IN A-12*
text objects, *PPT A-14*
title slides, *IN C-6*
Envelopes and Labels dialog box, *WD A-14*
Erase Pen, *PPT A-10*
event posters, *PPT A-12–17*
  formatting, *PPT A-16–17*
  inserting text objects, *PPT A-14–15*
  inserting WordArt and clip art objects, *PPT A-12–13*
Excel. *See also* charts; pie charts
  creating charts, *IN A-10–11, IN C-4, IN C-12*
  creating invoices, *IN A-4–5*
  creating price lists, *IN A-16–17*
  linking charts with Word summaries, *IN A-14–15*
  linking invoices with letters in Word, *IN A-8–9*
Expand Dialog button, *IN B-8*
exploding pie chart slices, *IN B-12, IN B-13*

► F

field names, *AC A-3*
fields
  adding to tables, *AC A-8*
  common, *AC A-6*
  dates entered as, *IN B-6*
  merge. *See* merge fields
  selecting for tables, *AC A-6*
Fill Color list arrow, *IN A-12, IN A-13*
fills
  clip art objects, *PPT A-10*
  presentation backgrounds, *IN C-19*
  reports, *AC A-16*
Filter By Selection button, *AC A-8*
font styles, changing, *PPT A-18*
Format Cells dialog box, *EX A-5*
Format Painter, *WD A-9*
Format Painter button, *WD A-8, WD A-9, WD A-18*
formatting
  budgets, *EX A-10-11*
  copying formats, *WD A-9*
  documents. *See* business cards; formatting documents; resumes; sales letters
  label sheets, *WD A-14–15*
  paragraphs, *WD A-18*
  presentations, *PPT A-16–17*
  removing from resumes, *WWW A-16, WWW A-17*
  reports, *AC A-10, AC A-11, AC A-16, AC A-17*
  values, *EX A-12*

formatting documents, *IN A-12, WD A-1–24*
  business cards. *See* business cards
  copying formats, *WD A-9*
  resumes. *See* resumes
  sales letters. *See* sales letters
form letters, creating, *IN B-6–7*
formulas
  copying, *IN A-10, IN A-16*
  entering, *IN C-4*
Free Rotate button, *WD A-16, WD A-17*

► G

graphics. *See* clip art objects; WordArt objects
grouping clip art objects, *PPT A-10, PPT A-11*
Groups dialog box, *IN C-15*

► H

hard page breaks, inserting, *IN B-14*
heading styles, *WD A-6, WD A-7*

► I

Increase Font Size button, *PPT A-14*
Infoseek, *WWW A-4–5*
input masks, *IN B-5*
  changing, *IN B-4*
Insert Chart button, *IN C-18*
Insert Clip Art button, *IN C-8, PPT A-8, PPT A-10, PPT A-12*
inserting. *See also* entering; entering data; entering data in databases; entering text; entering labels
  charts in presentations, *IN C-14–15*
  clip art objects in presentations, *IN C-18, PPT A-8, PPT A-9, PPT A-12–13*
  fields in tables, *AC A-8*
  hard page breaks, *IN B-14*
  pie charts into Word summaries, *IN A-14*
  text objects in presentations, *PPT A-14–15*
  WordArt objects. *See* inserting WordArt objects
  Word tables in slides, *IN C-16–17*
inserting WordArt objects, *WD A-16*
  documents, *IN B-14, WD A-16*
  presentations, *IN C-18, PPT A-12–13*
insertion point, moving, *IN A-18, PPT A-4*
Insert Microsoft Word Table button, *IN C-16*
Insert Table button, *WD A-4, WD A-5*
Insert WordArt button, *IN A-18, IN C-16, PPT A-12, WD A-16*

Internet Explorer, *WWW A-4, WWW A-6, WWW A-18*
Internet Searches box, *WWW A-6*
invoices
  creating in Excel, *IN A-4–5*
  linking with letters, *IN A-8–9*

► J

job opportunity searches, *WWW A-12–15*
job search databases, *IN B-2–9*
  analyzing job search results, *IN B-8–9*
  job application form letter, *IN B-6–7*
  setting up, *IN B-4–5*

► L

label forms, *IN B-18*
labels
  business cards, *WD A-10, WD A-11*
  creating, *IN B-18, IN B-19*
  enhancing, *EX A-4-5*
  entering. *See* entering labels
  formatting, *WD A-14–15*
  right aligning, *EX A-16*
  wrapping, *EX A-12*
Labels Options dialog box, *IN B-18*
lecture presentations, *PPT A-18–19*
letterhead, *WD A-16–17*
letters
  creating in Word, *IN A-6–7*
  form, creating, *IN B-6–7*
  linking with invoices, *IN A-8–9*
  sales. *See* sales letters
linking
  charts with presentations, *IN C-6, IN C-7*
  documents. *See* linking documents
linking documents, *IN A-1–24*
  Excel charts and Word summaries, *IN A-14–15*
  invoices and letters, *IN A-8–9*
  presentations, *IN C-8, IN C-9*
loan amortization, *EX A-12–15*
  evaluating options, *EX A-14–15*
  worksheets, *EX A-12–13*
logos, *WD A-12–13*

► M

Mail Merge, *IN B-6–7*
Mail Merge button, *IN B-6*
main documents, creating, *IN B-6–7*

margins
  outside printable area of page, *IN A-12*
  sizing, *WD A-8*
Merge and Center button, *EX A-5, IN A-4*
merge fields, *IN B-7*
  entering in form letters, *IN B-6*
merging, *IN B-6*
  cells, *EX A-5*
  Mail Merge, *IN B-6–7*
  records, *IN B-18*
modifying styles, *WD A-6–7*
Modify the query design option button, *AC A-14*
moving. *See also* navigating
  charts, *IN A-10, IN C-18*
  Chart Wizard dialog box, *IN A-10*
  clip art, *PPT A-8, PPT A-9*
  insertion point, *IN A-18, PPT A-4*
  picture toolbar, *PPT A-8, PPT A-9*
  text objects, *PPT A-14, PPT A-16*
  WordArt objects, *PPT A-12, WD A-12, WD A-13, WD A-16*

N

names
  fields, *AC A-3*
  styles, *WD A-6*
navigating
  between database cells, *AC A-4*
  between records, *AC A-12*
Netscape Navigator, *WWW A-4*
Net Search button, *WWW A-4, WWW A-5*
networks, ClipArt folder, *AC A-16*
New button, *PPT A-12*
New Database button, *AC A-4, AC A-12*
New Office Document button, *AC A-4, IN A-4, IN A-6, IN C-4, PPT A-4*
New Slide dialog box, *PPT A-4*
Next Slide button, *IN C-8, IN C-16, PPT A-8, PPT A-10*
Normal style, *WD A-6*
Numbering button, *WD A-18*

O

Office Assistant, *IN A-6, IN A-10*
Office Links list arrow, *IN B-8, IN B-10, IN B-12, IN B-14, IN B-18*
Open button, *IN C-10*
opening workbooks, *IN A-4*
organizational charts, creating, *IN C-14, IN C-15*
Outline view, *PPT A-3*
Outline View button, *IN C-6, IN C-12, PPT A-4, PPT A-18*

P

page breaks, hard, inserting, *IN B-14*
Page Layout View button, *WD A-4, WD A-5*
Page Setup dialog box, *WD A-8*
Page width option button, *IN A-18*
paragraphs, formatting, *WD A-18*
Paste button, *AC A-12, IN A-10, IN B-4, IN B-8, IN C-10, IN C-18, WD A-4, WD A-5, WD A-12*
Paste Function button, *IN B-18*
Paste link option button, *IN A-14, IN A-18*
Paste Special command, *IN C-12*
Paste Special dialog box, *IN C-19*
pasting
  labels in tables, *WWW A-8*
  row headings in tables, *WWW A-10*
percentages
  calculating, *EX A-8*
  formatting values as, *EX A-12*
Percent Style button, *IN A-10*
Picture toolbar
  displaying, *IN C-6*
  moving, *PPT A-8, PPT A-9*
pie charts
  copying, *IN C-14*
  creating, *IN B-8, IN B-9, IN B-12–13*
  exploding slices, *IN B-12, IN B-13*
  moving, *IN C-18*
planning budgets, *EX A-16–17*
posting resumes on Web sites, *WWW A-18–19*
PowerPoint. *See also* career options presentations; event posters; presentations; sales presentations; slides; training presentations
  copying Word text to, *IN C-19*
  pasting charts as links, *IN C-6*
presentations, *IN C-1–24, PPT A-1–24. See also* slides
  animation effects, *IN C-16, PPT A-6, PPT A-7*
  career options presentations. *See* career options presentations
  charts linked to, *IN C-6, IN C-7*
  class party presentation, *IN C-18–19*
  displaying, *PPT A-18*
  enhancing appearance, *IN C-19*
  event posters. *See* event posters
  lecture presentations, *PPT A-18–19*
  previewing, *PPT A-10*
  sales presentations. *See* sales presentations
  training presentation. *See* training presentations
  updating, *IN C-10–11*
  Word booklets linked to, *IN C-8, IN C-9*

previewing
  presentations, *PPT A-10*
  reports, *AC A-10, AC A-16*
price lists
  creating in Excel, *IN A-16–17*
  setting up in Word, *IN A-18–19*
primary key, designating, *AC A-18*
Primary Key field, *AC A-5*
Print button, *AC A-10, AC A-16*
printing
  budgets, *EX A-10–11*
  comparison tables, *WWW A-10–11*
  documents, *WD A-14*
  formatting presentations, *PPT A-16–17*
  reports, *AC A-10, AC A-11, AC A-16, AC A-17*
Print Preview button, *AC A-10, AC A-16*
programs. *See also specific programs*
  displaying, *IN C-4*
Promote (Indent Less) button, *PPT A-4*

Q

queries, *AC A-8–9*
  building, *AC A-10*
  creating, *AC A-14, AC A-15, AC A-18, AC A-19, IN B-8–9*
  modifying, *AC A-14, AC A-15*
  sorting, *AC A-14*
query tables
  creating, *IN B-16–17*
  scrolling, *AC A-10*

R

Random Transition effects, *IN C-10, IN C-11*
Recolor dialog box, *IN C-15*
Recolor Picture button, *IN C-6, IN C-14*
records, *AC A-3*
  copying, *AC A-12*
  deleting, *AC A-12*
  entering, *AC A-12*
  merging, *IN B-18*
  moving between, *AC A-12*
Region field, *AC A-5*
relationships, tables, *AC A-6*
Relationships dialog box, *AC A-7*
relative cell references, *EX A-7*
Remove Filter button, *AC A-8*
Remove Single Field button, *AC A-4*
removing. *See also* deleting
  borders from charts, *IN A-10*
  formatting in resumes, *WWW A-16, WWW A-17*

Report Design view, *AC A-16*
Report Layout view, *AC A-19*
reports
  creating, *AC A-18, AC A-19*
  fills, *AC A-16*
  formatting and printing, *AC A-10–11, AC A-16, AC A-17*
  previewing, *AC A-10, AC A-16*
  styles, *AC A-16*
Report Wizard, *AC A-10*
Restore Dialog Box button, *IN C-12*
Restore dialog box button, *IN A-10*
resumes, *WD A-2–9, WWW A-16–19*
  creating, *WWW A-16–17*
  enhancing, *WD A-8, WD A-9*
  entering text, *WD A-4–5*
  modifying styles, *WD A-6–7*
  posting on Web sites, *WWW A-18–19*
  printing, *WD A-8, WD A-9*
  removing formatting, *WWW A-16, WWW A-17*
right aligning labels, *EX A-16*
rotating
  text objects, *PPT A-16*
  WordArt objects, *WD A-16, WD A-17*
row headings, copying and pasting, *WWW A-10*
Run button, *AC A-9, AC A-10, AC A-14, IN B-8, IN B-10, IN B-16*

S

sales letters, *WD A-16–19*
  creating letterhead, *WD A-16–17*
  entering and formatting, *WD A-18–19*
sales presentations, *IN C-2–11*
  creating presentation and adding charts, *IN C-6–7*
  creating source materials, *IN C-4–5*
  modifying and creating Word booklets, *IN C-8–9*
  updating, *IN C-10–11*
Save button, *IN B-12*
saving worksheets in updated format, *IN B-8*
scrolling query tables, *AC A-10*
Select All Fields button, *AC A-6, AC A-8, AC A-10, AC A-14, AC A-16*
selecting
  fields for tables, *AC A-6*
  multiple clip art objects, *PPT A-8, PPT A-9*
Select Single Field button, *AC A-4, AC A-10, AC A-11, AC A-16, IN B-4*
shadows, WordArt, *WD A-12, WD A-13*
shapes, adding text, *IN A-12*
Show/Hide button, *WD A-4*

Show Table dialog box, *AC A-14*
Simple Query Wizard, *AC A-14*
sizing
   charts, *IN A-10*
   clip art, *AC A-16, PPT A-8, PPT A-9*
   margins, *WD A-8*
   text objects, *PPT A-16*
   WordArt objects, *IN A-6, PPT A-12, WD A-16*
sizing handles, *PPT A-8, PPT A-9*
Slide Master view, *IN C-8*
slides. *See also* presentations
   black and white, *PPT A-18–19*
   event posters. *See* event posters
   individual, modifying, *PPT A-8–9*
   lecture presentations, *PPT A-18–19*
   title, entering text, *IN C-6*
Slide Show button, *IN C-10, IN C-16, PPT A-6, PPT A-10, PPT A-11*
Slide Show view, *PPT A-10*
Slide Sorter toolbar, *PPT A-6, PPT A-7*
Slide Sorter view, *PPT A-10, PPT A-18*
Slide Sorter View button, *IN C-10, PPT A-6, PPT A-10*
Slide View button, *IN C-6, IN C-8*
Sort Ascending button, *AC A-12, IN A-16, IN B-12, IN B-14*
sorting
   queries, *AC A-14*
   tables, *AC A-12*
   worksheet data, *IN A-16, IN A-17*
Spelling and Grammar button, *WD A-4, WD A-5, WD A-18*
Spelling button, *PPT A-4*
straight line depreciation, *EX A-14*
study abroad programs, *WWW A-2–11*
   comparison table for, *WWW A-8–11*
   identifying, *WWW A-6–7*
   search for, *WWW A-4–5*
styles
   documents, modifying, *IN A-6*
   fonts, changing, *PPT A-18*
   modifying, *WD A-6–7*
   names, *WD A-6*
   reports, *AC A-16*
summaries
   creating in Word, *IN A-12–13*
   linking with charts, *IN A-14–15*
summer job opportunity search, *WWW A-12–15*
Symbol dialog box, *WD A-10, WD A-11, WD A-18*

T

Table AutoFormat, *IN A-18*
tables
   adding fields, *AC A-8*
   comparison. *See* comparison tables
   copying, *IN B-14*
   creating, *AC A-4–7, AC A-12–13, IN C-4*
   entering data, *IN C-4*
   query. *See* query tables
   relationships, *AC A-6*
   sorting, *AC A-12*
   Word. *See* Word tables
Table Wizard, *AC A-4*
templates, presentations, *IN C-6*
text
   adding to shapes, *IN A-12*
   centering, *AC A-16, WD A-10, WD A-11, WD A-14*
   wrapping, *IN A-10*
Text Box button, *IN A-12, IN A-13, PPT A-14*
text objects
   borders, *PPT A-14*
   entering text, *PPT A-14*
   inserting in presentations, *PPT A-14–15*
   moving, *PPT A-14, PPT A-16*
   rotating, *PPT A-16*
   sizing, *PPT A-16*
titles, chart axes, entering, *IN A-10, IN A-11*
title slides, entering text, *IN C-6*
totals, calculating, *EX A-6–7*
training presentations, *PPT A-2–11*
   creating outline, *PPT A-4–5*
   design, *PPT A-4*
   editing and showing, *PPT A-10–11*
   modifying individual slides, *PPT A-8–9*
   transition and animation effects, *PPT A-6–7*
transition effects, *IN C-10, IN C-11, PPT A-6, PPT A-7*

U

Undo button, *PPT A-10*
ungrouping clip art objects, *PPT A-10, PPT A-11*
Update Now command, *IN C-10*
updating
   presentations, *IN C-10–11*
   price lists in Excel, *IN A-18*
URLs, copying, *WWW A-8*

V

values
   entering in workbooks, *IN A-4*, *IN A-5*
   formatting, *EX A-12*
   replacing existing values, *EX A-8*
video database, *IN B-16–19*
   creating, *IN B-16–17*
   creating labels and charts, *IN B-18–19*
View button, *AC A-4*, *AC A-5*, *AC A-8*, *AC A-14*
viewing. *See* displaying
View list arrow, *AC A-10*, *AC A-16*, *IN B-16*, *IN C-4*

W

"what if?" questions, *EX A-8-9*
Whole page option button, *IN A-14*
Whole Page view, *IN A-14*, *WD A-18*
Word. *See also* documents
   adding tables to slides, *IN C-16–17*
   copying text to PowerPoint, *IN C-19*
   creating booklets linked to presentations, *IN C-8*, *IN C-9*
   creating company profiles, *IN B-14–15*
   creating letters, *IN A-6–7*
   creating summaries, *IN A-12–13*
   linking Excel charts with summaries, *IN A-14–15*
   linking invoices and letters, *IN A-8–9*
   setting up price lists, *IN A-18–19*
WordArt button, *IN B-14*, *WD A-12*
WordArt Gallery, *WD A-12*, *WD A-13*, *WD A-16*
WordArt objects
   copying, *WD A-12*, *WD A-13*
   creating, *IN A-6*, *IN C-16*
   inserting. *See* inserting WordArt objects
   logos, *WD A-12–13*
   moving, *PPT A-12*, *WD A-12*, *WD A-13*, *WD A-16*
   rotating, *WD A-16*, *WD A-17*
   shadows, *WD A-12*, *WD A-13*
   sizing, *IN A-6*, *PPT A-12*, *WD A-16*
WordArt Shape dialog box, *PPT A-13*
WordArt toolbar, *WD A-13*
Word tables
   adding to slides, *IN C-16–17*
   modifying, *IN C-16*
workbooks
   entering labels and values, *IN A-4*, *IN A-5*
   opening, *IN A-4*
worksheets
   budgets. *See* budgets
   entering data, *IN A-16*
   loans, *EX A-12–13*
   saving in updated format, *IN B-8*
   sorting data, *IN A-16*, *IN A-17*
World Wide Web (WWW), *WWW A-1–24*
   job opportunity search using, *WWW A-12–15*
   resume posting on. *See* resumes
   study abroad program search using. *See* study abroad programs
wrapping text, *IN A-10*
WWW. *See* World Wide Web (WWW)